VISIONS OF THE END TIMES

Religious Pluralism and Public Life
SERIES FOREWORD

WELCOME TO YOU, AS you join us in exploring religious pluralism—a topic both simple and complex.

Simply put, North America, like much of the world, is home to many different religious traditions. Though our traditions have different histories and philosophies, we share a common life. Thus, we must work together to navigate questions about politics, ethics, education, environment, possible futures, and more. Naturally, our different perspectives come into conversation and, sometimes, conflict. Conversation helps us discover new facets of problems and solutions. Conflict challenges us to learn skills of resolution: listening, waiting, translating, compromising, collaborating.

But living into religious pluralism can be complex. How exactly do we bring theologies into conversation? Can we face historical hurts and ruptures? When we honestly encounter one another, what happens to our traditions? Do we remain distinct? Teach one another new ideas and practices? Adopt a unifying spirituality that holds a place for all? And in its light creatively re-interpret our own sacred texts and rituals? Answers to these questions are likely situational, emerging out of our collaborations, conversations, and conflicts over specific issues.

Thus, this book series, Religious Pluralism and Public Life, begins with issues-oriented discussions. These exchanges uncover deeper theological and cultural challenges for scholars and activists of different traditions to explore together. By reading, discussing, and even writing to series contributors, you, the readers, become part of the discussion.

Thank you for joining us.

Laura Duhan-Kaplan
Harry O. Maier

VISIONS OF THE END TIMES

Revelations of Hope and Challenge

EDITED BY
Laura Duhan-Kaplan,
Anne-Marie Ellithorpe,
AND Harry O. Maier

☙PICKWICK *Publications* • Eugene, Oregon

VISIONS OF THE END TIMES
Revelations of Hope and Challenge

Religious Pluralism and Public Life 2

Copyright © 2022 Wipf and Stock Publishers. All rights reserved. Except for brief quotations in critical publications or reviews, no part of this book may be reproduced in any manner without prior written permission from the publisher. Write: Permissions, Wipf and Stock Publishers, 199 W. 8th Ave., Suite 3, Eugene, OR 97401.

Pickwick Publications
An Imprint of Wipf and Stock Publishers
199 W. 8th Ave., Suite 3
Eugene, OR 97401

www.wipfandstock.com

PAPERBACK ISBN: 978-1-6667-3695-3
HARDCOVER ISBN: 978-1-6667-9589-9
EBOOK ISBN: 978-1-6667-9590-5

Cataloguing-in-Publication data:

Names: Duhan-Kaplan, Laura, editor. | Ellithorpe, Anne-Marie, editor. | Maier, Harry O., 1959–, editor.

Title: Visions of the end times : revelations of hope and challenge / edited by Laura Duhan-Kaplan, Anne-Marie Ellithorpe, and Harry O. Maier.

Description: Eugene, OR : Pickwick Publications, 2022 | Series: Religious Pluralism and Public Life 2 | Includes bibliographical references.

Identifiers: ISBN 978-1-6667-3695-3 (paperback) | ISBN 978-1-6667-9589-9 (hardcover) | ISBN 978-1-6667-9590-5 (ebook)

Subjects: LCSH: Eschatology. | Eschatology—Bible teaching. | Apocalyptic literature—History and criticism. | Bible—Criticism, interpretation, etc.

Classification: BS646 .V58 2022 (print) | BS646 .V58 (ebook)

11/01/22

Scripture quotations marked KJV are from the King James or Authorized Version, originally published 1611, revised 1769, copyright @ 1975 American Bible Society.

Scripture quotations marked NABRE are from the New American Bible, revised edition, copyright © 2010, 1991, 1986, 1970 Confraternity of Christian Doctrine, Inc., Washington, DC. All Rights Reserved.

Scripture quotations marked NASB are from the New American Standard Bible, copyright © 1960, 1971, 1977, 1995, 2020 by The Lockman Foundation. All rights reserved.

Scripture quotations marked NRSV are from the New Revised Standard Version of the Bible, copyright @ 1989 by the Division of Christian Education of the National Council of the Churches of Christ in the U.S.A. Used by permission. All rights reserved.

Scripture quotations marked NRSVUE are from the New Revised Standard Version, Updated Edition, copyright © 2021 National Council of Churches of Christ in the U.S.A. Used by permission. All rights reserved worldwide.

Scripture quotations marked RSV are from the Revised Standard Version of the Bible, copyright @ 1952, 1971 by the Division of Christian Education of the National Council of the Churches of Christ in the U.S.A. Used by permission. All rights reserved.

TO A HOPEFUL FUTURE

Contents

Contributors | xi
Acknowledgments | xiii
Abbreviations | xiv

Introduction | 1
   Harry O. Maier, Laura Duhan-Kaplan and Anne-Marie Ellithorpe

Humans, the End Times Are in Your Hands: A Literary Reading of the Book of Zechariah | 10
   Laura Duhan-Kaplan

"Here at the End of All Things": The Poetry of Lament as Expression of the End | 21
   Patricia Dutcher-Walls

The Prophecy of Neferty: Recounting National Trauma as Apocalyptic Synthesis | 34
   David A. Falk

Why the Book of Revelation Matters | 44
   Harry O. Maier

Parody, Burlesque, and Identity in the Apocalypse of John | 55
   Emily Jarrett

Come Out of Babylon: Heavy Metal Music and the Book of Revelation | 63
   Trevor Malkinson

My Way or the Highway to Hell | 70
   Patricia Gruben

The "Evil Child" and the Age/Agency of Cinema's Young Antichrists: Damien's Legacies from *The Omen* to *Good Omens* | 80
  James Magee Jr.

Apocalypsis: With Love for This World and the Next | 103
  Jack Marsh

Skipping to the End: A Look at Messianic Zionism in Modern-Day Israel | 112
  Catherine Keene Merchant

A Spiritual Ecology of Apocalypse | 124
  Jason M. Brown

"That You Might Stand Here on the Roof of the Clouds": Finding Hope in a Cauldron of Encounter, War, and Conflict in Nineteenth-Century New Zealand | 138
  Graham Bidois Cameron

Friendship and Apocalyptic Visions: Christian, Jewish, and Māori Teachings | 153
  Anne-Marie Ellithorpe

The Transhuman Apocalypse: Utopia or Dystopia? | 165
  Kiara Falk

The End of (Our) Time: Reflections on Barth's Theology of Dying and the Thereafter | 174
  Roger L. Revell

Belief in the Day of Judgment: Its Impact on the Development of the Human Soul | 191
  Syed Nasir Zaidi

"Do You Not See How Powerful He Is?" The End, Metanoia, and Visual Imagery in the *Shepherd of Hermas* | 200
  Giulia Marchioni

Leonard Cohen: Dance Me to the End of Love | 210
  Lorraine Ashdown

The Eschatology of Everyday Life: Creation, Confession, and Friendship in Saint Augustine | 216
  Dylan Harvey

Contributors

Lorraine Ashdown, MDiv, DipIIS, is a minister at Bowen Island United Church

Jason M. Brown, PhD, lecturer at Simon Fraser University and adjunct instructor with Western Washington University, teaches a range of courses in the environmental humanities.

Graham Bidois Cameron (Ngāti Ranginui), MTh, is a doctoral student at Otago University and co-chair in restorative justice at Te Herenga Waka (Victoria University of Wellington).

Laura Duhan-Kaplan, PhD, is director of Inter-Religious Studies and professor of Jewish studies at Vancouver School of Theology.

Patricia Dutcher-Walls, ThD, recently retired as dean and professor of Hebrew Bible at Vancouver School of Theology, continues professional work and teaching for the church and academy.

Anne-Marie Ellithorpe, PhD, is a research associate at Vancouver School of Theology, author of *Towards Friendship-Shaped Communities: A Practical Theology of Friendship*, and co-chair of the Religious Reflections on Friendship seminar unit of the American Academy of Religion.

David A. Falk, PhD, is a research associate at Vancouver School of Theology and author of *The Ark of the Covenant in its Egyptian Context: An Illustrated Journey*.

Kiara Falk, MA, is a research affiliate at Vancouver School of Theology in bioethics, Enlightenment philosophy, and posthumanism, and is the author of "Predatory Spirituality: Vampire Religion in America."

Patricia Gruben is a filmmaker who has recently retired as associate professor in the School for the Contemporary Arts at Simon Fraser University.

Dylan Harvey, MA, is a graduate student specializing in sociology and political philosophy.

Emily Jarrett, MATS, MDiv, is an employee of the government of British Columbia.

James Magee Jr., MATS, MA, is a research affiliate with Vancouver School of Theology researching the various intersections of Bible, religion, film, and constructs of childhood.

Harry O. Maier, DPhil, is a professor of New Testament and early Christian studies at Vancouver School of Theology and a research fellow at the Max Weber Center for Advanced Cultural and Social Studies at the University of Erfurt, Germany.

Trevor Malkinson, MDiv, MA (philosophy), is an ordained minister in the United Church of Canada.

Giulia Marchioni, PhD in Preservation of Cultural Heritage, is an art historian at the Cultore di Materia in image anthropology and a high school teacher of art history.

Jack Marsh, PhD, studies theology at University of St. Andrews and is the author of *Saying Peace: Levinas, Solidarity, Eurocentrism* and co-editor of *Normativity, Meaning, and the Promise of Phenomenology*.

Cathy Merchant, MA, MDiv, is founder of the Living Interfaith Sanctuary multifaith congregation in Vancouver.

Roger Revell, PhD, is a research fellow in the Faculty of Theology and Religion at the University of Oxford and a chaplain to students in the university.

Syed Nasir Zaidi, PhD in Islamic Philosophy and Theology, is a spiritual care practitioner at Vancouver General Hospital, a sessional lecturer at Vancouver School of Theology, a Muslim chaplain at the University of British Columbia, and a religious and spiritual health consultant at Az-Zahraa Islamic Centre.

Acknowledgments

WE THANK ALL WHO helped this volume move from concept to completion. The Inter-Religious Studies Program and the Vancouver School of Theology hosted the conference where first drafts of these chapters were shared and discussed. VST President Richard Topping offered ongoing enthusiastic support. Graduate editorial assistant Cathy Merchant copyedited and formatted papers with care and thoughtfulness. George Callihan and Matthew Wimer, our editors at Wipf & Stock, provided helpful support. And, last but not least, family and friends listened as we worried over the book's many details.

LAURA DUHAN-KAPLAN, ANNE-MARIE ELLITHORPE,
and HARRY O. MAIER

Vancouver School of Theology, British Columbia, Canada
Traditional, ancestral, and unceded territories of the Musqueam people

Abbreviations

BZNW	Beihefte zur Zeitschrift für die neutestamentliche Wissenschaft
CBQ	*Catholic Biblical Quarterly*
CD	Barth, Karl. *Church Dogmatics*. Translated by G. W. Bromiley. 14 vols. Peabody, MA: Hendrickson, 2010.
JBL	*Journal of Biblical Literature*
JSTOR	*Journal for the Study of the Old Testament*
OTL	Old Testament Library
Wb	A. Erman and W. Grapow, eds. *Wörterbuch der ägyptischen Sprache*. 7 vols. Berlin: Akademie, 1926–1931.

Introduction

Harry O. Maier, Laura Duhan-Kaplan, and Anne-Marie Ellithorpe

WHAT DO YOU THINK of when you read the words apocalypse and apocalyptic? War, global warming, mass extinction, heat domes, sea-level rise, mass migration of displaced people, COVID, genocide, the discovery of unmarked graves of children at former residential schools? Maybe you think of TV evangelists and religious fanatics. Perhaps they prompt pessimistic thoughts you would rather avoid. The terms *apocalypse* and *apocalyptic* have entered common English usage to describe calamities of every kind. In a more restricted sense, they are terms that describe a kind of ancient Jewish and Christian literature and a particular kind of experience usually generated by a crisis. In 1979, the Yale Hebrew Bible professor John J. Collins advanced precise definitions of these terms as they apply to the study of the past.[1] Apocalypse is a cognate of the Greek word *apokalyptein*, which means to reveal; apocalyptic can describe revelatory literature of this sort, but also has a broader meaning that can describe literature that depicts a present or coming crisis usually associated with God's judgment. Biblical scholars use these words to describe certain kinds of Jewish and Christian canonical and extracanonical literature. Be that as it may, when people see the words apocalypse and apocalyptic, disaster, destruction, and despair come to mind.

The title of this collection of essays, *Visions of the End Times*, might lead one to expect that it is about the end of the world and stern warnings about the future. This is not what this book is about. In May 2017 Vancouver

---

1. Collins, "Introduction."

School of Theology hosted a conference with the same title. In part, this book is a collection of the revised essays of most of its participants. Presenters offered a variety of perspectives to explore ways past and present people conceive(d) the future and how those visions have influenced the way people live. Those perspectives included different religious traditions, Indigenous cultures, biblical writings, ancient history, popular culture, science, and politics. As the subtitle of this collection, *Revelations of Hope and Challenge*, suggests, the book's contributors seek to move beyond an examination of the disasters that often accompany end time visions to consider the hope such visions often inspire.

What does it look like to combine ancient and contemporary senses of the end times, and to offer both hope and challenge? Martin Luther King's last speech in Memphis, Tennessee, on April 3, 1968, "I've Been to the Mountaintop," offers an excellent example. King says,

> I've been to the mountaintop . . . . And I've looked over. And I've seen the Promised Land. I may not get there with you. But I want you to know tonight, that we, as a people, will get to the Promised Land. So, I'm happy, tonight. I'm not worried about anything. I'm not fearing any man. *Mine eyes have seen the glory of the coming of the Lord.*[2]

Here King uses biblical imagery to unveil truths about King's present and offer a revelation of the future. King names the blight of racism and the need for workers to strike for just wages. He tells his audience to boycott products and to withdraw money from banks that promote injustice. Earlier in the speech, King says,

> It's all right to talk about "long white robes over yonder," in all of its symbolism. But ultimately people want some suits and dresses and shoes to wear down here! It's all right to talk about "streets flowing with milk and honey," but God has commanded us to be concerned about the slums down here, and his children who can't eat three square meals a day. It's all right to talk about the new Jerusalem, but one day, God's preacher must talk about the new New York, the new Atlanta, the new Philadelphia, the new Los Angeles, the new Memphis, Tennessee. This is what we have to do.[3]

Apocalyptic prophecy, King suggests, must be used to address real-time challenges and hopes. In this book, we take King's teaching seriously. Each

---

2. King, "I've Been to Mountaintop."
3. King, "I've Been to Mountaintop."

of the essays explores its subject matter as a means to articulate the vision it promotes, the hopes it seeks to create, and the challenges it seeks to address.

In "Humans, the End Times Are in Your Hands: A Literary Reading of the Book of Zechariah," Laura Duhan-Kaplan, VST's director of Inter-Religious Studies and professor of Jewish Studies, examines a call to visionary hope conveyed by the sixth-century BCE prophet Zechariah. Duhan-Kaplan presents a literary reading of Zechariah in which the prophet uses three genres to deliver a three-part message. By sharing apocalyptic dreams, Zechariah calls on his audience to have faith in the power of the spirit. Using symbolic morality plays, he urges them to choose an area of activism and step up to it. And, finally, using eschatology, he reminds them of the power of hope.

Focus on the Hebrew Bible continues with "'Here at the End of All Things': The Poetry of Lament as Expression of the End" by Patricia Dutcher-Walls, professor emerita of Hebrew Bible and former dean of VST. Dutcher-Walls focuses on the power of apocalyptic speech to convey crisis and sorrow. She examines a poem from the first chapter of the book of Lamentations, in which Daughter Zion laments the destruction of Jerusalem that occurred in 586 BCE. After identifying the poetic elements of Lamentations, Dutcher-Walls considers similarities and differences between Lamentations and other Jewish apocalyptic literature. Like apocalyptic literature generally, Lamentations was generated by a crisis and transcends historical time. Unlike that genre, however, its narratives are clearly linked with historical events. Dutcher-Walls explores trauma theory to understand Lamentations' apocalypse-like historical writing. The essay ends with an argument for the influence of Lamentations on the laments of 4 Ezra, a first-century apocalypse written in the wake of the destruction of the second temple in 70 CE.

The author of 4 Ezra writes *as if* he is the sixth-century BCE scribe Ezra, predicting the eventual destruction of the very temple he is rebuilding. Thus, he is engaging in *ex eventu* prophecy, describing events after the fact using a literary style that suggests prediction. In "The Prophecy of Nerferty: Recounting National Trauma as Apocalyptic Synthesis," David Falk, an Egyptologist and postdoctoral research associate at VST, turns our attention to the third and second millennium BCE to explore another *ex eventu* prophecy, the *Prophecy of Neferty*. The Egyptian king Snefru (c. 2575–2551 BCE) summons the sage Neferty to entertain him with speeches that prophesy the future. Neferty describes the political situation in Egypt over five hundred years later during the reign of Anemenhat I (1991–1962 BCE). The book is political propaganda disguised as prophecy. Most scholars agree that apocalyptic is a type of literature that was created in the Levant during the third century BCE. Falk, however, argues that the *Prophecy* is exemplary of apocalyptic *avant le lettre*. It contains numerous apocalypse-like elements: the prediction of political crisis and military conflicts, natural catastrophes, threats from foreign peoples, and the promise of a saving figure to set everything right (Anemenhat I, of course). Later scribes reproduced and altered the *Prophecy* to make it mean new things relevant to their contemporary situations. Falk's analysis offers a case study in ways in which prophecies about coming events are usually about the present, and the way prophetic texts often depart from their original intentions as they are reinterpreted by successive generations to consider new ways of looking at the future.

The next three essays focus on the Book of Revelation and its engagement with empire. Harry Maier, VST's professor of New Testament and Early Christian Studies, in "Why the Book of Revelation Matters," describes the ways Revelation has been used by liberal and fundamentalist Christians to envision a gradualist creation of a just social order, predict an imminent social demise, and—more recently by the American religious right—promote American nativism and imperialist politics. Maier critiques these approaches and reads Revelation for the ways it champions countercultural Christian witness.

In "Parody, Burlesque, and Identity in the Apocalypse of John," Emily Jarrett, a VST graduate, discusses the Apocalypse as a burlesque, a literary subgenre of parody, of the Roman Empire. Revelation uses apocalyptic to ironize Rome's emperors and its economic power in order to convince its first century audience to avoid economic and social entanglement with them, so far as that is possible. Revelation's characters and events imitate imperial emperors and powers. Its visions create a theatrical spectacle for its audience to observe the Roman Empire and its villainous disguises even as it champions resistance to them.

Maier and Jarrett look to Revelation for counter-imperial witness. So does VST alumnus and United Church of Canada minister Trevor Malkinson in "Come Out of Babylon: Heavy Metal Music and the Book of Revelation," but in a perhaps more unexpected way. Malkinson surveys some of the ways heavy metal lyrics draw directly on or form analogies with Revelation's political critique of injustice. Heavy metal music is a genre that regularly uses vivid apocalyptic language to represent chaos and destruction. Because of this, people often associate metal with violence and despair. Malkinson rejects this assessment, arguing rather that heavy metal music is a raised fist against injustice, motivated by hope for an exodus from imperialism and into transformation. He calls on progressive mainline churches to rediscover the book of Revelation as a resource to address injustice and to form Christian identity.

Patricia Gruben, a filmmaker and retired professor of film studies at Simon Fraser University, examines the kind of thinking we often associate with the book of Revelation—fundamentalist Christian belief that the book gives a timetable of what is about to happen in this last generation before Christ's second coming. In "My Way or the Highway to Hell," Gruben examines the use of Revelation promoted by the End Time Ministries of American fundamentalist Christian Irvin Baxter in his weekly television show, podcasts, radio shows, and website. Gruben deploys her expertise in film studies as she considers Baxter's way of turning the rich and complex myths of the Bible into a formulaic set of rigid doctrines and literal beliefs that delivers the answers to life's questions on a platter. Baxter's teaching, she says, advances American exceptionalism in a historically simplistic way. And its preoccupation with chaos and destruction evidences an avoidance of reality and, paradoxically, a denial of death.

As Gruben notes, many people get their understanding of the book of Revelation from movies and TV shows. James Magee Jr., a VST and Trinity Western University alumnus, looks at one of those sources in detail. He surveys the figures of the evil child and the young antichrist in cinema from the 1950s until 2019. He traces the box office success of movies about the boy antichrist such as *The Omen* and *Damien* and their relation to best-selling publications of dispensationalist ideas, of the sort promoted by Erwin Baxter in the 1970s. In movie representations of "evil kids," Magee discovers a more complicated depiction of the antichrist. Here, child antichrists resist the fate the book of Revelation destines them to play and thereby transform a genre usually associated with Satan's victory into an expression of hope and resistance against evil.

The book of Revelation is not the only example of apocalyptic in the New Testament. In "Apocalypsis: With Love for This World and the Next," Jack Marsh, postdoctoral student at the University of St. Andrews and adjunct instructor of philosophy at Messiah University in Pennsylvania, considers three different New Testament apocalyptic traditions found respectively in 2 Peter, Paul's letters, and the Apocalypse. Each presents a different call to what Marsh describes as "prophetic practice . . . correlated with a proper apocalyptic attitude." His essay identifies some ways these texts invite us to address and resolve contemporary challenges. Marsh notes that cataclysm, despair, cynicism, and skepticism are often associated in popular apocalyptic thinking. He argues, however, that *biblical* apocalyptic points us toward individual, social, and environmental engagement. Its traditions ask us to consider the afterlives we imagine and the roles they invite us to play in being co-creators with God of the present.

Other writers, however, are more cautious about the contemporary use of biblical apocalyptic. For, example, there may be no place on earth that is the focus of more end times visions than Jerusalem. Cathy Merchant, a Mahayana Buddhist, interfaith leader of the Living Interfaith Sanctuary, and Vancouver School of Theology graduate, chronicles the rise of Messianic Zionism in Israel and its influence on contemporary Israeli politics. This form of Zionism has resulted in the formation of several ultranationalist religious sects who focus on the coming of the Messiah and the building of a third temple on the Temple Mount, which is currently managed by an Islamic trust. Merchant relates the intergenerational transmission of the trauma of the Shoah to the Messianic Zionists' conviction that the Bible mandates Israeli control of all the historic lands of biblical Israel. Merchant argues that Messianic Zionist use of apocalyptic to advance nation building arises from a selective reading of Israel's Bible and results in injustice against Palestinians.

Environment, colonization, and utopian hopes in science are all areas where apocalyptic ideas can help people understand and respond to changing conditions. Jason Brown, lecturer in Forestry at Simon Fraser University and VST research associate, describes and critiques the goals and strategies amongst different kinds of environmental groups to avoid environmental collapse. He presents Josephus's profiles of various first-century Jewish groups, i.e., Pharisees, Sadducees, Essenes, Zealots, the Jesus movement. He uses them analogically to show differences between contemporary environmental movements that advocate individual action, cooperation with corporations, withdrawal, revolution, or a middle way that deploys insights from each group. Finally, he cites Indigenous wisdom and promotes a middle way that seeks insights from different environmental groups to solve the climate crisis. Although environmentalists usually use the term apocalypse to warn against a coming calamity, Brown draws on its alternative meaning as a revelation of something new to inspire a fresh start.

Next, Graham Cameron, a Māori doctoral student in the Department of Theology and Religion at Otago University and co-chair in Restorative Justice at Te Herenga Waka, chronicles the role apocalyptic played in the emergence in the nineteenth century of Indigenous Christianity amongst his Pirirākau people, a subtribe of the Ngāti Ranginui iwi (tribe) in Aotearoa/New Zealand. His central focus is on the growth of Pai Mārire, a nonviolent millenarian movement led by the prophetic Ngāti Ruanui visionary Te Ua Haumene. Cameron describes the visions Te Ua started receiving in 1862 and the founding of a prophetic response to the violent expropriation of Indigenous land. He celebrates Te Ua and Pai Mārire faith that inspired

Pirirākau to millenarianism, a path toward an indigenizing, contextual Christian faith dedicated to justice and hope.

Anne-Marie Ellithorpe, VST research associate, also explores positive apocalyptic visions informing Indigenous resistance in Aotearoa. In "Friendship and Apocalyptic Visions: Christian, Jewish, and Māori Teachings," Ellithorpe identifies apocalyptic literature as providing an imaginative counter to contemporary perceptions of the world. Apocalyptic literature, she writes, can help shape our social imaginary to value visions of friendship, justice, and peace and to resist colonization. Ellithorpe highlights themes of friendship, justice, and peace in late medieval Cistercian theology, the biblical books of Revelation and Isaiah, and the work and words of Māori leaders and prophets Tohu Kākahi and Te Whiti o Rongomai, who founded the Parihaka community in response to expropriation of Indigenous land. Ultimately, Ellithorpe hopes, apocalyptic visions of friendship will reshape our practices and promote justice and peace.

In "The Transhuman Apocalypse: Utopia or Dystopia," bioethicist and VST Research Affiliate Kiara Falk peers critically into a future imagined by the transhumanist movement. In this future, humanity is improved through genetic engineering, cybernetics, nanotechnology, and technological enhancement. Falk critiques the movement's utopian ideals, saying they rest on an intolerance of human difference, especially of those who do not conform to the Enlightenment ideal of the rational, physically able, autonomous self. Falk warns against the dystopian apocalyptic future transhumanists would bring if they were able to produce their "brave new world." Her criticism of transhumanism is itself a kind of apocalypse, namely a revelation of and prophetic warning against the sinister ideology that accompanies transhumanist blind belief in scientific progress.

Biblical apocalyptic has been used for millennia to speculate about the nature of the afterlife. Augustine, for example, used it to speculate how old people will be in the new Jerusalem of Rev 21:1—22:5, and whether people who were bald or overweight will have full heads of hair and be thin. What about life before the fall? Would Adam and Eve have died if they had not fallen from grace in the garden of Eden? No, says the traditional Christian answer, because death is a consequence of their sin. At first glance, this may seem like a trivial question. Not so, argues Roger Revell, a postdoctoral researcher at the University of Oxford, who examines the twentieth-century German theologian Karl Barth's answer to the question. Not only would Adam and Eve have died if they had not sinned, says Barth, but death would have been God's gift to them. Barth of course knew that Gen 3 is not history, but rather a way to help people reflect on what it means to be human. Death, for Barth, is not an entry into an afterlife that transforms the best features of our present lives into something better in a sequence of time without end. Instead, it is the doorway to transfiguration in time-transcending eternity. Revell explores and assesses the contours of this idea, noting the way Barth grounds his reasoning in Scripture and how the Bible played an important role in his teaching of the otherness of God and creation's relationship with God. Finally, Revell considers the insights this offers for ways we might live in time and space on this side of the grave.

Dr. Syed Nasir Zaidi, Islamic chaplain and theologian, offers a Qur'anic perspective on the way a spiritual understanding of death can transform a person's life. In his essay "Belief in the Day of Judgment: Impact on the Soul's Development," he explains the Qur'anic view that earthly life is an opportunity to prepare for an expanded life of the soul. Teachings about the day of judgment, properly interpreted, offer practical guidance on how to prepare. Through prophetic poetry and stories, the Qur'an inspires believers to deepen their awareness of God, develop their conscience, loosen their attachment to wealth, and balance fear with hope.

Italian art historian and VST research associate Giulia Marchioni combines textual analysis, material culture research, and iconographical study in her essay on *Shepherd of Hermas*. The *Shepherd* was written in Rome in the second century CE and was one of the most widely read writings in the early church. During several visions the eponymous shepherd appears to the protagonist Hermas to reveal Hermas's shortcomings as well as those of his Roman congregation. The work uses the apocalypse genre to exhort its audience to both personal transformation and cohesion to their group. Marchioni notes that funerary images in ancient Italian catacombs frequently feature solitary shepherds, often associated with biblical motifs such as faithful leadership and trust in God. Marchioni asks whether the popular *Shepherd of Hermas* also influenced viewers' thoughts when they saw catacomb shepherd depictions. If so, the iconic shepherds could have invited catacomb visitors to recall the conversion of the deceased while they were still alive, along with their own hopes for eternal life and need to adhere closely to the church.

With "Leonard Cohen: Dance me to the End of Love," United Church of Canada minister Lorraine Ashdown looks at a different personal dimension of apocalypse, as she engages Cohen's music and poetry as revelation. She uses the words apocalypse/apocalyptic to describe Cohen's work under a variety of aspects: as cataclysm, warning, and redemption. She contests one journalist's description of Cohen as "gloom-monger" and concludes instead that Cohen's apocalyptic reveals him to be a wise, mystical prophet. His eclectic beliefs drawn from Buddhism, Christianity, and his native Judaism inform his reverence for human beings as spiritual beings.

Augustine of Hippo (354–431) is perhaps the single most important figure who has shaped the interpretation of biblical apocalyptic in the western Christian tradition. Augustine's thinking was motivated in part by his impatience with those who looked to Revelation for predictions of the military disasters roiling the Roman Empire. In "The Eschatology of Everyday Life: Creation, Confession, and Friendship in Saint Augustine," Dylan Harvey, a graduate student at Ryerson University, brings the lens of Western European phenomenology to Augustine's treatment of last or ultimate things in the *Confessions*. The *Confessions* is a revelation both of Augustine's internal life and of the orientation toward death that arises from the knowledge of being created *ex nihilo*. Harvey speaks of the related anxiety of knowing social relationships are temporary. Drawing on Augustine's accounts of spiritual friendship, Harvey shows how shared recognition of the *nihil* can inspire friends to turn together towards the presence of an immutable God.

There is an urgency to these essays. A global pandemic, dire warnings of global warming tipping points, tribalism in politics, the gulf between rich and poor, religious intolerance, and racism are only a few of our contemporary challenges. Each one is so big, it can paralyze. Put together, they can lead to despair. We are all too aware of negative end times visions. Terms like apocalypse and apocalyptic recur repeatedly in the media on any given day; the revelations that media present are almost always those that challenge rather than give hope. May these essays help readers reflect on their own end times visions and on what kind of world they hope to form.

BIBLIOGRAPHY

Collins, John J. "Introduction: Towards the Morphology of a Genre." *Semeia* 14 (1979) 1–20.

King, Martin Luther, Jr. "I've Been to the Mountaintop." American Rhetoric, Apr. 3, 1968. https://www.americanrhetoric.com/speeches/mlkivebeentothemountaintop.htm.

Humans, the End Times Are in Your Hands

A Literary Reading of the Book of Zechariah

Laura Duhan-Kaplan

What is the message of the Biblical prophet Zechariah? Many Jews know him as a prophet with a miraculous vision. They are most familiar with a famous quotation that ends every Jewish prayer service: "On that day, God will be One and God's name will be One" (Zech 14:9).[1] One day, God will bring about a change in human nature. Religious traditions formerly at odds will reconcile, and interreligious wars will end. Many Christians meet Zechariah through his influence on the book of Revelation.[2] Thus, they focus on his fiery predictions of God's all-out war. One day, God will purify the earth and establish there a lasting divine kingdom. But a careful, comprehensive reading of the book of Zechariah shows that Zechariah does not believe in waiting for divine intervention. Rather, he urges people to take action. At times, he says, God organizes regional politics so that there is a chance for peace. But then, people must seize the moment, acting in their communities with justice and integrity. This is the only way to create a sustainable society, one not fractured by conquest and revolt.

---

1. See Rosenstein, *Siddur Eit Ratzon*, 110, for the text and commentary. For a range of possible interpretations of the phrase, see Duhan-Kaplan, "Zechariah's Interfaith Vision."

2. Jauhiainen, *Use of Zechariah*, 142–53. Jauhiainen identifies eighty-one hints to Zechariah in Revelation. Of these, he argues, seven are unequivocal allusions and fourteen evoke biblical language or motifs that appear only in Zechariah.

Of course, Zechariah presents these ideas in the literary style of biblical prophecy. He speaks in dreamtime metaphors, symbolic performances, and intertextual allusions. His writing is so challenging that classical commentator Rabbi David Kimchi, in frustration, wondered if it represents a deteriorated form of prophecy.[3] Thus, readers need a guide to decode Zechariah's work. Here, I provide such a guide. First, I locate the book in historical time. I note that, based on historical information, scholars usually identify two distinct sections. Then, I depart from historical scholarship to move into a more literary analysis. Through that lens, I identify three distinct sections, based on style and theme. Finally, I explore a key message of each section, using three different hermeneutic lenses. Throughout, I argue that the three sections comprise an integrated message of faith, justice, and hope.

HISTORICAL CONTEXT AND THE STRUCTURE OF THE BOOK OF ZECHARIAH

Was Zechariah a real person? Most likely, he was. A superscript at the beginning of his book tells us that he began to prophesy in 520 BCE. The date places him sixty-six years after the Babylonian army invaded the southern Israelite kingdom of Judah in 586 BCE. The invasion destroyed the capital city of Jerusalem; devastated the land; forcibly exiled the educated, landed, and wealthy citizens; and left the poor without urban infrastructure or healthy rural fields.[4]

Zechariah speaks of destruction, but he focuses on restoration. In 539 BCE, only nineteen years before he began to prophesy, Babylonia fell to Persia. The Persian Emperor Cyrus encouraged Jews to rebuild Judah's political and religious institutions. A conservative nationalist group accepted the challenge but made only a tiny start. Finally in 522 BCE—just two years before the start of Zechariah's prophetic career—the new Emperor Darius re-funded the revival project.[5] The rebuilding started for real, and Zechariah became part of it. Zechariah supports the revival but advocates for a more liberal approach. For example, for him, rebuilding Jerusalem's walls is not a priority but creating a welcoming society is.

Clear historical references in Zechariah chapters 1–8 confirm this dating. Names of people and places check out. So do the controversial public issues Zechariah discusses. Thus, most historical scholars agree: a historical

---

3. Kimchi, *Rabbi David Kimchi's Commentary*, 3. For the Hebrew, see *Mikra'ot Gedolot*, 504.

4. Hooker, "Jewish Temples."

5. Zakheim, *Nehemiah*, Kindle loc. 539.

prophet called "Zechariah" wrote it. But chapters 9–14 are vague. Few historical references check out. So, historical scholars divide the book into two halves and speculate about their relationship. Have these two distinct books been edited into one? If so, then who wrote part 2 and when? Who edited them together and why? But these scholars draw no definitive conclusions.[6] As they should; there is in fact no scholarly consensus on how prophetic books were composed, performed, or edited.[7] Thus, I begin by reading the book of Zechariah as it is presented, a unified whole with an integrated message. On this reading, the historical ambiguity of chapters 9–14 appears as a deliberate invitation to imagination and hope.

The biblical book of Zechariah includes fourteen short chapters. It makes its case in fewer than five thousand words.[8] Yet its literary style includes all genres of prophetic writing. Oracles of comfort. Oracles of doom. Moral rebuke. Dreams. Travel to heavenly realms. Performance art. Poetry. Using these styles, the book explores all the main themes of biblical prophecy.[9] Utopia. Dystopia. Morality. Politics. Economics. History. Spirituality. The genres and themes are not haphazardly edited together. Rather, the book divides neatly into three sections. Each section focuses on a theme and presents it through a particular genre of prophetic writing. Using apocalypse (chs. 1–6), Zechariah calls on his audience to have faith in the power of the spirit. Using symbolic morality play (chs. 7–11), he urges them to choose an area of activism and step up to it. Finally, using eschatology (chs. 12–14), he reminds them of the power of hope.

APOCALYPSE: UNDERSTANDING SPIRITUAL POWER

In everyday conversational English, we use the word *apocalypse*. There, it refers to a big game-changing event that destroys and then rebuilds human society. But in Biblical scholarship, apocalypse has a different meaning. Here, apocalypse means "revelation." In one motif typical of apocalyptic literature, human beings ascend to the heavenly realms. An angelic escort shows them hidden secrets of world governance, such as morality, destiny, and meteorology.[10] This apocalyptic motif, some scholars say, is influenced

---

6. Assis, "Structure of Zechariah 8," 1; Brettler, *How to Read Bible*, loc. 2706–43.
7. Brettler, *How to Read Bible*, loc. 1970–84.
8. Kranz, "Word Counts."
9. For a slightly different list of those themes, see Brettler, *How to Read Bible*, loc. 2005–10.
10. Collins, "Introduction."

by Babylonian cosmology.[11] So it is not surprising that Zechariah, returning from Babylonia, would use it to express his insights.

Zechariah describes his heavenly tour in detail in chapters 1–6. He describes it as an extended night vision. In fact, it reads like a series of loosely disconnected dream scenes.[12] Four horsemen report that the earth is at peace. Four horns represent divine powers on the move. A young man with a measuring tape learns that Jerusalem will become a city without walls, protected only by God's glory. The high priest Joshua and the political governor Zerubbabel are anointed to lead side by side. A golden menorah (lampstand) is fed oil directly from two olive trees. A flying scroll has driven thieves and liars out of the community. And a flying tub has removed evil. And, finally, four horse-drawn chariots, representing the four winds, emerge from the mountains ready to advance.[13]

In his visions, Zechariah sees the spiritual forces that direct our world. But he does not see them directly. He sees them only symbolically. So, he has to keep asking his angelic guide to interpret the symbols. But the interpretations are sometimes as cryptic as the symbols. For example, after Zechariah sees the menorah (4:2–3), his guide explains its meaning. "Not by might, and not by power, but by my spirit, says the LORD of hosts" (Zech 4:6).[14] But what does God's "spirit" mean here? What is it that will be more effective than might and power? Is it, as classical commentators have suggested, God's personal direction of regional affairs?[15] The spiritual talents of Persian[16] or Judean[17] leaders? The community's attention to words of the Torah?[18] Based on contemporary liturgical use of Zechariah's menorah vision, I will suggest another possibility: communal commitment to justice is more effective than might or power.

Jews read Zechariah's vision of the menorah (Zech 2:14—4:7) in synagogue on Shabbat during the holiday of Hanukah.[19] This holiday was invented in 164 BCE to celebrate the victory of Judean rebels over the

---

11. Boyarin, "Talmudic Apocalypse and Christology"; Collins, *Daniel*, 16.

12. Moses Maimonides argues that most prophets see their oracles in symbolic dreams. See "Mishneh Torah," 7:1–7.

13. This summary is influenced by Von Rad, *Message of the Prophets*, 252–53.

14. Scripture translations are the author's own.

15. Malbim in *Mikra'ot Gedolot*, 529.

16. Rashi in *Mikra'ot Gedolot*, 528.

17. Fishbane, *Haftarot*, 228.

18. Targum Yonatan in *Mikra'ot Gedolot*, 528.

19. Fishbane, *Haftarot*, 366.

invading Syrian-Greek Seleucid army.[20] The Maccabees, a priestly family who led the revolt, established the Hasmonean dynasty. But, by the year 200 CE, the Hasmoneans had partnered with Rome.[21] And Rome had overrun Judea. Jews were dispersed around the Mediterranean region.[22] They had very little political power. Certainly not enough to restore a temple in their former capital city. But they did have enough intellectual and spiritual power to re-envision their tradition. So, rabbinic teachers of that era reinterpreted Hanukah to suit the politics of their own time. They told the following allegorical story about the Maccabees. After winning their war, the Maccabees inspected the temple. But they found only one day's worth of pure, high-priest-approved oil. Still, oil from that little jar fueled eight full days of menorah light.[23] What is the moral of the story? Our generation does not have Maccabean might or Hasmonean political power. We no longer have high-priest approved oil. But, we have access to something better and brighter. God's spirit flows to us directly from the created world.

Zechariah himself prophesies almost nine hundred years before the Talmudic rabbis. But their spiritual interpretation of his vision is helpful. Zechariah writes in a time of restoration. So, he is not worried about a Jewish community without religious or political power. He wants Jews to live well *with* political power. As he puts it: in our time, God is arranging regional dynamics in our favor. Finally, the horrific war is over. Persia's version of peace encourages local self-government and regional cooperation. So, we have a chance now to help create a non-militarized world. But to succeed, our leaders must follow a strict ethical code. We must insist they show integrity, generosity, and concern for the oppressed. Our guide will be the mantra: "Not by might, not by power, but by my spirit."

MORALITY: PRACTICAL ACTIONS FOR JUSTICE

Like all biblical prophets, Zechariah places moral teaching at the center of his work. Literally! Moral themes dominate the middle of his book, chapters 7–11. There, he criticizes mechanical approaches to religion. The true spirit of religion, he says, is to practice the essentials of justice. Do not defraud the widow, the orphan, the stranger, and the poor. Instead, live in truth and faith. Then, the whole world will see our utopia and want to join our religion. Next, Zechariah criticizes materialistic business leaders. Greedy empires will fall in dramatic acts of divine justice. Developers who exploit the forests of Lebanon will suffer when the forests burn. Finally, Zechariah also scolds corrupt

---

20. Waskow, *Seasons of Our Joy*, 88–90.
21. Goldenberg, *Origins of Judaism*, 120–37.
22. Jaffee, *Early Judaism*, 25–53.
23. Sefaria, "Talmud: Babylonian," *Shabbat* 21b.

and apathetic political leaders. With symbolic public theatre, he predicts the end of "shepherds" who abuse their flocks. But he does not specify who those shepherds are.[24] Thus, subtly, he challenges his entire audience to choose an area of activism. To show how he does this, I present his performance from chapter 11 in a contemporary idiom.[25]

Imagine yourself a fan of Zechariah. Picture a scene in ancient Judea—or even right now, in your home town. You've arrived at Speakers' Corner, because you heard the prophet Zechariah is going to perform just as the afternoon market opens. You know the performance is going to be political.

Zechariah does not disappoint! He opens with a short poem, an oracle of doom. He says, "Big empires and small countries: there is nowhere to hide. Whoever you are, I'm talking to YOU! Yes, you, shepherds! Literal shepherds working hard to make a living by managing flocks. Metaphorical shepherds, too, those responsible for managing the communal affairs of the working people." And you, the audience member, know this will be a performance filled with double entendre, words and skits with multiple meanings.

Next Zechariah invokes God. Now you know this is going to be a religious performance too. Zechariah says, "God told me, 'Go tend those sheep. Go tend them, because their shepherds are not taking care of them, only looking to sell them out and line their own pockets.' So, I said to God, 'Okay, I'll do the job with double commitment and double skill; maybe I can be a role model for those poor people.' Then I got two shepherd's crooks, not just one."

Zechariah picks up two staffs, one in each hand, and waves them in the air. He continues, "I named one 'Favor' and the other 'Unity.' And I got to work. But during just my first month, I saw three other shepherds simply give up, leaving the sheep to die. I was so disgusted and impatient, too, because my help was so useless. So I broke my staff Favor!" Zechariah breaks his staff with a loud crack, and you gasp! He says, "I broke it because—know this, people!—God doesn't favor any of you. Everyone will have the same fate."

Zechariah continues. And now you, the audience, can guess where he's going when he says, "At that point, my employers realized I had been there to give them a message from God. With my job done, it was time to go. So I said, 'Pay me, if you want to.' And they handed me a check, paying me at a slave-wage pay level. I donated it to the temple. But I saw how little they valued me, and I realized: human fellowship and interpersonal respect don't exist anymore in this society. So I broke my staff Unity."

---

24. Berrigan, *Minor Prophets, Major Themes*, 333–84, interprets shepherds as warring capitalist leaders; Klein, *Zechariah*, notes forty different interpretations of who the shepherds are.

25. My interpretation is inspired by Nelson, "Priestly Purity."

Zechariah breaks it with a loud crack, but this time, you don't gasp; you just applaud. But he holds up his hand; he's not finished yet. And he says, "Then God told me: 'Go, outfit yourself like one of these useless shepherds. Because that's the only kind of shepherd you've got here. The kind that ignores the lost, the injured, and the frail. And feasts on the healthy, ripping them apart. Well, the time is coming when those people won't be able to plan or act. Let the sword descend!'"

And you, a member of the audience, clap and shout!

You say to your friend, "I'm disgusted with those big businesses paying less than minimum wage. Zechariah's sure got their number."

And your friend says, "I thought he was talking about the city council. They are making an absolute mess of the affordable housing initiative."

Someone overhears you and says, "It made me think of the schools I'm sending my kids to. Where there's no sensitivity to diversity, and no peace-oriented teaching to help the kids create a sustainable community."

Someone else says, "The real barrier to peace isn't schools, it's the military industrial complex. The army and its cronies getting rich off us and paying no attention to national security."

And even though you all heard something different, you can agree on a few things. Change has to come; change is coming; it's going to be big; and it's going to involve a terrible upheaval. If you are an activist, you say, "Now is the time to choose my cause and commit to it!" If you are a religious person, accustomed to speaking of God, you say, "God is coming!" And, in Zechariah's understanding of spirituality as moral activism, you are both saying the same thing. Faith and activism are two facets of hope.

ESCHATOLOGY: DRAMATIC HOPE

Eschatology is study of the eschaton, i.e., the "end times." Perhaps, psychologically speaking, eschatology comes from disappointment with lived time. In real time, life is a jumble of events, both good and bad, over which we have limited control. So, it can be comforting to imagine that our messy reality is a brief anomaly. True time began with the *arche*, a perfect ancient utopia. And it will end with the eschaton, a perfect future utopia.[26] In between lies the short, sad human story of greedy warring empires.[27] But that story will soon end, and our children will be free from suffering.

In chapters 12–14, Zechariah describes an end-times scenario. The region's final war is waged against Jerusalem. Foreign invaders capture the city, plunder the houses, and rape the women. Two-thirds of the city's people perish. But survivors extend compassion, experience healing, and

---

26. Grossman, "Lectures on the Humanities."
27. Maier, "Lectures on Revelation."

receive true prophecy. God then moves mountains, reroutes rivers, flattens deserts, and recreates the cycle of day and night. On that day, a spirit of healing prevails. Survivors from all nations recognize their spiritual kinship. Together, they pray for rain in Jerusalem's restored temple. The world is so holy, even horses wear priestly sashes.

Zechariah narrates these eschatological oracles in a future tense. However, I do not read them as future predictions. Instead, I read his description of destruction in the past tense. The book identifies its own historical setting: after the return from Babylonian exile. In that context, the oracles of destruction seem to describe past events: the horrors of Babylonia's invasion of Judah. I read Zechariah's description of restoration as one possible future, written in the subjunctive tense. Why? For three reasons. First, the eschatological discussion appears after the book's moral rebuke and call to action. Clearly, for Zechariah, restoration is contingent upon the people's return to justice. The oracles of restoration, then, seem to describe a possible future. Second, the book is a call to hope. Thus, it invites us to see beyond a linear chain of cause and effect into a realm of spiritual promise. Finally, the events Zechariah describes are less important than the way he describes them. Using intertextual allusions to creation, exodus, and earlier prophets, he plays with our sense of time. Thus, he invites us to move beyond the boundaries of our ordinary sense of history.

In his intertextual play, Zechariah draws on the Hebrew Bible's complex presentation of human experiences of time. Because of that complexity, scholars have argued variously that biblical time is open-ended, cyclical, or linear.[28] And, in fact, these different senses of time do animate different stories. Open-ended time begins with creation. God fills the world with prototype plants and animals. They scatter seeds, reproduce, and start the wild, evolving genetic lottery that brings innovation into the world.[29] Cyclical time is represented in the exodus, particularly as the crossing of the Red Sea is read in midrash.[30] Oppression will always give way to liberation. Linear time appears in eschatological visions. Isaiah's vision of the lion and the lamb together, for example, teaches that the world will transform into its perfected state of peace. In the biblical view, no paradigm of time should lead to despair.[31] Open-ended uncertainty and cyclical patterns can be as redemptive as an ultimate utopia.[32]

28. For arguments that biblical time is linear, see Schorsch, "Judaism and Linear History"; Cahill, *Gifts of the Jews*. For arguments that it is circular, see Von Rad, *Message of the Prophets*; Yerushalmi, *Zachor*. For arguments that it is open ended, see Dempster, "Geography and Genealogy," 68; Shamash, "Hope in Troubled Times."

29. Duhan-Kaplan, "Tazria."

30. Neusner, *Introduction to Rabbinic Literature*.

31. Duhan-Kaplan, "Jewish Time."

32. Held, "Hope Is the Essence."

In this spirit, Zechariah (14:6–9) weaves motifs from creation, exodus, and earlier prophets into a theology of hope.

In the creation story of Gen 1, the world begins in darkness. God's first creation is light. God then divides light from dark, initiating an alternating cycle of evening and morning (Gen 1:1–5). This cycle of days becomes the container that gives a rhythm and stability to all creation. Still, the world has seen many bad days in this fixed cycle. Some have come from seemingly intractable divisions between people, stubborn as the cycle of day and night. So, Zechariah sees that God could rework this cycle any time. God could try something new, a different open-ended experiment, a beginning of wild new potentials. God could create a world without the old divisions. "In that [new first] day, there shall be a continuous day . . . of neither day nor night, and there shall be light at eventide" (Zech 14:6).[33]

On that new kind of day, the world might even see a new exodus. Not an identical one but a flexible one, adapted particularly to a new order. At the crossing of the Red Sea, "the waters were split, and the Israelites went into the sea on dry ground, the waters forming a wall for them on their right and on their left" (Exod 14:22).[34] When that happened, "mountains skipped like rams, hills like sheep" (Ps 114:4).[35] On the new day, Zechariah says, mountains and water could move in unexpected ways. They could once again provide people with what they need to survive: abundant water for an arid land, even in the dry summer season. Jerusalem's Mount of Olives could split, leaving a huge gorge. And then, "in that day, fresh water shall flow from Jerusalem, part of it to the Eastern Sea, and part to the Western Sea, throughout the summer and winter" (Zech 14:8).[36] Such a flow of water could transform agricultural life, making farming more accessible to everyone. This could lead to a more equitable distribution of work, wealth, and power. Perhaps no one would sell themselves into indentured servitude again. Thus, the water, starting as a stream as narrow as "the antenna of a grasshopper," could become a "flowing river" of healing, purifying waters.[37]

And, on that new kind of day, a leader could appear who has "the spirit of the LORD . . . wisdom and insight . . . counsel and valor . . . devotion and reverence" (Isa 11:2).[38] It is possible that this leader would neither evoke nor invoke the familiar bitter national and ethnic divisions. They might represent no particular human group, only the unifying presence

33. NJPS translation in Berlin and Brettler, *Jewish Study Bible*.
34. Berlin and Brettler, *Jewish Study Bible*.
35. Berlin and Brettler, *Jewish Study Bible*.
36. Berlin and Brettler, *Jewish Study Bible*.
37. Sefaria, "Talmud: Babylonian," *Yoma 77b–78a*.
38. Berlin and Brettler, *Jewish Study Bible*. Zechariah himself signals his knowledge of the earlier prophets in 1:4–6.

of God. It could be as if "God will be One and God's name will be One" (Zech 14:9). Or, as *Targum Yonatan* understands it, the entire world could have a shared mystical experience, and all problems of intercultural communication could end.[39]

Radical hope? Yes. It is possible, says Zechariah, to create a sustainable society marked with justice, peace, and holiness. But something different and special will emerge only if people do the work. Zechariah speaks into his own historical time, but his words reach into our time too. We must seize the moment, develop the spirit, let go of greed, strengthen acts of justice, imagine the impossible, and take hope seriously. This, Zechariah teaches, is the divinely revealed guide to ending the troubles of human history.

BIBLIOGRAPHY

Assis, Elie. "The Structure of Zechariah 8 and Its Meaning." *Journal of Hebrew Scriptures* 12 (2012). https://doi.org/10.5508/jhs.2012.v12.a12.

Berlin, Adele, and Marc Zvi Brettler. *The Jewish Study Bible*. 2nd ed. Oxford, UK: Oxford University Press, 2014.

Berrigan, Daniel. *Minor Prophets, Major Themes*. Eugene, OR: Wipf & Stock, 2009.

Boyarin, Daniel. "The Talmudic Apocalypse and Christology." Lectures at Vancouver School of Theology, Vancouver, Can., July 2016.

Brettler, Marc Zvi. *How to Read the Bible*. Philadelphia: Jewish Publication Society, 2010. Kindle.

Cahill, Thomas. *The Gifts of the Jews: How a Tribe of Desert Nomads Changed the Way Everyone Thinks and Feels*. New York: Anchor, 1998.

Collins, John J. *Daniel: With an Introduction to Apocalyptic Literature*. Grand Rapids: Eerdmans, 1984.

———. "Introduction: Towards the Morphology of a Genre." *Semeia* 14 (1979) 1–20.

Dempster, Stephen G. "Geography and Genealogy, Dominion and Dynasty: A Theology of the Hebrew Bible." In *Biblical Theology: Retrospect and Prospect*, edited by Scott J. Hafemann, 66–82. Downers Grove, IL: InterVarsity, 2002.

Duhan-Kaplan, Laura. "Changing Geographies in Uncertain Times: Prophetic Guidance from Zechariah." Workshop at OHALAH: Association of Rabbis and Cantors for Jewish Renewal, Boulder, CO, Jan. 2018.

———. "Hanukkiah: I'm Here to Tell You Resistance Never Ends." Laura Duhan-Kaplan, Dec. 13, 2017. http://www.sophiastreet.com/2017/12/13/hanukkiah-zechariah-resistance/.

———. "Jewish Time: Cyclical, Linear, or Open-Ended?" Laura Duhan-Kaplan, Jan. 26, 2018. http://www.sophiastreet.com/2018/01/26/jewish-time-cyclical-linear-open-ended/.

———. "Tazria: Seeds of Torah." Laura Duhan-Kaplan, 2008. http://www.sophiastreet.com/tazria-seeds-of-torah/.

———. "Zechariah's Interfaith Vision." Dec. 2009. http://www.sophiastreet.com/zechariahs-interfaith-vision/.

---

39. *Mikra'ot Gedolot*, 616. *Targum Yonatan* is an interpretive Aramaic translation attributed to the second-century scholar Yonatan ben Uzziel.

Fishbane, Michael. *Haftarot: The JPS Bible Commentary*. Philadelphia: Jewish Publication Society, 2002.
Goldenberg, Robert. *The Origins of Judaism: From Canaan to the Rise of Islam*. Cambridge, UK: Cambridge University Press, 2007. Kindle.
Grossman, Allen. "Lectures on the Humanities." Brandeis University, Waltham, MA, Spring 1977.
Held, Shai. "Hope Is the Essence of Jewish Thought." Lecture at OHALAH: Association of Rabbis and Cantors for Jewish Renewal Conference, Boulder, CO, Jan. 2018.
Hooker, Richard. "The Jewish Temples: The Babylonian Exile (597–538 BC)." Jewish Virtual Library, n.d. https://www.jewishvirtuallibrary.org/the-babylonian-exile.
Jaffee, Martin. *Early Judaism*. New York: Prentice Hall, 1995.
Jauhiainen, Marko. *The Use of Zechariah in Revelation*. Tübingen, Germ.: Mohr Siebeck, 2005.
Kimchi, David. *Rabbi David Kimchi's Commentary upon the Prophecies of Zechariah*. Translated by A. M'Caul. London: James Duncan, 1938.
Klein, George L. *Zechariah: An Exegetical and Theological Exposition of Holy Scripture*. New American Commentary 21. Nashville: B&H, 2008.
Kranz, Jeffrey. "Word Counts for Every Book in the Bible." Overview Bible, May 29, 2014. http://overviewbible.com/word-counts-books-of-bible/.
Maier, Harry O. "Lectures on Revelation." Vancouver School of Theology, Vancouver, Can., Spring 2016.
Maimonides, Moses. "Mishneh Torah, Foundations of the Torah." Sefaria, c. 1176–1178. https://www.sefaria.org/Mishneh_Torah,_Foundations_of_the_Torah?tab=contents.
Mikra'ot Gedolot: Trei Asar [Rabbinic commentaries on the twelve minor prophets]. Jerusalem: Mekor HaSefarim, 1998.
Nelson, Richard. "Priestly Purity and Prophetic Lunacy: Hosea 1:2–3 and 9:7." In *The Priests in the Prophets: The Portrayal of Priests, Prophets, and Other Religious Specialists in the Latter Prophets*, edited by Lester L. Grabbe and Alice Ogden Bellis, 115–33. London: T&T Clark International, 2004,.
Neusner, Jacob. *Introduction to Rabbinic Literature*. New Haven, CT: Yale University Press, 1999.
Rosenstein, Joseph G. *Siddur Eit Ratzon*. Highland Park, NJ: Shiviti, 2006.
Scheindlin, Raymond P. *A Short History of the Jewish People*. Oxford, UK: Oxford University Press, 1998.
Schorsch, Ismar. "Judaism and Linear History." JTS, Jan. 22, 1994. http://www.jtsa.edu/judaism-and-linear-history.
Sefaria. "Talmud: Babylonian." Sefaria, 3rd–8th c. https://www.sefaria.org/texts/Talmud.
Shamash, Susan. "Hope in Troubled Times." Lecture at Vancouver School of Theology, Vancouver, Can., Feb. 24, 2015.
Von Rad, Gerhard. *The Message of the Prophets*. Translated by D. M. G. Stalker. New York: Oliver and Boyd, 1965.
Waskow, Arthur O. *Seasons of Our Joy: A New-Age Guide to the Jewish Holidays; A Celebration of Modern Jewish Renewal*. Boston: Beacon, 1982.
Yerushalmi, Yosef Hayim. *Zachor: Jewish History and Jewish Memory*. Seattle: University of Washington Press, 1996.
Zakheim, Dov S. *Nehemiah: Statesman and Sage*. Jerusalem: Maggid, 2016. Kindle.

"Here at the End of All Things"
The Poetry of Lament as Expression of the End

Patricia Dutcher-Walls

The title of this chapter comes from the climactic scene of the third *Lord of the Rings* film, as Frodo and Samwise crawl to an outcrop of rock while Mt. Doom explodes all around them. In exhaustion and grief in the face of both the destruction of the ring and their apparent imminent deaths, Frodo comforts the weeping Samwise with the words, "I'm glad to be with you, Samwise Gamgee, here at the end of all things."[1]

It is a quote that the persona of Daughter Zion in Lam 1 might understand, except that she would add that there is no one to comfort her as the end comes upon her.

> For these things I weep, my eyes flow with tears,
> for a comforter is far from me, one to revive my courage;
> my children are desolate, for the enemy has prevailed.
> (Lam 1:16 NRSV)

In this essay I explore briefly the image of the end of Jerusalem/Daughter Zion as a thematic source for end-times imagery that emerged in apocalyptic literature of Judaism. My method here will use a historical framework for placing the imagery of the end of the city within the literature of the intertestamental and early rabbinic periods. I am not prepared to make any claims of use of Lamentations as a direct source for later apocalyptic literature as a whole, although I will explore one more direct relationship.

1. Jackson, "Return of the King."

I merely suggest intertextual connections between poetic description in Lamentations about the end of Jerusalem during the Babylonian conquest and the end as envisioned in later apocalyptic thought.

The definition of apocalypse that I will be using places my exploration within ongoing scholarship on the genre. I draw largely on the work of John J. Collins, eminent biblical scholar who has published extensively in the field. Early on in the emerging study of apocalyptic literature, Collins suggested a definition of apocalypse that has remained useful for identifying the common elements of the genre, even as many scholars note the wide-ranging variety of elements within such literature in the several centuries on either side of the beginning of the Common Era. Collins proposed this definition:

> A common core of constant elements permits us, then, to formulate a comprehensive definition of the genre: "Apocalypse" is a genre of revelatory literature with a narrative framework, in which a revelation is mediated by an otherworldly being to a human recipient, disclosing a transcendent reality which is both temporal, insofar as it envisages eschatological salvation, and spatial insofar as it involves another, supernatural world.[2]

Collins also distinguishes several subtypes within the genre: for example, apocalypses that focus on an otherworldly journey are distinguished from those that contain a historical review as a prelude to the eschatological vision; ones that feature cosmic and political eschatology are differentiated from those that contain speculation about personal outcomes.[3]

LAMENTATIONS: SOME PRELIMINARY MATTERS

I read the book of Lamentations as an extended picture of the destruction of Jerusalem by the Babylonian Empire in 586 BCE, the precipitating event that lies behind the poetry of the book. In five poems that were probably originally independent, imagery and language convey the emotional impact of the events of siege, destruction, and exile on the people themselves. The terms of outright suffering are intense and repeated.

A brief review of the work of biblical scholars in treating critical issues about Lamentations highlights the following:

- The deep imagery of the book finds echoes in two genres of ancient poetry. First, the lament form, found often in the Psalms, gives

---

2. Collins, "Introduction," 9.
3. Collins, "Introduction," 13.

expression to the grievances and emotions of personal or community suffering, anger at God for allowing such suffering to happen, pleas for help and intervention by God, and imprecations against enemies. A second form is the *qinah* (dirge), a poem created for the public mourning of the death of an individual. Between a lament that seeks redress and restoration for a situation of suffering and a *qinah* that expresses grief and mourning at a death, the five poems of lament in the book find their poetic roots.[4]

- The phrase "daughter Zion" may be terminology that evoked protective care for a beloved city; the term may have been used as a term of tenderness when mourning the death of the city.[5]
- In the honor and shame cultures of the ancient world, a political defeat was understood as deep shame that brought on intense mocking by political enemies, which is a source for the language of mocking and shame in the poems.
- The representation of a city as a woman whose "lovers" have abused and abandoned her rests on a politically astute wordplay. In the international treaties of the ancient world, the political and economic loyalty of a vassal toward an empire was described as "love" for the overlord; that is, to maintain political loyalty between treaty partners was to "love" the state's overlord or allies. Historically, Judah's political allies proved incapable of helping resist the Babylonian empire—Judah's "lovers" had betrayed and abandoned the besieged state.
- This same understanding of covenant loyalty that expressed the theological relationship between God and God's people helps to comprehend the theology of punishment that underlies the poetry. Judah's rebellion against God's ways—its obstinate refusal to keep loyalty—was a breaking of its covenant with God. Its punishment was harsh confirmation that God was still concerned with the fate of Israel.[6]

For the purposes of space, I can highlight only a few of the intense laments of Daughter Zion and her narrator in Lam 1 (NRSV):

> [1] How lonely sits the city that once was full of people!
> How like a widow she has become, she that was great among
> the nations!

---

4. Berlin, *Lamentations*, 23–24.
5. Berlin, *Lamentations*, 12.
6. Berlin, *Lamentations*, 18.

She that was a princess among the provinces has become
    a vassal.
² She weeps bitterly in the night, with tears on her cheeks;
she has no one to comfort her; among all her lovers
all her friends have dealt treacherously with her, they have
    become her enemies.
³ Judah has gone into exile with suffering and hard servitude;
she lives now among the nations, and finds no resting-place;
her pursuers have all overtaken her in the midst of her distress.

⁷ Jerusalem remembers, in the days of her affliction and
    wandering,
all the precious things that were hers in days of old.
When her people fell into the hand of the foe, and there was
    no one to help her,
the foe looked on mocking over her downfall.

¹⁰ Enemies have stretched out their hands over all her precious
    things;
she has even seen the nations invade her sanctuary,
those whom you forbade to enter your congregation.
¹¹ All her people groan as they search for bread;
they trade their treasures for food to revive their strength.
Look, O Lord, and see how despised I have become.
¹² Is it nothing to you, all you who pass by? Look and see
if there is any sorrow like my sorrow, which was brought was
    brought upon me,
which the Lord inflicted on the day of his fierce anger.

¹⁵ The Lord has rejected all my warriors in the midst of me;
he proclaimed a time against me to crush my young men;
the Lord has trodden as in a wine press youthful daughter
    Judah.
¹⁶ For these things I weep; my eyes flow with tears;
for a comforter is far from me, one to revive my courage;
my children are desolate, for the enemy has prevailed.

²⁰ See, O Lord, how distressed I am; my stomach churns,
my heart turns within me, because I have been very obstinate.
In the street the sword bereaves; in the house it is like death.
²¹ They heard how I was groaning, with no one to comfort me.
All my enemies heard of my trouble; they are glad that you
    have done it.
Bring on the day you have announced, and let them be as I am.

²² Let all their evildoing come before you; and deal with them
as you have dealt with me because of all my rebellions;
for my groans are many and my heart is faint.

INDIRECT RELATIONSHIPS BETWEEN LAMENTATIONS AND APOCALYPSE-LIKE THINKING

When we consider the relationship of the poetry of Lamentations to the genre of apocalypse-like thinking, I want to be very careful. I am not asserting any linear relationship between them, yet I want to propose that the book of Lamentations, especially chapter 1, and the crisis behind the book, provide both indirect relationships to and, at least in one case, a direct source for apocalypse-like thinking. I will note several indirect aspects of the relationship before exploring one direct intertextual connection.

The first point of relationship is the indirect impact of the event to which Lamentations refers—the destruction of Jerusalem and its attendant virtually complete disruption of the institutions and assumptions of Judahite life. In the quoted verses of Lam 1, we of course have a description of an end fully accomplished—Jerusalem is destroyed and is at the end of all its known realities. The conquest and destruction of Jerusalem proved to its inhabitants and the people of Judah as a whole that "the end of all things" could in fact happen and had happened. Social world studies of ancient Israel remind us that the "end" may have been more final for the elite sectors of society that lived in Jerusalem itself and who were killed or deported. The peasants were left on the land by the Babylonian conquerors to continue producing the economic surplus that an empire always expects from conquered territories (2 Kgs 25:8–12). But for those killed in the siege and destruction of the city, and for those deported into exile, the end had happened. Daughter Zion laments the end of her existence in deep bitterness and isolation. To say that the realization of an *actual* "end of all things" in the destruction of Jerusalem lies behind the inception of apocalypse-like thinking might seem a tautology but worth asserting, nonetheless.

This leads to a second point of indirect relationship between Lamentations and apocalypse-like thinking. Collins notes about the apocalyptic texts he studied: "All the texts considered . . . can be said to have been written for a group in crisis, if only because the entire Jewish people can be said to have been in crisis for most of the period in question."[7] The initial and perhaps single most disruptive crisis in the history that lies behind the

---

7. Collins, "From Prophecy to Apocalypticism," 158.

rise of what we are calling apocalypse-like thinking was the destruction of the capital city, sanctuary, and dynasty of the state of Judah. The ongoing impacts of that traumatic "end" resonate through the experiences of later oppressive regimes, political disorder, imperial hegemonies, and other crisis situations. Collins continues, "All the apocalypses we have considered . . . are born out of a sense that the world is out of joint. The visionaries look to another world, either in the heavens or in the eschatological future, because this world is unsatisfactory. . . . Typically, the appeal for divine intervention is necessitated because the world is believed to be in the grip of hostile powers."[8] To use the language of post-traumatic stress disorder, the destruction of Jerusalem in 586 BCE provided the initial trauma, which is then triggered by all the later traumas.[9]

In making the case for one further point of indirect relationship, I recognize a different attitude to historical events between Lamentations and apocalyptic literature. In Lam 1, the time horizon is still that of normal time; a "day" or "time" has arrived, and another day of vengeance is looked for. These days are of the same type as the days of judgment promised in prophets such as Amos—the day of the Lord, which is darkness and not light (Amos 5:18–20). So, this is a historical "end" that has arrived. This sense of time and history is distinct from the sense of the end of history or eras beyond history characteristic of apocalypses. Collins notes one common element of apocalypses as *"eschatological upheavals* which disturb the order of nature or history."[10] In the revelations contained in such literature, ordinary history may end in an apocalyptic crisis. "The temporal axis of the revelation provides a context in which the transcendent eschatological salvation is seen to contrast sharply with previous history and the afflictions of the eschatological crisis."[11]

However, Lamentations is not in itself a historical genre. The first chapter of Lamentations most probably emerged within a generation of the actual historical situation of the destruction of Jerusalem, and the intense grief and lament that followed are expressed in the genre of poetry. Poetry already creates a distance between the event and the literary vehicle of that poetic form. The language and imagery of poetry are artistic expressions, not historical genres. Berlin notes, "Metaphor and simile are hallmarks of poetry . . . there is widespread acknowledgement that metaphor abounds in the Bible's poetic

8. Collins, "From Prophecy to Apocalypticism," 159.

9. A full exploration of a collective identity of trauma would be useful here, though outside the focus of this essay. I would refer interest in this topic to Alexander, "Toward a Theory."

10. Collins, "Introduction," 7 (emphasis original).

11. Collins, "Introduction," 12.

discourse."[12] Trauma studies may again prove helpful for the analysis of the poetry of a book like Lamentations. Specifically in response to trauma, symbolization is seen as part of the psychological responses that may help the survivors respond to what happened.[13]

The move to poetic expression in response to trauma and crisis in a chapter like Lam 1 can be seen to parallel the intense use of figurative language in apocalypses. The characteristics of the genre outlined by Collins include much about otherworldly realities in both time and space,[14] perforce needing figurative language, including such forms as "visions, auditions, otherworldly journeys."[15] Whatever specific historical references may be behind Lam 1 that get expressed in poetry, for apocalypses, any historical specificity is further lost or even concealed in the apocalyptic genre. By the allegorization and symbolization inherent in the genre, the historical is deliberately lifted into either a nonspecific and thereby more generalized contextualization or is lifted onto a transcendent realm. There may be various reasons for the veiling of historical reality, specific referents and events, and the tradents who created the highly symbolic language. Collins notes, "In all the Jewish apocalypses the situation of the historical author is to some degree concealed."[16] What I am noting here is the use of evocative, poetic language and highly figurative speech in both the initial poetic responses to the "end of all things" when Jerusalem was destroyed and what emerges in apocalypse-like expressions.

A DIRECT LINK? LAMENTATIONS 1 AND 4 EZRA

To these indirect connections of later apocalyptic to the trauma of the destruction of Jerusalem, however veiled, I would like to add one possibly more specific tie between the descriptions of the suffering of Daughter Zion in Lam 1 and a particular apocalyptic book. The book I will focus on is 4 Ezra. Most scholars consider this book a Jewish response to the second destruction of Jerusalem in 70 CE, written probably in the last decade of the first century. It is now located as the middle section of 2 Esdras, which has given it a Christian framework, but 4 Ezra is a Jewish work. Its extant form is in Latin, but most scholars assume there was a Greek version and

---

12. Berlin, "Introduction to Hebrew Poetry," 311.
13. O'Connor, "How Trauma Studies," 2:213–19.
14. Collins, "Introduction," 6–8.
15. Collins, "Introduction," 11.
16. Collins, "Apocalyptic Technique," 99.

perhaps an original Hebrew version. "*4 Ezra* narrates Ezra's dialogues with the angel Uriel, his reception of various apocalyptic visions, and his activity in rewriting the twenty-four books of the Hebrew Scriptures along with seventy secret, apocalyptic books."[17]

Four Ezra consists of seven episodes of a conversation between Ezra and Uriel. The first three explore the questions of theodicy in response to the destruction of Jerusalem, and in the last four visions, Uriel attempts to provide answers to Ezra's challenges of God's justice.

> The author answers the problem of . . . the apparent lack of God's faithfulness to his election and covenant with Israel by affirming a future reversal where Israel's oppressors will be destroyed and God's Messiah will restore Israel. He responds to the problem of God's apparent injustice in the damnation of many and the salvation of only a few by reemphasizing the possibility of obedience to the law for salvation and the revelation that the "Few" were actually a great multitude, and by Ezra's example of restoring and proclaiming the law in episode 7.[18]

My interest for this chapter is episode 4, in which Uriel reveals a vision to Ezra of a woman lamenting bitterly for the death of her son. Ezra tries without success to console her. In the vision, she is transformed into a beautiful city. Uriel interprets the vision for Ezra.

> In Uriel's interpretation, the woman's . . . bearing of a son represents Solomon's building of the city and offering of sacrifices; her bringing up her son with much care represents the period of residence in Jerusalem; and the son's death represents the destruction of Jerusalem. . . . Finally, the transformation of the woman represents the reality and existence of God's own city, the true, imperishable, heavenly Zion.[19]

In episode 4, the woman explains her lament and bitterness, and then Ezra attempts to distract her from her own sufferings by recounting his understanding of the destruction of the city of Jerusalem. He describes in some detail the sufferings of that time. In the context of the book's response to the second destruction of Jerusalem, this description would apparently be a description of the historical event that preceded the book by about thirty years. However, what I would like to highlight here are the parallels

---

17. Stewart, "Narrative World, Rhetorical Logic," 374.
18. Stewart, "Narrative World, Rhetorical Logic," 388.
19. Stewart, "Narrative World, Rhetorical Logic," 384.

between the description of the destruction of the city in 4 Ezra and the destruction of the city in Lamentations 1.

While I cannot trace the parallels in specific vocabulary because one text exists in Hebrew and the other in Latin, the parallels in the imagery and language in describing the impact of the destruction of the city on Daughter Zion in Lam 1 and the bereaved woman in Ezra 4 are remarkable. I highlight four types of parallels between the texts in the following tables.

1. Language about the impact of the city's destruction on Daughter Zion and the woman

Lam 1	2 Esd 9:38–42, 10:19–24
[2] She weeps bitterly in the night, with tears on her cheeks [8] she herself groans, and turns her face away	[9:38] she was mourning and weeping with a loud voice, and was deeply grieved at heart
[16] For these things I weep; my eyes flow with tears [21] They heard how I was groaning, with no one to comfort me [22] for my groans are many and my heart is faint	[9:41] I may weep for myself and continue to mourn, for I am greatly embittered in spirit and deeply distressed

One interesting parallel reflected in this first table is the use of voices to describe the suffering and destruction experienced by Daughter Zion in Lam 1 and the woman in 2 Esdras. Lamentations 1 uses both the voice of the narrator and that of Daughter Zion to convey the utter hopelessness of the situation from two complementary perspectives. Even though Ezra does not know it while the vision is occurring, the bereaved woman's lament is almost inarticulate about how much she has suffered. Later in the recounting of the vision, Ezra takes the part of the narrative voice that accurately describes the city's suffering. This means in both accounts of the trauma of the city, both the city/woman itself and the narrator's voice can accurately describe the suffering of the conquest and destruction.

2. The impact on Jerusalem politically and internationally during and after the destruction

Lam 1	2 Esd 9:38–42, 10:1–24
[3] Judah has gone into exile with suffering and hard servitude	[20] how many are the adversities of Zion?
[7] in the days of her affliction and wandering	[7] For Zion, the mother of us all, is in deep grief and great distress.
[9] her downfall was appalling, with none to comfort her	
[12] Look and see if there is any sorrow like my sorrow	[20] the sorrow of Jerusalem
[2] all her friends have dealt treacherously with her, they have become her enemies	[23] and given over into the hands of those that hate us
[3] she lives now among the nations, and finds no resting-place	
[4] all her gates are desolate	
[5] Her foes have become the masters, her enemies prosper	
[7] when her people fell into the hand of the foe, and there was no one to help her	
[14] the Lord handed me over to those whom I cannot withstand	
[6] From daughter Zion has departed all her majesty	[23] the seal of Zion has been deprived of its glory

It is clear in this second table that Lam 1 expresses more clearly and deliberately the status of Jerusalem among the other states threatened by the Babylonian Empire at the time of the conquest of the city. Expected aid from Judah's treaty partners did not materialize; her "lovers" abandoned her. As well, Lam 1 laments more deliberately the conquest by hated foreigners. In Lamentations, the fluidity of identity between the city and Daughter Zion continues in these impacts.

3. The impact on the temple/sanctuary/festivals

Lam 1	2 Esd 9:38–42, 10:1–24
¹⁰ she has even seen the nations invade her sanctuary	²¹ our sanctuary has been laid waste, our altar thrown down, our temple destroyed
⁴ The roads to Zion mourn, for no one comes to the festivals	²² our harp has been laid low, our song has been silenced, our rejoicing has been ended, the light of our lampstand has been put out
¹⁰ Enemies have stretched out their hands over all her precious things	²² the ark of our covenant has been plundered
¹⁰ those [enemies/nations] whom you forbade to enter your congregation	²² our holy things have been polluted
¹⁷ Jerusalem has become a shunned woman [alt., "a filthy thing"] among them	²² the name by which we are called has been almost profaned

It is noteworthy that the cultural language of honor and shame (pollution, profanation) clusters around the impacts on the temple, with its festivals and artifacts. As the temple was the center of the ancient theological and cultural system of honor and shame, this is not surprising.

4. The impact on populations within the city

Lam 1	2 Esd 9:38–42, 10:1–24
¹⁶ my children are desolate, for the enemy has prevailed	²² our children have suffered abuse
⁴ her priests groan ¹⁹ my priests and elders perished in the city	²² our priests have been burned to death, our Levites have gone into exile
⁴ her young girls grieve, and her lot is bitter ¹⁵ the Lord has trodden as in a wine press youthful daughter Judah	²² our virgins have been defiled and our wives have been ravished

Lam 1	2 Esd 9:38–42, 10:1–24
[6] Her princes have become like stags that find no pasture; they fled without strength before the pursuer	[22] our righteous men have been carried off
[5] her children have gone away, captives before the foe	[22] our little ones have been cast out
[15] he proclaimed a time to crush my young men	[22] our young men have been enslaved
[18] my young women and young men have gone into captivity	
[15] The Lord has rejected all my warriors in the midst of me	[22] our strong men made powerless

The one-to-one correspondences in the lists of the population groups who have been disastrously impacted by the city's conquest, destruction, and trauma are clear.

CONCLUSIONS

Of course, the destruction of a city in the ancient world no matter the time period presents similarities in effect and affect, so the description in 4 Ezra may have only coincidental parallels to Lamentations. However, given the extensive parallels between the two descriptions, categories of impacts, and imagery, I think the possibility exists that the authors of 4 Ezra used Lam 1 as a source for the portrayal of the city's destruction. The event of 586 BCE had been repeated in 70 CE—the portrayal in Lam 1 very probably served at least as a model for the description voiced by Ezra, if not a direct source.

If this is the case, then I have described two points of connection between Lamentations and apocalypse-like thinking. First, I explored the possibility that the event behind Lamentations was a general historical parallel for the suffering, the "end," that contributes to the creation of the apocalypse-like thinking. Beyond that, I noted the use of evocative, expressive language and highly figurative speech in both the initial poetic responses to "the end of all things" when Jerusalem was destroyed and in what emerges in apocalypse-like expression. Without proposing more than an indirect relationship here, it is evident that in response to crisis, trauma, and disaster, the move to expression in poetry and symbolic language bears observation. Second, a close examination of the parallels in language and imagery in Lam 1 and in the visionary description of the destruction of Jerusalem in 2 Esd 9–10 establishes the possibility of a more direct connection. This suggests an afterlife for the sorrowful poetry of Daughter Zion. The lament and devastation of Daughter Zion survived to be told another day, once again describing "the end of all things" that had come upon the people.

BIBLIOGRAPHY

Alexander, Jeffrey C. "Toward a Theory of Cultural Trauma." In *Cultural Trauma and Collective Identity*, edited by Jeffrey C. Alexander et al., 1–30. Berkeley: University of California Press, 2004.

Berlin, Adele. "Introduction to Hebrew Poetry." In *The New Interpreter's Bible*, 4:301–315. Nashville: Abingdon, 1996.

———. *Lamentations: A Commentary*. OTL. Louisville, KY: Westminster John Knox, 2002.

Collins, John J. "The Apocalyptic Technique: Setting and Function in the Book of Watchers." *CBQ* 44 (1982) 91–111.

———. "From Prophecy to Apocalypticism: The Expectation of the End." In *The Encyclopedia of Apocalypticism*, 1:129–61. New York: Continuum, 2000.

———. "Introduction: Towards the Morphology of a Genre." *Semeia* 14 (1979) 1–20.

Jackson, Peter, dir. *The Return of the King*. Burbank, CA: New Line, 2003.

O'Connor, Kathleen M. "How Trauma Studies Can Contribute to Old Testament Studies." In *Trauma and Traumatization in Individual and Collective Dimensions*, edited by Eve-Marie Becker et al., 2:210–22. Göttingen, Germ.: Vandenhoeck & Ruprecht, 2014.

Stewart, Alexander E. "Narrative World, Rhetorical Logic, and the Voice of the Author in 4 Ezra." *JBL* 132 (2013) 373–91.

The Prophecy of Neferty

Recounting National Trauma as Apocalyptic Synthesis

David A. Falk

Even though apocalyptic was not formally recognized as a genre until the Christian era, scholarly consensus today agrees that the earliest form of apocalyptic literature dates to the postexilic period.[1] Yet, when the genre form was fleshed out, John J. Collins observed that apocalyptic was "not a purely modern form."[2] C. C. McCown in 1925 recognized that ancient Egypt had its own form of apocalyptic literature and *ex eventu* prophecy.[3] This chapter will focus on the *Prophecy of Neferty* as an example of Egyptian apocalyptic literature and discuss the prophetic aspects of the text and its relationship to Egyptian society.

As we discuss the use of apocalyptic literature, we should introduce the concept of *reception history*. Reception history is the history of meanings that have been ascribed to historical events. It is the attempt of people to make sense of events as they unfold as well as people in the present looking back and giving meaning to those events. As we look at one particular piece of apocalyptic literature, the *Prophecy of Neferty*, we are going to see one set of events interpreted according to an *ex eventu* prophecy; that prophecy later become disassociated from its original events; and then the apocalyptic prophecy was reused and recontextualized, not once but twice, to different sets of circumstances.

---

1. Himmelfarb, *Apocalypse*, 3.
2. Collins, "Apocalyptic Genre," 84.
3. McCown, "Hebrew and Egyptian Apocalyptic," 368–69 and 381–82.

While Levantine cultures had a strong religious tradition of foretelling the future with omens, portents, and prophets, ancient Egyptian culture differed markedly in this regard. Much of this can be attributed to the concept of Maat, which is best described as "order" and is one of the organizing principles of Egyptian society.[4] The king was seen as a divine figure who maintained the order of the world on behalf of the gods, so when society was operating as it should everything was supposed to remain the same. Even though individuals kept personal family histories to establish claims to titles or property (e.g., the tomb of Mes),[5] the Egyptians generally did not maintain long narratives recording sequences of events. Typically, the reception history that expressed the Egyptian ideal was that everything is working as it should with nothing ever changing.

With that in mind, Egyptian society did not have a strong tradition of prophecy as a means to predict the future. The common person believed in prophetic portents in dreams for one's personal life, e.g., *Papyrus Chester Beatty 3* (BM 10638) "dream book"; however, the direction of larger historic movements was believed to be within the control of the king who had dominion over the cosmic order. As such, predicting change may have been subversive because of its potential to undermine the king as maintainer of cosmic order. Hence, conspicuously absent from Egyptian literature is the genre of prophetic literature or even omen texts like one would find in Akkadian literature, which is why the prophetic texts of the Middle Kingdom (including the *Prophecy of Neferty*) provide for us an interesting exception.

The *Prophecy of Neferty* was an early second-millennium BCE text written as political propaganda recounting events that took place in the late third millennium retrojected to the court of King Sneferu (ca. 2613–2589 BCE). The text was written during the reign of Amenemhat I (ca. 2029–2000 BCE), first king of Dynasty 12, and predates the book of Daniel by at least 1400 to 1800 years. Yet, this text takes on a role in Egyptian history that is more than just political propaganda; over the centuries, the prophecy transforms into a kind of apocalyptic.

At the end of Dynasty 11, King Mentuhotep IV (ca. 2036–2039 BCE) was unable to rule, possibly from some form of incapacity. His vizier Amenemhat ruled in place of Mentuhotep IV, declared a renaissance, and upon Mentuhotep's death usurped the throne. But because Amenemhat was not from the royal family, his reign had to be legitimized by extraordinary means. One way to legitimize his reign was to show that his rule

---

4. Bárta, "Ancient Egyptian History," 2.
5. Kitchen, *Historical and Biographical*, 425.

was prophetically predicted, and therefore his rule was preordained by fate (XIIIa–b)[6] and divinely sanctioned.[7]

Consistent with the definition of apocalyptic literature defined by the SBL Genre Project, the *Prophecy of Neferty* is "revelatory literature with a narrative framework" that is mediated by a human recipient, "disclosing a transcendent reality" and envisaging "eschatological salvation" while involving the world of the supernatural.[8] The narrative of the *Prophecy of Neferty* begins in the court of Sneferu, who wanted to be entertained by an accomplished man who could relieve his boredom with eloquent words. Sneferu's nobles present before the King Neferty, who was a lector priest who had impressive skills and was wise and wealthier than his peers (a sign of good character). And Neferty asked the king if he wanted to hear "concerning what has happened [or] concerning what is to happen" (IIm). The king replied that he wanted to hear the future, for "today has already happened and it is gone" (IIn). As Neferty begins, the king pulls out writing materials to take notes, thus showing the king as a literate and wise ruler not desiring to miss a single excellent word. Neferty then foretells the misery that was supposedly to beset Egypt during the First Intermediate Period (ca. 2185–2069 BCE), which took place prior to the accession of the Middle Kingdom monarchs Mentuhotep IV and Amenemhat I.

The First Intermediate Period is often perceived as a time of decline and turmoil in Egypt. It was a time of civil war, when the traditional ruling house of Egypt (Herakleopolitans) warred against the princes of Thebes. Contrast this situation to the Old Kingdom, when many smaller catastrophes beset the period towards its end; however, these smaller traumas did not spell an immediate fall for the monarchy. The Old Kingdom was a time of climate change when the Neolithic Wet Period ended, causing the savannah of the Sahara to disappear and the Nile River to experience low water levels. Foreigners from the Sahara and the Sinai were forced to settle in the Nile Delta in search of food, putting pressure on the local population to compete over scarce hunting and fishing resources as the agricultural crops failed. The climate situation precipitated an economic crisis that caused the patronage system and, in turn, the centralized government to collapse.[9] The combination of these factors disturbed the delicate balance of Egypt's religious system and stratified social order.

6. Line numbers are cited from the critical edition of the text published by Helck, *Prophezeiung des Nfr.tj*.
7. Callender, "Middle Kingdom Renaissance," 146.
8. Collins, "Introduction," 9.
9. Malek, "Old Kingdom," 107.

The author of the *Prophecy of Neferty* took the pessimism of national trauma from the end of the Old Kingdom and First Intermediate Period and aggregated them to carve out a perceived dark age to contrast the utopian thinking established by the apparatus of Middle Kingdom bureaucracy.[10] The prophecy foretold the destruction of the Egyptian world of the Old Kingdom and unveiled the inauguration of a new world where Maat would be restored. The prophecy was written in poetic form using symbolism, couplets, compressed language, amphiboly, and contextualization. The apocalypse starts and ends with an arch describing the moral catastrophes that predicated physical catastrophes and then "predicts" its consummation through the coming of Ameny, a king from the south who would unite the two lands (XIIIa).

The first depiction we see in the prophecy is a call to mourning (IIIf). The text states that lying would become ubiquitous and that evil would be spoken without consequence. Nobles would no longer rule the land, and the social order would be reversed. In a stratified society like ancient Egypt, the upheaval of the social strata had consequences that extended beyond the transcendence of class structures. The moral decay led to no one caring for the land, which caused the land to languish and perish, resulting in famine. But this was only the beginning of woes.

After this, the sun disk would be obscured and men would not be given its light to see (Vc). The word for sun in this instance is *itn*, which during the Amarna period will be worshiped in the pantheism of Akhenaten. Storm clouds would hover over the land, and the people would fall into despair at the absence of the sun. Neferty at this point stressed that he was prophesying that which would take place: "I will say what is before my face. I am not foretelling what has not come" (Vf). Neferty is saying that none of these prophecies are conditional and they cannot be avoided; everything will come to pass as he said. Like other apocalyptic literature, Neferty assumed that the future can be unveiled only by those who have the divine power to see it.[11]

The text then predicts that the Nile River would dry up and that the waters of Egypt could be crossed on foot (VIa). This event is described in Egypt as "the meeting of the two banks";[12] it is symbolic of drought and the arrest of decay. However, a low Nile also meant famine, as agricultural production was dependent upon high water levels. Egypt was primarily a river nation, so a low Nile had further consequences beyond famine. And

---

10. Kemp, *Ancient Egypt*, 243–44.
11. Ortlund, "Review of *Polemical Preacher*," 104.
12. CT 168, in De Buck and Gardiner, *Egyptian Coffin Texts*, 3:28a–c.

as the primary mode of transportation was by boat, drought could cripple the infrastructure of the country. The wheel would not arrive in Egypt until the Second Intermediate Period, so without the river the transport of goods was limited.

At the same time, the South wind would *ḥsf*—"battle against"—the North wind (VIe). There are two winds that are recognized in Egypt: a hot, dry wind from the South and a humid, cooling wind from the Mediterranean in the North. These winds were believed to carry with them sand, locusts, and birds, and in this text they also represent Egyptian factional infighting. With the powers of Egypt clashing, confused, and no one dominating, foreign birds would infiltrate into the Delta region (VIf).[13]

Earlier we discussed how the end of the Neolithic Wet Period forced nomadic peoples to settle in the Delta where there were fish and fowl. However, these natural resources were also used by the Egyptians during times of drought when agricultural production failed. The allusion to foreign birds was a metaphor for Asiatic and Libyan foreigners who created tension over the allocation and distribution of natural resources.

Those tensions had important implications because these foreigners had not yet assumed any sort of dominance. The text says that the entry of these foreigners drove the *rmṯ*—"the (native) people"—out for *g3w*, "lack/defect" (VIg). It is interesting to note that *g3w* is a term that is an amphiboly meaning both "lack" of resources and "defect" in the moral sense,[14] so that the meaning here could be taken to be either that of "the people were driven out for lack (of resources)" or "the people were chased out by defect (of their own moral character)." The text further describes foreigners entering the border forts while guards slept and overpowering the drowsy watchmen (VIIe-i), which adds credence to a dual reading of *g3w*. The text is not describing a literal sudden takeover by the Asiatics but reflects a slow infiltration of foreigners taking over abandoned fortifications.

However, the Asiatics did not have political control over Lower Egypt at any time before the writing of the prophecy, so *Neferty* may reflect local growing concerns that were retrojected to have existed at the end of the third millennium.[15] While the evidence suggests that both Libyan and Semitic tribesmen had entered into Egypt by the time of the First Intermediate Period, the text is particularly focused upon the incursion of the Asiatics and their negative impact. They were said to have their way with the land and that their herds, "goats of a foreign land will drink from the rivers of Egypt" (VIIIa), because no one would be willing to stop them (VIIIb-c).

---

13. Cf. Rev 18:2–3.
14. *Wb* 5:152; Faulkner, *Concise Dictionary*, 287–88.
15. Redford, *Egypt, Canaan, and Israel*, 68.

Following this, lines VIIId-IXf describe the moral state of Egypt, unveiling the undercurrents of Egyptian society. Men would arm themselves with weapons of war (VIIIf). They sought blood as food (IXa), laughing "gleefully over suffering" (XIb), a couplet poetically amplifying the sense of cruelty. There would be an attitude of selfishness "caring only for himself" (IXc) as well as callousness: "A man rests to his side and turns his back while one man kills another" (IXe). There would even be upheaval in the structure of the family, where a brother becomes the enemy and a son kills his father.

In the next ten lines, *Neferty* gives us examples where the social order is reversed and the land itself suffers because the land is not spared from the apocalyptic events. The nobleman loses his wealth, while the foreigner becomes prosperous (Xe). The land becomes "desolate," while too many rulers are in charge. The weak becomes mighty. The lowly becomes exalted. The follower becomes a freeman. People live in tombs. Paupers gain wealth. Beggars eat bread. Slaves are exalted. The land is "ruined," but taxation is equally "immense." Grain becomes a precious commodity, and yet it is being distributed as if there were no tomorrow. The inference is that the grain is not being devoted towards offerings to the gods, which in the eyes of pious Egyptians should be the priority, and therefore the sun god Re abandons mankind. The sun itself goes into hiding, and the whole land becomes plunged into darkness (XId-f). No one can tell what time of day it is, no one can see their shadow, and Re will only appear muted in the sky like the moon (XIg).[16]

Yet, the reality of the First Intermediate Period seems to differ from the image portrayed in the literature of the Middle Kingdom. John Gee argues that far from being a time of collapse, the period was one of unprecedented wealth, personal piety, and charity as a noble ideal.[17] Gee suggests that writings like the *Prophecy of Neferty*, *Admonitions of Ipuwer*, and the *Instruction of Merikare* are the results of our efforts "to read our own day into the past."[18] While it is certainly arguable whether those national traumas may have occurred during the First Intermediate Period, it is inarguable that these traumas did not occur during the Middle Kingdom when these texts were composed. Apocalyptic as justification of the status quo could certainly explain the origin of some portion of these texts, but for these texts to resonate they must tap into some angst, which is a form of collective aggregate trauma.

As collective farming reached into the former hunting grounds of the Fayum, some must have noticed that game, fowl, and fish were no longer as

---

16. Compare with Isa 13:10, Joel 2:10, Matt 24:29, Mark 13:24, Rev 8:12.
17. Gee, "Did Old Kingdom Collapse," 72.
18. Gee, "Did Old Kingdom Collapse," 64.

plentiful as they had been. Some must have noticed that the old regime was unable to maintain its hold upon the institutions of Egypt. And the times when drought had struck the Nile during the end of the Old Kingdom must have resulted in tens of thousands of lives being lost; few families would have escaped the consequences of living on knife-edge agriculture. Far from simply being our own day retrojected into the past, this form of apocalyptic took real events from Egypt's past and extrapolated upon them in order to establish new relationships with the reader.

For the new rulers of Dynasty 12, that new relationship was to portray Amenemhat's dynasty as the defender of Maat from the chaos of what came before. And like most apocalyptic, *Neferty* not only predicted the destruction of the old world order but pointed to a king who would come in order to save Egypt. In typical ancient Near Eastern style, that king was said to be the slayer of Asiatics, Libyans, and rebels. He will be assisted by the uraeus on his brow—the belief that the king was assisted by the cobra goddess to drive out impurity before him. He would build a fortress, Inbu-Heqa, on the eastern frontier to stop the inflow of foreigners, and drive those that remain to begging for water. With the new king, order and Maat would be restored and chaos driven off. The name of this king just happens to be "Ameny" (XIIIa), an abbreviation of Amenemhat I.[19]

However, the texts do not limit the reader to a strictly propagandist reading. The use of the future unfulfilled prophetic in this apocalyptic is meant to lead the reader but does not limit the reader, and likewise the reader is not misreading the author by ascribing a futurist intent. Rather, the writer plays with amphiboly, intentionally leading the reader to recontextualize the future as a means to recount.

However, the history of the text is more complicated than both its origins and recounting of national trauma. There are twenty-two fragments of the prophecy that are extant today.[20] The corpus dates to the New Kingdom. Eighteen copies were ostraca, one copy was a papyrus, and two copies were student writing tablets. The texts date between early Dynasty 18 and the Ramesside Period. The corpus is large enough to apply a lower text critical approach that implies the existence of an urtext.[21] The earliest extant copy (*Papyrus Petersburg 1116*) shows textual variants that have diverged from the Ramesside Ostraca. However, it is equally important to note that the variants are limited to updates in grammar and orthography, while the content of the text was not altered in a way that significantly changed its meaning. Thus, there is no indication that later religious or cultural concerns were written back into the text through any sort of redaction process.

19. Leprohon, *Great Name*, 60.
20. Helck, *Prophezeiung des Nfr.tj*, 1–2.
21. Helck, *Prophezeiung des Nfr.tj*, 59–60.

In fact, the final line of *Neferty* reads, "It was with diligence that this speech was copied," which is a scribal note, or perhaps even a scribal reminder, indicating that accurately copying the text without significant alteration was an important part of the text's tradition. Moreover, this implies that most of the surviving ostraca fragments were reader copies as opposed to documents written for scribes. Literacy was perhaps more common across the strata of Egyptian society than it was in other Levantine cultures.

Another implication is that there may have been renewed interest in *Neferty* following the reign of the Hyksos. During the Second Intermediate Period (ca. 1666–1550 BCE) and long after Dynasty 12, the Hyksos, a group of Asiatic Semites, ruled the delta region of Egypt. Unlike the Asiatic incursions of the First Intermediate Period where these ethnic groups had no real power, the Hyksos assumed their rule of Avaris when the Theban rule from Iti-Tawy collapsed. During their hundred-year rule, the Hyksos stripped the country of resources growing rich from trade with the Mediterranean. They desecrated native Egyptian tombs and monuments. And as the Hyksos lost their grip and their reign became increasingly repressive, they lived down to the meanest reputation of the foreigner.

The irony is that by the beginning of Dynasty 18, four hundred years after the text was written, the *Prophecy of Neferty* was no longer connected with Amenemhat I but with Ahmose (a king from the southern Theban 17th Dynasty) who was now seen as the liberator and unifier of Egypt. As a device for the recounting of national trauma, *Neferty* was no longer prophecy *ex eventu* but prophecy consummated. With new divine mandate, the kings of the New Kingdom enslaved[22] and brutally repressed the Asiatic populations of the Delta, just as Amenemhat I had done.[23] The kings of Dynasties 18 and 19 built fortresses along the eastern frontier of Egypt, along the northern coast of the Sinai, and elevated Egypt into a power that would dominate the region for three hundred years. In light of the national trauma of Hyksos oppression, the Egyptians of early Dynasty 18 had recontextualized *Neferty*.

However, many of the reader copies date to the Ramesside period, which was two hundred fifty years after the events of Ahmose and the Hyksos. During the reign of Amenhotep III, the Asiatic population seems to have had a reprieve from general persecution and could even hold high office; e.g., Aperel became vizier under Amenhotep III and Akhenaten,[24]

---

22. Biography of General Ahmose son of Ibana, line 14, in Sethe, *Urkunden des 18. Dynastie*, 4.10–13.

23. Callender "Middle Kingdom Renaissance," 147.

24. Zivie, *Lost Tombs of Saqqara*, 133–37.

and Yanammu became a high state official under Akhenaten.[25] Akhenaten transformed Egyptian religion into a view that was essentially a monolatrous pantheism,[26] while Semitic populations brought with them henotheism as part of a Western Semitic tradition.[27]

After the Amarna Period, the Egyptians exercised *damnatio memoriae* desecration targeted against Asiatics.[28] Images of Asiatics at Akhet-Aten had been hacked out, while similar images of Nubians beside the desecrated images were left unharmed. This desecration would have taken place between the abandonment of Akhet-Aten by Tutankhamun in his third regnal year (ca. 1332 BCE) and the destruction of monuments of Aten by Seti I (ca. 1303 BCE).[29] After the remonstrance of Tutankhamun, non-polyteist worldviews and cultures became lumped together with Akhenaten's heresy. This led to the rise of post-Amarna tensions against Asiatics; it is possible that the Egyptians had a subsequent conflict with the resident Semitic population in Egypt, which prompted a second Ramesside recontextualization of *Neferty* that dates to the mid-thirteenth century BCE.

In conclusion, the *Prophecy of Neferty* exhibits not only the characteristics of apocalyptic literature that texts a thousand years later would also exhibit but reveals some insight into how apocalyptic develops. Through *Neferty*, we can gain insight into how one text developed from aggregated national trauma that had been extrapolated and retrojected for an idealistic purpose to becoming recontextualized by readers in new contexts. Apocalyptic then as a genre cannot be restricted to merely a historicist or preterist reading. Instead, it is a genre pregnant with amphiboly where reader and text constantly form new relationships, the intent of which is to recount by gleaning new insights from the ancient words. It seems that for the author of the *Prophecy of Neferty*, the best way to remember the past was to look to the future.

BIBLIOGRAPHY

Aldred, Cyril. *Akhenaten and Nefertiti*. London: Thames & Hudson, 1973.
Assmann, Jan. *From Akhenaten to Moses: Ancient Egypt and Religious Change*. New York: American University in Cairo, 2014.

25. Redford, "Egypt and Asia," 43.
26. Assmann, *From Akhenaten to Moses*, 13.
27. *P. Sallier I*, 1,2–1,3, in Gardiner, *Late-Egyptian Stories*, 85:8–10. Gunn and Gardiner, "New Renderings," 40.
28. Aldred, *Akhenaten and Nefertiti*, 202.
29. Dodson, *Amarna Sunset*, 135–37.

Bárta, Miroslav. "Ancient Egyptian History as an Example of Punctuated Equilibrium: An Outline." In *Towards a New History for the Egyptian Old Kingdom: Perspectives on the Pyramid Age*, edited by Peter Der Manuelian and Thomas Schneider, Harvard Egyptological Studies 1, 1–17. Boston: Brill, 2015.

Callender, Gae. "The Middle Kingdom Renaissance (c. 2055–1650 BC)." In *The Oxford History of Ancient Egypt*, edited by Ian Shaw, new ed., 137–71. New York: Oxford University Press, 2003.

Collins, John J. "Apocalyptic Genre and Mythic Allusions in Daniel." *JSTOR* 21 (1981) 83–100.

———. "Introduction: Towards the Morphology of a Genre." *Semeia* 14 (1979) 1–20.

De Buck, Adriaan, and Alan H. Gardiner. *The Egyptian Coffin Texts*. 7 vols. Chicago: University of Chicago Press, 1935–1961.

Dodson, Aidan. *Amarna Sunset: Nefertiti, Tutankhamun, Ay, Horemheb, and the Egyptian Counter-Reformation*. New York: American University in Cairo Press, 2009.

Enmarch, Roland. *The Dialogue of Ipuwer and the Lord of All*. Oxford, UK: Griffith Institute, 2005.

Erman, Adolf, and Hermann Grapow. *Wörterbuch der aegyptischen Sprach*. 5 vols. Berlin: Akademie-Verlag, 1971.

Faulkner, Raymond O. *A Concise Dictionary of Middle Egyptian*. Oxford, UK: Griffith Institute, 1962.

Gardiner, Alan H. *Late-Egyptian Stories*. Brussels: Fondation Égyptologique, 1973.

Gee, John. "Did the Old Kingdom Collapse? A New View of the First Intermediate Period." In *Towards a New History for the Egyptian Old Kingdom: Perspectives on the Pyramid Age*, edited by Peter Der Manuelian and Thomas Schneider, Harvard Egyptological Studies, 60–75. Boston: Brill, 2015.

Gunn, Battiscombe, and Alan H. Gardiner. "New Renderings of Egyptian Texts: II. The Expulsion of the Hyksos." *Journal of Egyptian Archaeology* 5 (1918) 36–56.

Helck, Wolfgang. *Die Prophezeiung des Nfr.tj*. Wiesbaden, Germ.: Harrassowitz, 1970.

Himmelfarb, Martha. *The Apocalypse: A Brief History*. West Sussex, UK: Wiley-Blackwell, 2010.

Kemp, Barry J. *Ancient Egypt: Anatomy of a Civilization*. 2nd ed. NY: Routledge, 2006.

Kitchen, Kenneth A. *Historical and Biographical*. Vol. 3 of *Ramesside Inscriptions*. Oxford, UK: Blackwell, 1980.

Leprohon, Ronald J. *The Great Name: Ancient Egyptian Royal Titulary*. Atlanta: SBL, 2013.

Malek, Jaromir. "The Old Kingdom (c. 2686–2160 BC)." In *The Oxford History of Ancient Egypt*, edited by Ian Shaw, new ed., 83–107. New York: Oxford University, 2003.

McCown, C. C. "Hebrew and Egyptian Apocalyptic Literature." *Harvard Theological Review* 18 (1925) 351–411.

Ortlund, Eric. "Review of *A Polemical Preacher of Joy: An Anti-Apocalyptic Genre for Qoheleth's Message of Joy*, by Jerome N. Douglas." *Themelios* 40 (2015) 103–4.

Redford, Donald B. "Egypt and Asia." In *Ancient Egypt*, edited by David P. Silverman, 42–43. New York: Oxford University Press, 1997.

———. *Egypt, Canaan, and Israel in Ancient Times*. Princeton, NJ: Princeton University Press, 1992.

Sethe, Kurt. *Urkunden der 18. Dynastie* 1. Leipzig: Hinrichs'sche, 1906.

Zivie, Alain. *Lost Tombs of Saqqara*. Cairo: American University of Cairo Press, 2007.

Why the Book of Revelation Matters

Harry O. Maier

A TALE OF TWO ENDINGS

THE TWENTIETH-CENTURY GERMAN NEW Testament scholar Ernst Käsemann once said that apocalyptic is the mother of theology.[1] What he meant is that the Christian religion the New Testament helped to create was in part a response to the non-return of Jesus and the result of a need to wrestle with the meaning of the life, death, and resurrection of Jesus in the world in expectation of his advent or the disappointment of his delayed second coming. It is arguable that there are no theologians in heaven (or certainly more of them in hell!). The reason is that with the beatific vision, the time for theologizing passes away to give way to praise and worship and communion with the divine. The need to give reason for the hope that lies within us is no longer there, as the need for interpretation passes when we no longer see in a glass dimly, but see face to face (1 Cor 13:12). All is a new creation; the old things have passed and the new have arrived (2 Cor 5:17). Hence, for Käsemann, theology arises as a consequence of time and is something the people of God do in the meantime as they seek to understand the faith with which they hope for the reconciliation of all things.

This chapter considers the way one form of New Testament apocalyptic, namely that found in the book of Revelation, has resulted in particular ways that Christians have thought about time and space and social identity. Revelation was written in a particular time and place for a specific audience, but once it became canonized and read alongside other biblical texts from both the First and Second Testaments, it took on a life that extended beyond

---

1. Käsemann, "Beginning of Christian Theology," 40.

its original historical intentions. This chapter charts two ways that the book of Revelation has moved beyond its original context to influence conceptions of history; two ways, taking up Käsemann, that theology has been made in the meantime and the places we are to inhabit while we await history's completion. One, which I will call the gradualist account, uses the Apocalypse to dream of a millennium in which humans and God cooperate with each other and orchestrate a shared solution to the world's problems and establish a utopia. The other, which I call the revolutionary account, finds in Revelation a picture of a dramatic divine intervention in history that solves humanity's problems by sweeping away an old order in order to inaugurate a new one.[2] Both these modes—the gradualist and the revolutionary—use the Apocalypse to establish a grand historical narrative; both dream of a new heaven and a new earth but envision their arrival in dramatically different ways. I propose that classical liberal Christian theology is especially fond of the gradualist account, and that American Fundamentalism and some forms of Evangelicalism represented specifically by premillennial dispensational Christianity (let me stress, I do *not* mean Evangelicalism in general, which is a socially diverse and complex social phenomenon, with varieties of eschatological beliefs) has come to champion the revolutionary one.[3]

I will argue that both these uses of Revelation to understand history are flawed—sometimes tragically—and share the same basic problem that makes them strange bedfellows: namely, they suffer from the error and perhaps even idolatry of trying to predict the future and, as a consequence, betray what is the content of a this-worldly Christian incarnational faith. It is an incarnational reading of the book of Revelation that I will propose at

---

2. The gradualist account often goes by the name of progressive millennialism or postmillennialism and is based on Rev 20:4–6 (see below), citing two victories of Christ over evil and two reigns (Rev 19:11—20:6; 20:7–10), the first for the eponymous thousand years. The revolutionary account, often named premillennialism or catastrophic millennialism, advances the idea that an inevitable descent of humankind into evil will be interrupted only by Christ's return after which Christ alone will install the millennium. For discussion, see Ashcraft, "Progressive Millennialism," and Gallagher, "Catastrophic Millennialism."

3. The term *dispensational premillennialism* refers to a belief that history is divided up into a series of seven outpourings or dispensations of the Holy Spirit and that the church is presently living at the end of the fifth dispensation, namely on the eve of the sixth dispensation, a seven-year period called "the great tribulation" when an evil figure (the antichrist) will persecute the church and whose reign will end upon Jesus's return to inaugurate the millennium of Rev 20:4–6. It is *pre*millennial because it occurs *before* the thousand-year reign. The logical relation of dispensational premillennialism to Evangelicalism is that all dispensationalists are Evangelicals but not all Evangelicals are dispensationalists. Those Evangelicals who are not dispensationalists do not read Revelation as the timetable of an imminent future.

the end of this chapter in a partially polemical aim of disputing the spiritualization of Christian faith found in both the liberal and Fundamentalist modes. Both the gradualist and the revolutionary reading of Revelation are steeped in narrative, and so is mine. I look to Revelation for a different kind of story: one that does not look for grand blueprints for making history, but rather finds in it a call to costly witness and testimony and to engage in revelatory speech amidst the small lived stories of believers in practices of daily life. I write of Christians here. I do not address myself to other faith traditions and their uses of apocalyptic, which are specific to their own ways of thinking about the world and space and time. In other words, I am addressing a kind of family feud.

USING REVELATION TO READ HISTORY: THE GRADUALIST ACCOUNT

In its earliest version, the gradualist account of history was the result of the confluence of three things: the incorporation of the book of Acts and the book of Revelation in the New Testament canon, the expansion of Christianity through the Roman Empire, and Constantine's endorsement of the church as a legitimate imperial institution. In the book of Acts, we see an explosive expansion of Christianity wherever the apostles travel. The narrative ends with Paul in Rome under house arrest, awaiting trial before the emperor to whom he will preach the gospel. It is an optimistic narrative, which is signaled by the fact that there is no report of Paul's martyrdom, which the author of Acts would have believed happened shortly after his imprisonment.

The other narrative, the one found in Revelation, at first seems not gradualist in its orientation because it envisions an end to a persecuting empire through the return of Jesus. But in Rev 20:4–6 (RSV), it envisions a thousand-year reign of Christ:

> Then I saw thrones, and those seated on them were given authority to judge. I also saw the souls of those who had been beheaded for their testimony to Jesus and for the word of God. They had not worshiped the beast or its image and had not received its mark on their foreheads or their hands. They came to life and reigned with Christ a thousand years. (The rest of the dead did not come to life until the thousand years were ended.) This is the first resurrection. Blessed and holy are those who share in the first resurrection. Over these the second death has no power, but they will be priests of God and of Christ, and they will reign with him a thousand years.

When these words were incorporated into a New Testament canon alongside the book of Acts, the thousand-year reign of Christ was interpreted by some to mean that Christians were to help to establish the historical conditions for the return of Jesus. In the fourth century, the church historian Eusebius (283–339 CE), who witnessed the rise of Constantine (306–337 CE) and the empire-wide endorsement of Christianity, interpreted the emperor's reign as the inauguration of a Christian millennium or new age. This idea of an earthly millennium achieved through political means was a powerful way of conceiving the union of church and state to create a more blessed and just union of ecclesial and political power.[4]

For our purposes here, we pick up the story 1300 years later, in the sixteenth and seventeenth centuries, when Puritans fled religious persecution in England and settled in new American colonies, bringing with them a similar gradualist narrative. Arriving on a new continent with unending natural abundance, they believed that they had been providentially appointed to create a theocratic society and government to create the historical conditions for Christ's millennial reign.[5] In the eighteenth century, the first evangelical awakening wedded conversion with notions about God blessing Protestant America to create a belief in the United States as a redeemer nation.[6] In due course, this theocratic vision was transformed into a secular idea of American manifest destiny where, again, it was believed that a historical process of divine design had established the United States to realize a utopian global order of democracy with America at the helm.[7]

Nineteenth-century American Christians, buoyed by technological progress and a second wave of evangelical revival, interpreted the book of Revelation's promised millennium as the product of cooperation between God and humans.[8] Optimism about such cooperation and progress helped to shape the early social gospel movement, which understood the historical role of the church as advocating for the poor in order to create social institutions and laws that would reflect Christ's spiritual reign on earth.[9] The United Church of Canada, to name but one Canadian Christian institution affected by this movement, at its inception was caught up in this form of optimism. Its activist role in politics and in the post-World War

---

4. For further discussion, see Markus, *End of Ancient Christianity*.
5. For an account, see Stoll, *Protestantism, Capitalism, Nature*.
6. Tuveson, *Redeemer Nation*.
7. Bloch, *Visionary Republic*.
8. For discussion, see Moorhead, "Between Progress and Apocalypse."
9. For discussion of the link, especially in the nineteenth-century, early period of the social gospel, see Evans, *Social Gospel*, 21–47.

II period continued the nineteenth-century gradualist historical narrative further through its support of social democratic ideals and policies.[10] The United Church, as well as Canada's other mainstream churches (Anglican, Presbyterian, and Roman Catholic), are complex institutions with their own histories. Nevertheless, one may generalize that at least one strand of the governing ideology of the Canadian Protestant tradition can be traced to nineteenth-century liberal theology optimism about human enlightenment, civilization, and human progress.

The genetic trace of this optimism continues in new models of evolutionary and progressive Christianity and idealistic forms of spirituality that celebrate human potential and God's spirit animating humanity's better achievements. Albeit not at first glance but nevertheless visible upon close scrutiny, one encounters in these progressive models the book of Revelation's effects. The gradualist interpretation of Revelation morphs into the idea that we are becoming Christ or realizing christic consciousness by degrees through a slow evolutionary process of societal and individual improvement as well as intentional cooperation with evolutionary becoming.[11] It is sobering in the light of this to consider how blind we can be to history and the potential for destruction that lies in our ideals. For example, it was the same postmillennialist vision that motivated the entire residential school movement, by a group of people who were no less convinced that they were helping to further a Christ-directed movement of history.[12]

USING REVELATION TO READ HISTORY: THE REVOLUTIONARY ACCOUNT

The revolutionary application of the book of Revelation is the one we are most familiar with today, thanks to its wide distribution in American

10. For an account of the historical roots of the United Church of Canada, its relation at its foundation to currents of the North American social gospel, its historical relation to currents of North American liberal theology, and its relationship with the government to promote certain kinds of institutions, see Airhart, *Church with the Soul*.

11. For representative, popular accounts, see Sanguin, *Darwin, Divinity, and Dance*; Fox, *Coming of Cosmic Christ*, for evolution, 253n1; Pannikar represents a more academic approach, for which see *Christophany*, 143–90. None of these authors relate their thinking to the book of Revelation or postmillennial currents of thought, but I would argue that from a historical and cultural perspective it is implicit.

12. For the residential school system (in Canadam a joint venture between the government of Canada and Anglicans, Roman Catholics, Presbyterians, and the United Church of Canada), the churches' relation to the social gospel movement parallels with the residential school model in the United States and with international analogues in the nineteenth and twentieth centuries. See Truth and Reconciliation Commission of Canada, *History, Part 1*, 133–48.

culture.[13] Here, history is not the gradual achievement of a set of social goods and utopia, but rather is the arena for a divine disruption of the world. This model, too, had its proponents in the early church. Early Christian chiliasm (named after the Greek word for thousand, *chilia*) expected a violent overthrow of the civil order with the return of Jesus and his thousand-year reign. Here it is not the millennial reign of Rev 20:4–6 but Rev 19:11–16 that the revolutionary reading of Revelation focuses upon:

> Then I saw heaven opened, and there was a white horse! Its rider is called Faithful and True, and in righteousness he judges and makes war. His eyes are like a flame of fire, and on his head are many diadems; and he has a name inscribed that no one knows but himself. He is clothed in a robe dipped in blood, and his name is called The Word of God. And the armies of heaven, wearing fine linen, white and pure, were following him on white horses. From his mouth comes a sharp sword with which to strike down the nations, and he will rule them with a rod of iron; he will tread the wine press of the fury of the wrath of God the Almighty. On his robe and on his thigh, he has a name inscribed, "King of kings and Lord of lords."

Use of Revelation to predict a violent overthrow of the social order has recurred repeatedly within Western history. It, too, has its secular models found in the Fascist idea of the need violently to overthrow the racially impure who govern history or the Marxist Maoist idea of a violent end of capitalism.[14] *Premillennialism* is the term used to describe this model, because it sees history not getting gradually better but spiraling downward and believes that God alone, not humans, can bring about the utopian millennium. In politics, the form of millennium on offer comes about through a radical intervention that disrupts the slide toward destruction. Thus, in the premillennialist model of the book of Revelation, a world careening on a road of greater chaos can be set right only by a divine wresting of the historical wheel from human hands to set things straight.

In the later nineteenth century, a large number of churches embraced the premillennialist model. and it became the dominant model in some parts of Protestantism, thanks to a massive mailing of tracts to churches in the

---

13. See O'Leary, *Arguing the Apocalypse*, 134–71, for an account of the emergence and wide distribution of this point of view in popular American Christianity.

14. For millennialism and National Socialism, see Redles, "National Socialist Millennialism"; for Marxism, see Lowe, "Chinese Millennial Movements." Boer, *Criticism of Earth*, discusses Marx's and Engel's respective treatments of the book of Revelation and argues for their critical assessment of it.

early years of the last century.[15] Some strange allegiances have resulted. In the 1980s, American premillennialists made a Faustian bargain with political conservatism in the belief that by the spread of American democracy and capitalism throughout the world and the defeat of Communism, the church could securely preach the gospel in order to bring Christ to all nations, which would then trigger the second coming.[16] There are many forms of premillennialism. A more radical form of this movement, the dominionist movement, to which Sarah Palin and Ted Cruz have close ties, believes that God has established America to be the place where God has prepared the elect to oppose a coming evil world order.[17] This extraordinarily pessimistic view of history revels in conspiracy theory and sees the devil under every stone even as it engages in shrewd calculation to use the devil to outsmart him.

Many people will be familiar with a less radical form of premillennialism that has entered mainstream popular culture through the influence of a best-selling novel by Tim LaHaye and Jerry B. Jenkins entitled *Left Behind: A Novel of the Last Days*.[18] *Left Behind* is the first of a twelve-volume series that offers a fictionalized account of the end of the world loosely based on the book of Revelation. Its main title, *Left Behind*, refers to the premillennialist belief in the "rapture": the conviction that, at the time of a coming great tribulation when the beast or antichrist will rule the world and persecute the church, God will transport true believers into heaven and thus save them from inevitable calamity.[19] With eighty million sales, LaHaye and Jenkins have made a personal fortune from their series. Its success has spawned a variety of religious films based on the novels, as well as the 2014 secular film *Left Behind*, starring Nicholas Cage, and HBO TV series *The Leftovers* (2014–17).

---

15. For an account of its genesis, cultural influence, and means of distribution, see Boyer, *When Time Shall Be*.

16. O'Leary, *Arguing the Apocalypse*, offers a general overview of millennial rhetoric in American conservative Christianity. For America's temporary role to assist in God's plans for global evangelism before the second coming, see Pat Robertson (candidate for the presidency in 1988), *New World Order*, in which he claimed his bid for power was a means for God to install a Christian leader to make American strong as part of God's premillennial plan for missionaries to evangelize the world. For analysis of the cognitive dissonance of this trend with further literature, see Wilcox et al., "Reluctant Warriors."

17. Barron, *Heaven on Earth*, offers an excellent account. For Sarah Palin, Ted Cruz, and dominionist theology, see Carlson, "Dominionism Rising."

18. For a general orientation, including critical reception, a list of the books of the series, and the dates of the publication, see "*Left Behind* Wiki."

19. For the origins, popularity, and critical review of this belief, see Rossing, *Rapture Exposed*.

These are bold narratives. Probably most mainstream Christian readers of this chapter can recognize themselves in varying degrees in the postmillennial script, and find the premillennial in varying degree odd, dangerous, and/or entertaining. It is worth remembering that another set of readers would find the opposite to be true, namely that the postmillennial model is fraught with error and threatens Christian faith.

AN INVITATION TO INCARNATIONAL HISTORY

What if we turned to Revelation not for a blueprint of history—neither the evolutionary progressive Christianity account nor the revolutionary pessimistic one—but for a different "picture of the end time"? There would be no bold claims about whether history is on a divinely appointed incline upward or a devilishly inspired one downward, but rather an assertion about identity in the midst of time. In other words, we would not stand outside of time to predict a big story about history's ultimate outcome; rather we would immerse ourselves within time and live faithfully a smaller story with the moments that we are given in our short span of years. This alternative way of reading Revelation offers a fully incarnational model of Christian faith. It does not ask what Revelation can tell us about "time" in the absolute sense but what it reveals—unveils, as the Greek term *apocalypsis* means—about the meantime, the daily, the lived, and the experienced. It makes the claim that it is here, right now, where God belongs and lives and calls us to faithfulness.

On this account, we look to the characters of the book of Revelation for our guidance, that is, the creatures who inhabit the world of Revelation's text. Foremost amongst these, as we all know, are martyrs. In popular usage, the term *martyr* is a word that describes suffering or dying for what one believes in. But the term in Greek means "to witness" (*martyrein*). Revelation is filled with characters who witness (Rev 1:2,9; 2:13; 6:9; 11:3, 7; 12:1, 17; 17:6; 19:10; 20:4; 22:16; 22:18; 22:20), that is, who give full-throated voice, most usually in hymns and praise to *the* witness, Jesus of Nazareth (Rev 1:5; 3:14), who testified to God even before his executioners. In fact, the book of Revelation is far less interested in ultimate blueprints for history than it is in faithful witness. Its overall apocalyptic narrative is designed in the first place to convince its listeners of the need and demand for faithful witness. When we ask "What is it they are to witness to, and what are they to talk about?," the answer for its audience of Christ followers is the slain Lamb of God (Rev 5:6, 12; 7:14), even the Lamb of God slain since the foundation of the world (Rev 13:8; 2:16; 19:15, 21). This is not a macabre fascination with death, but rather a revelation of God as one whose almightiness is known not in a divine wielding of omnipotent domination over time and space, but rather in self-sacrificing and self-emptying love for creation. The crucified Jesus, symbolically represented as the slain Lamb, is *the* faithful witness in Revelation (1:4; 3:14; 19:11). In the book of Revelation, when God slays—*the only time God slays*—is by the sword of truth that comes out of Jesus's mouth (Rev 1:16; 2:12; 19:15, 21). The most violent text of the New Testament is in fact one that is paradoxically couched in nonviolence, namely in Jesus's faithful testimony before evil. It wagers that the mightiest thing is not the sword or even the pen, but rather potent speech in faithfulness to God.

In Rev 19:10, first John learns from his angelic interpreter that Jesus is the witness (*martyr*), and then he receives instruction about prophetic testimony, a testimony he shares with Jesus: "I am a fellow servant with you and your comrades who hold the testimony of Jesus (*tēn matyrian Iēsou*) . . . . The testimony (*martyria*) of Jesus Christ is the spirit of prophecy" (Rev 19:10). The verse is both provocative and syntactically interesting. It is provocative because it replaces a big story of historical prophecy of the outcome of time and space with prophetic speech that is testimonial. And it is syntactically interesting because of the possibilities of meaning of the possessive noun "of Jesus." The possessive here can mean bearing testimony/witness to/about Jesus, sharing his testimony by way of imitation (presumably referring to Jesus's testimony in his trial—John 18:33–38; in Mark 15:1–5; Matt 27:11–14; Luke 23:1–12 he remains silent before Pilate), or a testimony that comes from him; or it can be purposely ambiguous to imply all these possibilities. In each case, it is a call to a kind of speech and life that are in solidarity with Jesus in his life, death, and resurrection. Whatever the arc of history may turn out to be, it is this prophetic witness in the historical conditions that we find at the heart of faithful Christian life.

To live out this faithful witness is world ending in the sense that it calls into question every form of distortion that destroys creation and keeps us from being fully human. It confesses that the one who is coming to judge the living and the dead comes in every act of faithful witness and speech as a coming of life and death, the presence of God, in world-ending and world-making discipleship. Here in this model, there is no spiritualization of the Christian message, whether it take the form of a secularization of the gospel that would convert potent religious speech into social justice slogans or notions of progressive theology or evolutionary notions in which biblical speech becomes a metaphorical expression of wishful thinking. Nor is it a spiritualization of the gospel that imagines this world as little more than an antechamber to eternity or, worse, a manipulative means to realize a predetermined end of a nationalistic history. No. Such a costly testimony, just like the people of Israel and God's self-revelation in Jesus of Nazareth, meets

God in the here and now, under the conditions of history whatever they may be, in the particularity of everyday life.

Neither postmillennial, gradualist idealism nor premillennial, revolutionary pessimism is the reason why Revelation matters. After the bloodiest century in history brought about in part by the colonialist enterprises of the modern period, enterprises that—albeit in a different form—continue to bathe the world in blood, it is important to be cautious about historical stories that confidently anticipate big endings. The Apocalypse's importance lies elsewhere. As a Christian who longs to sing the song of the Lamb (Rev 5:9–10), I believe incarnational life in imitation of God's self-emptying is the apocalyptic form of living this present moment calls us to, and there is not a second a waste. I long to hear this hallelujah in my church, to give voice with my brothers and sisters in the hymn before the throne, in a song that has no end.

BIBLIOGRAPHY

Airhart, Phyllis D. *The Church with the Soul of a Nation: Making and Remaking the United Church of Canada*. Montreal: McGill-Queen's University Press, 2014.

Ashcraft, W. Michael. "Progressive Millennialism." In *The Oxford Handbook of Millennialism*, edited by Catherine Wessinger, 44–65. Oxford, UK: Oxford University Press, 2011.

Barron, Bruce A. *Heaven on Earth? The Social and Political Agendas of Dominion Theology*. Grand Rapids: Zondervan, 1992.

Bloch, Ruth H. *Visionary Republic: Millennial Themes in American Thought, 1756–1800*. Cambridge: Cambridge University Press, 1985.

Boer, Roland. *Criticism of Earth: On Marx, Engels and Theology*. Historical Materialism Book 35. Leiden: Brill, 2012.

Boyer, Paul. *When Time Shall Be No More: Prophecy Belief in Modern American Culture*. Cambridge, MA: Belknap, 1992.

Carlson, Frederick. "Dominionism Rising: A Theocratic Movement Hiding in Plain Sight." Political Research, Aug. 18, 2016. www.politicalresearch.org/2016/08/18/dominionism-rising-a-theocratic-movement-hiding-in-plain-sight.

Evans, Christopher H. *The Social Gospel in American Religion: A History*. New York: New York University Press, 2017.

Fox, Matthew. *The Coming of the Cosmic Christ*. San Francisco: HarperOne, 1988.

Gallagher, Eugene V. "Catastrophic Millennialism." In *The Oxford Handbook of Millennialism*, edited by Catherine Wessinger, 27–43. Oxford, UK: Oxford University Press, 2011.

Käsemann, Ernst. "The Beginning of Christian Theology." *Journal for Theology and Church* 6 (1969) 17–46.

"*Left Behind* Wiki." https://leftbehind.fandom.com/wiki/Left_Behind_(series).

Lowe, Scott. "Chinese Millennial Movements." In *The Oxford Handbook of Millennialism*, edited by Catherine Wessinger, 307–25. Oxford, UK: Oxford University Press, 2011.

Markus, R. A. *The End of Ancient Christianity*. Cambridge: Cambridge University Press, 1990.

Moorhead, James H. "Between Progress and Apocalypse: A Reassessment of Millennialism in American Religious Through, 1800–1880." *Journal of American History* 71 (1984) 524–42.

O'Leary, Stephen. *Arguing the Apocalypse: A Theory of Millennial Rhetoric*. Oxford, UK: Oxford University Press, 1994.

Pannikar, Raimon. *Christophany: The Fullness of Man*. New York: Orbis, 2004.

Redles, David. "National Socialist Millennialism." In *The Oxford Handbook of Millennialism*, edited by Catherine Wessinger, 529–48. Oxford, UK: Oxford University Press, 2011.

Robertson, Pat. *The New World Order*. Dallas: Word, 1991.

Rossing, Barbara R. *The Rapture Exposed: The Message of Hope in the Book of Revelation*. Oxford, UK: Westview, 2004.

Sanguin, Bruce. *Darwin, Divinity, and the Dance of the Cosmos: An Ecological Christianity*. Kelowna, Can.: Coppershouse, 2007.

Stoll, M. *Protestantism, Capitalism, and Nature in America*. Albuquerque: University of New Mexico Press, 1997.

Truth and Reconciliation Commission of Canada. *The History, Part 1: Origins to 1939; The Final Report of the Truth and Reconciliation Commission of Canada*. Vol. 1 of *Canada's Residential Schools*. Montreal: McGill-Queen's University Press, 2015.

Tuveson, E. I. *Redeemer Nation: The Idea of America's Millennial Role*. Chicago: University of Chicago Press, 1968.

Wilcox, C., et al. "Reluctant Warriors: Premillennialism and Politics in the Moral Majority." *Journal for the Scientific Study of Religion* 30 (1991) 245–58.

Parody, Burlesque, and Identity in the Apocalypse of John

Emily Jarrett

INTRODUCTION

IN THE BOOK OF Revelation, author John of Patmos uses parody and burlesque to help define Christian identity in opposition to empire. John contrasts the grotesque and the holy, and places a boundary between them. Here, I examine how the images of the dragon and the whore of Babylon function as parodies of the Roman Empire. These contrast with the images of the lion/lamb and the temple, which, though ironic, serve to amplify, not parody, God's sovereignty. Finally, I suggest John uses this contrast to take a position on an ongoing dispute within the early Christian community regarding Christian identity and appropriate public behavior, particularly as it relates to engagement with the Roman imperial cult.[1]

I propose that the parody found in the book of Revelation is more precisely a form of burlesque. Specifically, it is a travesty in which John satirises Rome and the imperial cult through the use of the vulgar. In contrast, John uses elevated language and reverent imagery to describe the "faithful" and the heavens. While he still amplifies these through parody, he does not undermine them with the use of the vulgar. Through this contrast, John also exaggerates both the spiritual and spatial boundaries between these opposing forces, thereby reinforcing his own claims regarding Christian identity and behavioral participation in the larger society.

1. Friesen, "Satan's Throne"; Campbell, *Reading Revelation*, 281–83.

BURLESQUE AS A SUBGENRE OF PARODY

In his book *Apocalypse Recalled*, Harry O. Maier considers Revelation's rhetorical uses of irony and argues that the work is a sustained parody of imperial power.[2] Here, I expand this view by considering Revelation as an example of burlesque. Burlesque is a subgenre of parody. Parody in general relies on irony, i.e., expressing meaning by using language that normally means the opposite. Burlesque focuses on the inversion of high culture and low culture. Through this kind of mockery, burlesque seeks to undermine the authority of higher classes, unmasking the authority as a self-interested fiction created by the powerful. Burlesque draws on established language and mores, but situates them in inappropriate contexts. Through these humorous counterscripts,[3] it offers a transgressive critique of the powerful. It leaves the subject of its critique recognizable but twists it so that it is seen as unworthy of respect. This subject is usually a cultural norm, public behaviors, or social institutions, not a specific individual.[4]

Burlesque pits dominant values against the values of the performers in a combative encounter. In one variation, often called "travesty," it juxtaposes the absurd, grotesque, or vulgar with dignified subject matter. In another, it absurdly amplifies and reveres the pathetic. Modern burlesque, for example, cleverly reconstructs the object of the male gaze as the subject of female and/or queer sexual agency.[5] Because burlesque has its historical roots in Greek theatre, even its literary form creates a visceral, visual spectacle whose humor relies on audience investment and participation.[6]

SPECTACLE IN ROMAN CULTURE

In Revelation, John invokes the Roman concept of the "spectacle." John draws on the spectacles of the Roman imperial cult, which showcased grand arts and liturgies.[7] Yet he draws more heavily on the Roman gladiatorial spectacle, which formed one of the centerpieces of city-culture. This spectacle of physical combat pitted the "heroes," usually Roman or Roman-looking gladiators, against foes pulled from the reaches of the Roman

---

2. Maier, *Apocalypse Recalled*, 164–97.
3. Hirst, "Diverse Voices."
4. Attordo, *Encyclopedia of Humor Studies*, 95.
5. Domino, "Burlesque, Parody, Idiocy, Zaniness," 3.
6. Domino, "Burlesque, Parody, Idiocy, Zaniness," 97–98.
7. An example is found in the art of the temples, wherein statues representing the conquered are depicted as women in varying states of undress, based on the level of cultural assimilation into the Roman Empire. See Grant, *Art in Roman Empire*.

Empire. According to Christopher A. Frilingos, in using the Roman spectacle as a template, John "permitted its audience to do what Mediterranean populations under the empire had already been trained to do: gaze on a threatening 'Other.'"[8] Partly, the popularity of the spectacle depends on a cultural distrust of the visual. On the one hand, the viewing of strange sights is enthralling. On the other hand, it leads to ambivalence. The strangeness of the sights calls their reality into question, and therefore they become objects of distrust.[9] In this way, fear of the other was an important aspect of the spectacles. The more monstrous the other, the greater the cultural anxiety. Thus, the spectacles showed the grotesque other subdued by Rome, through either a fighter's victory in the Coloseum or a visual representation of gods-supported victory in the temples.[10] These spectacles involved visual participation in public acts by people across the social and economic classes. Thus, John's writing makes strong use of public spaces, such as streets, temples, arenas, and the open spaces at city gates.[11]

THE DRAGON AND THE MARK OF THE BEAST

In Revelation, this other appears as grotesque, strange creatures that function as caricatures of the emperor and the Roman Empire.[12] This suggests that the grotesque, rather than the holy, is worshipped and revered.

> Then another portent appeared in heaven: a great red dragon, with seven heads and ten horns, and seven diadems on his heads. His tail swept down a third of the stars of heaven and threw them to the earth. Then the dragon stood before the woman who was about to bear a child, so that he might devour her child as soon as it was born. (Rev 12:3–4 NRSV)

The dragon is a parody. It stands in for imperial power, rendering Rome into the very otherness that it fears and seeks to conquer. The appropriate response to the grotesque or monstrous other is fear, uncertainty, and a desire to conquer and tame it. In Roman imperial expansion, the intent was to take the other and make it Roman, not to empower it by allowing it

---

8. Frilingos, *Spectacles of Empire*, 1.

9. Frilingos, *Spectacles of Empire*, 52. Frilingos also discusses how Roman and Greek writers specifically argued against too much visual stimulation, because the ease of visual deception leads not only to a distrust of the visual but also a distrust of the other senses and, ultimately, ambivalence about reality.

10. Frilingos, *Spectacles of Empire*, 45.

11. Frilingos, *Spectacles of Empire*, 46.

12. Frilingos, *Spectacles of Empire*, 9.

to remain on its own terms. But, ironically, despite clearly being monstrous, the dragon is not feared. Rather, it is trusted, worshipped, and revered. The mark of the beast, a perversion of the seal of God, marks allegiance to an inappropriate source of authority.[13] The mark enables the denizens of this vision's Babylon to engage in material culture and economic activity. Despite the monstrous nature of the beast, it is seductive. It draws people to give into its demands through the illusion of peace and prosperity, which is juxtaposed against the beastly desire to kill and consume.

THE WHORE OF BABYLON

> I saw a woman sitting on a scarlet beast that was full of blasphemous names, and it had seven heads and ten horns. The woman was clothed in purple and scarlet, and adorned with gold and jewels and pearls, holding in her hand a golden cup full of abominations and the impurities of her fornication; and on her forehead was written a name, a mystery: "Babylon the great, mother of whores and of earth's abominations." And I saw that the woman was drunk with the blood of the saints and the blood of the witnesses to Jesus. (Rev 17:3b–6 NRSV)

The whore is meant to be looked at and to be seen. The spectacle of her entrance evokes the spectacles of the Roman Empire. Yet she is not a stand in for the nature of spectacle. Rather, she is an allegory for the city of Rome itself and the perceived behaviors of those within. Babylon's fall is attributed both to fornication and to merchants growing wealthy from her. This associates the economic values of the Roman Empire with lascivious sexual deviancy.[14] At a distance, the whore appears as an elegant woman.[15] Yet, on closer sight, she is revealed in all her vulgar forms, combining the violence of the blood and the monstrosity she rides with her clear sexual deviancy. This makes the whore an example of classic burlesque travesty. The satire relies on the visual reinforcement of the behaviors and morals that are represented: extravagance, wealth, power, idolatry, and fornication. Together, these spell death for the faithful witnesses on whose blood she has become drunk. Paul Spilsbury sums up the visual spectacle of the whore of Babylon as he describes the effect of her entrance into the vision:

> This appalling picture of a prostitute riding on the back of the beast adds new depth to Revelation's depiction of evil. At its

---

13. Spilsbury, *Throne, Lamb, & Dragon*, 100; Rev 13:16–17.
14. Friesen, "Satan's Throne, Imperial Cults," 371.
15. Koester, *Revelation and End*, 146, 155.

most basic level the image of the prostitute, who is drunk on fornication and the blood of witnesses to Jesus, is a portrayal of the City of Rome.[16]

The parading of these figures through the streets reinforces the visual nature of the parody. Drawing on the cultural norm of the Roman spectacle, it uses visceral images in order to engage the reader as a theatrical audience. The visual nature is further reinforced by the textual focus on the eyes of the central characters and the descriptions of the spectators, both in heaven and on the ground.[17]

THE LAMB AND THE TEMPLE: REVERENCE WITH AMPLIFICATION

Unlike the dragon or the whore of Babylon, the lamb is not an image of Roman imperialism.[18] The lamb is functionally opposite to the grotesque, vulgar representations of empire, embodying instead meekness and humility. The lamb, however, is not a simple image, particularly as it associates the lion and the lamb within a single symbol. If a reader imagines the symbol as a visual mash-up of both animals in one, they might consider it an example of the monstrous. However, I prefer to imagine the symbol as simultaneously lion and lamb; the images are superimposed, rather than stitched together.[19] Readers hold in reverence both the humble image of the lamb and the triumphant image of the lion. This reverence continues through the transformation or superimposition of the images. Neither lion nor lamb prompt fear of the other as the beasts do. Thus, reverence towards the lion and the lamb is not a point of opposition or tension like the reverence shown to the beasts.

The temple and throne, symbols of God's power and sovereignty, are also looked upon with awe and reverence. Scripturally, this is the appropriate response when looking upon the holy. While the images are exaggerated in the context of the vision, the overpowering experience of God's presence and majesty in visions is not unique to Revelation. Rather, it is an established pattern going back to the Hebrew Bible, for example, in Isaiah's vision of God enthroned in the temple (Isa 6). These images do not juxtapose the expected with the unexpected as seen with the beast and the whore of Babylon. Instead, they amplify familiar biblical themes of the holy.

16. Spilsbury, *The Throne, Lamb, & Dragon*, 105.
17. Frilingos, *Spectacles of Empire*, 40.
18. Frilingos, *Spectacles of Empire*, 112; Friesen, "Satan's Throne," 197–99.
19. Stevenson, *Power and Place*, 232.

IDENTITY POLITICS

Gregory Stevenson identifies in Revelation two primary boundaries between the sacred and the profane: the boundary between heaven and earth, and the boundary between the temple and the world.[20] In both cases, John identifies the profane as that which is idolatrous, or sexually deviant.[21] Through the course of John's vision, the temple boundary shifts until, in the final edification, the new city becomes the temple. The sacred permeates the streets and even the walls, which are bathed in glory.[22] The gates mark the only permeable space in this boundary. However, fittingly, those outside are not able to enter in and must only leave their offerings at the gates themselves.

The book of Revelation also applies the division between the sacred and the profane to the general populace. It places two identities in contention: the people of God and the people of the world.[23] This is not a permeable boundary; "people of God" is a Christian identity that must be kept fully segregated from Roman contamination. As Stevenson says, "John seems concerned that many Christians have been led into idolatry and into an unholy alliance with certain aspects of the Roman Imperial society that call their identity into question."[24] The book of Revelation repeatedly places Roman forces in opposition to Christ followers, for it shows that "faith witness often leads to being slain (2:13; 6:9; 11:3, 7; 20:4) and the blood of all the faithful who have been slain on the earth laid at the foot of Rome (18:24; 17:6)."[25] One cannot be both faithful in one's witness and collude with Rome. The Christian's encounter with Christ must be decisive. Any faltering removes the individual or community from the side of the sacred, ejecting them across the border into the profane world.

John places the early Christian and Jewish communities on opposite sides of the physical boundaries of temple/world and heaven/earth.[26] In contrast to John's model for Christians, Jewish communities engaged with Roman leadership through partial participation in public life and open worship. John also uses Israel to show the dangers of backsliding. In his book, Jews have failed to meet their obligations, thereby breaking the covenant

---

20. Stevenson, *Power and Place*, 273–74.
21. Stevenson, *Power and Place*, 274.
22. Campbell, *Reading Revelation*, 298.
23. Stevenson, *Power and Place*, 224.
24. Stevenson, *Power and Place*, 230.
25. Stevenson, *Power and Place*, 281.
26. Stevenson, *Power and Place*, 225.

with Abraham.[27] God's favor, John suggests, can also be withdrawn from his readers if they do not fulfil their responsibilities. Of course, this criticism does not only apply to Judaism but also reflects the influence of the gentile communities from which many of the early Christians would have come.

CONCLUSION

Central to the text of Revelation is its parody of the Roman Empire. The text also relies on a clear conceptual and spatial delineation between the holy and profane. The parody, however, functions differently within the holy and profane spaces. The profane spaces play host to a burlesque of empire and Roman culture. By showing the audience to be under the thrall of the monstrous, this burlesque turns Rome into the barbaric other that the culture fears. The holy is expressed in amplified imagery of God's and Christ's sovereignty, showing them to be the natural authority that is counter to the Roman "other." Those who do not recognize this authority are left in thrall to the dragon and the whore, deceived by the visual spectacle that masks ill intent. This effective use of burlesque is part of John's argument against involvement with the economic and social machinations of empire. It shows not only that Roman authority is ultimately baseless but that the barrier between the appropriate and inappropriate is impermeable. On one side lies truth; on the other, misdirection and peril.

BIBLIOGRAPHY

Attordo, Salvatore, ed. *Encyclopedia of Humour Studies*. Thousand Oaks, CA: Sage, 2014.

Campbell, W. Gordon. *Reading Revelation: A Thematic Approach*. Foundations in New Testament Criticism Cambridge, UK: Clarke & Co, 2012.

Domino, Christophe. "Burlesque, Parody, Idiocy, Zaniness: Let's Be Serious." Translated by Simone Pleasance. *Critique d'Art* 23 (Spring 2004). https://journals.openedition.org/critiquedart/1733.

Friesen, Steven J. "Satan's Throne, Imperial Cults and the Social Setting of Revelation." *Journal for New Testament Studies* 27 (2005) 351–73.

Frilingos, Christoper A. *Spectacles of Empire*. Philadelphia: University of Pennsylvania Press, 2013.

Grant, Michael. *Art in the Roman Empire*. London: Routledge, 1995.

Hirst, Elizabeth. "Diverse Voices in a Second Language Classroom: Burlesque, Parody, and Mimicry." *Language and Education* 17 (2003) 174–91.

Koester, Craig R. *Revelation and the End of All Things*. Grand Rapids: Eerdmans, 2001.

Maier, Harry O. *Apocalypse Recalled: The Book of Revelation after Christendom*. Minneapolis: Fortress, 2002.

---

27. Campbell, *Reading Revelation*, 326–7.

Spilsbury, Paul. *The Throne, the Lamb & the Dragon: A Reader's Guide to the Book of Revelation*. Downers Grove, IL: IVP Academic, 2002.

Stevenson, Gregory. *Power and Place: Temple and Identity in the Book of Revelation*. BZNW 107. New York: De Gruyter, 2001.

Come Out of Babylon

Heavy Metal Music and the Book of Revelation

Trevor Malkinson

> A significant part of metal mythology revolves around the more apocalyptic strain of Christianity, especially the Book of Revelation.
>
> —Deena Weinstein

I'd like you to read some of the best heavy metal lyrics of all time:

> The second angel poured his bowl into the sea, and it became like the blood of a corpse, and every living thing in the sea died. The third angel poured his bowl into the rivers and the springs of water, and they became blood. The fourth angel poured his bowl on the sun, and it was allowed to scorch people with fire. And there came flashes of lightning, rumblings, peals of thunder, and a violent earthquake, such as had not occurred since people were upon the earth. The great city was split into three parts, and the cities of the nations fell. And every island fled away, and no mountains were to be found; and huge hailstones, each weighing about a hundred pounds, dropped from heaven on people, until they cursed God for the plague of the hail.

These, of course, are not actually heavy metal lyrics. They are sections from the book of Revelation, chapter 16 (NRSVUE). But they sound like metal lyrics. As I was going through seminary and reading more of the Bible in depth, I started to recognize that many images from the book of Revelation were found in the lyrics of heavy metal music. Songs like "The Four Horsemen" by Metallica and "Number of the Beast" by Iron Maiden were obvious ones.[1] As I researched this link further, I discovered that this connection was much more developed than I had imagined. The defining moment came when I discovered a thread on the website Reddit. The original poster of the thread asked if anyone knew of heavy metal songs with themes from the book of Revelation. By the thread's end there must have been seventy examples given. It blew my mind. What a treasure trove for the researcher this thread was! As I read the lyrics of the songs posted there, I saw that there was a much deeper connection between the ancient text and this contemporary art form than I had first realized.

Heavy metal has been a much maligned and persecuted musical genre over the past few decades. Many have viewed it as deviant and dangerous.[2] The Christian right in the United States has been a particularly persistent critic and foe.[3] But the more deeply I have looked into heavy metal music and its use of imagery from the book of Revelation, the more I discovered a very remarkable thing: heavy metal music is *doing the book of Revelation*. Heavy metal is not just drawing from the book of Revelation because there is cool imagery that makes for good album covers and T-shirts. Heavy metal music is doing a *faithful reenactment of the book of Revelation*. In its style, in its values, in its ethos, heavy metal is presenting the book of Revelation in musical form.

In fact, the book of Revelation and heavy metal share many characteristics when it comes to genre and style.[4] Both are ornate and complex. Both are not afraid to use the imagery of death, horror, destruction, and violence. Both intentionally invoke extreme experiences in their reader and listener. Both are big, bold, vivid, and designed to shock. Both are powerful, larger than life, and sometimes terrifying. Brian Froese writes that "Black Sabbath was writing music and poetry with the force of apocalyptic literary style."[5]

---

1. O'Hear and O'Hear, *Picturing the Apocalypse*, 239.

2. "Back in the 1980s, rock'n'roll was viewed as a dangerous, diabolical art-form, a vile, depraved sinkhole of sin and immorality from which innocent teenagers must be protected" (Brannigan, "Why Your Favorite").

3. Nekola, "More Than Just Music."

4. O'Hear and O'Hear, *Picturing the Apocalypse*, 3.

5. Froese, "Is It the End," 23.

POLITICAL THEMES

Harry Maier, in his book *Apocalypse Recalled*, explains what the book of Revelation is doing. Maier writes:

> [The author] John challenged the original audience of his Book of Revelation to think critically about their political culture. In particular, he exhorted his audience to look carefully at the economic order of the Roman Empire and the human and ecological misery it unleashed on the world as antithetical to the intentions of God for humankind and creation.[6]

The book of Revelation urges its audience to not give in to the ways of the empire's economic order and to persist even under situations of violence and persecution. Its vivid and extreme political language attempts to jolt readers into choosing their allegiance to the Lamb of God, no matter what obstacles they face.

We, too, live in a time of plutocracy and tyranny, where big money has captured the ruling apparatuses of many states. A tiny minority of people continue to accumulate obscene wealth, while the social welfare state is cynically dismantled and millions are left to fend for themselves. This all takes place against the backdrop of climate change and widespread ecocide. Thus, heavy metal also challenges its listeners to think critically about the current global world order, with its rampant injustice, inequality, and ecological destruction.

As Deena Weinstein says, "Allusions to injustice abound in heavy metal music."[7] We can think of a song like Metallica's "And Justice for All," with its lyrics about justice as "lost," "raped," and "gone." Heavy metal lyrics, says Peter Buckland, "engage socio-political issues like civil repression, economic inequality and exploitation, environmental degradation, euthanasia, execution, nuclear warfare, political corruption, religious corruption, surveillance, uncontrolled technological innovation, and war."[8] You can hear some of the political themes in these band names: Anthrax, Nuclear Assault, Celtic Frost, Sodom, Death Angel, Artillery, Destruction, Megadeth. These band names are not celebrating what they point to. Instead, they are screaming out against a world full of destruction and war. There are many songs about war in heavy metal music, but you would be hard pressed to find one that promotes or glorifies war. Most of the songs are about the madness of war and how average people suffer from its evils.

---

6. Maier, *Apocalypse Recalled*, xi.
7. Weinstein, *Heavy Metal*, 40.
8. Buckland, "When All Is Lost," 146.

VIVID SYMBOLS

The book of Revelation is a literary form of resistance against imperialism, empire, domination, and exploitation.[9] The author of Revelation uses the literary form of the apocalypse to "drive home the urgency" of his message that readers need to think critically about their political situation.[10] He often uses "vivid and terrifying symbols" to jolt his readers into waking up to the true reality of their situation. His core symbols of the dragon, the beast from the sea, the beast from the earth, and the whore of Babylon are designed to "unveil" and "reveal the true face of empire as monstrous, rapacious, violent and deceitful."[11]

Heavy metal music seeks to do the same for our own current world order. Its lyrics and album covers hold up a mirror to the hideous face of a world threatened by nuclear war and climate change, and stricken by greed, inequality, ongoing warfare, and ecological devastation. To portray both the depravity and gravity of this situation, heavy metal frequently uses images of evil from the book of Revelation and popular images drawn from other parts of the biblical canon associated with it. Heavy metal lyrics often speak in terms of a battle between good and evil. The beast, Satan, the antichrist, and so on "serve as a shorthand" for the kinds of forces that are currently destroying our world.[12]

In response to that threat, songs say, "Fire rains down,"[13] "the first trumpet blows,"[14] and "Doomsday Jesus, we need you now."[15]

HOPE

In Revelation, hope explicitly comes at the end of the text, with its famous vision of a new heaven and a new earth, and a new Jerusalem descending down to earth from heaven. But hope is found earlier, too. Throughout, the book of Revelation demands that its readers "reassess [their] political and economic allegiances"[16] and exhorts them to "come out" of Babylon (Rev 18:4). Greg Carey writes that Revelation is a kind of protest literature, in that "a great deal of Revelation's script involves avoidance, refusal

---

9. Carey, "Book of Revelation."
10. Maier, *Apocalypse Recalled*, xii.
11. Portier-Young, "Jewish Apocalyptic Literature," 153.
12. Weinstein, *Heavy Metal*, 41.
13. Lamb of God, "Reclamation."
14. DeMaio, "Revelation (Death's Angel)."
15. Wylde, "Doomsday Jesus."
16. Maier, *Apocalypse Recalled*, xi.

to participate, refusal to bow down before the Great Beast (Rev. 13:7–10; 14:9–11) . . . . John's counter-imperial script called Jesus loyalists to an extremely rigorous level of resistance."[17]

At first glance, it may look like apocalyptic hope is missing from heavy metal. Little in heavy metal music displays an openly utopic sensibility. Many lyrics sound dark and dystopic, expressing that a deep cry of pain lives beneath the surface of heavy metal's sonic power. Some even seem to "hail the apocalypse,"[18] welcoming destruction as the only way out of "humanity's . . . failed experiment."[19] But, in heavy metal, hope is found in the call to action. Heavy metal shares Revelation's call to resist and reject the dominant culture and its imperial empire. Heavy metal expresses a defiant "you will not defeat us" attitude toward the forces of death. It has a sense of determination and an ethos of standing up for who you are and what you believe in. Songs call on listeners to "wake up,"[20] "be brave,"[21] "fight,"[22] and "show the world that love is still alive."[23] Fans of heavy metal music and its commentators agree that the musical form is *empowering*.[24] It has been described as a "musical will to power,"[25] and the sheer volume and high energy of the music offers inspiration and vitality to those who listen to it. Juliet Forshaw writes that, in heavy metal, "the depiction of dystopia is useful in that it may motivate people to change what they don't like about the world."[26] Laura Wiebe Taylor offers a more detailed analysis: "Within metal's images of destruction and despair often lie the seeds of utopian possibility, particularly when such narratives locate the blame for oppressive and apocalyptic outcomes in human society and leave room for the chance of averting such disaster."[27]

CONCLUSION

Progressive churches today should re-embrace the book of Revelation and learn how to take up its robust call to persist in the face of tyrannical forces.

---

17. Carey, "Book of Revelation," 170–72.
18. Avatar, "Hail the Apocalypse."
19. Lamb of God, "Reclamation."
20. Saracen, "Horsemen of the Apocalypse."
21. Osbourne et al., "Children of the Grave."
22. Tipton et al., "Blood Red Skies."
23. Osbourne et al., "Children of the Grave."
24. Weinstein, *Heavy Metal*, 41; Heavy Metal and Religion, "Let Us Bow."
25. Heavy Metal and Religion, "Let Us Bow."
26. Forshaw, "Metal in Three Modes," 44.
27. Taylor, "Images of Human-Wrought Despair," 89.

The church should also take seriously the contemporary version of this call in heavy metal music. If we are to one day make it out of Babylon, we will need both heavy metal and the book of Revelation on our side.

BIBLIOGRAPHY

Avatar. "Hail the Apocalypse." Track 1 on *Hail the Apocalypse*, recorded by Avatar. Toronto: Entertainment One, 2014. https://genius.com/Avatar-hail-the-apocalypse-lyrics.

Brannigan, Paul. "Why Your Favorite Rock Band Is a Tool of Satan . . . and Must Be Stopped!" Louder, May 19, 2019. https://www.loudersound.com/features/satan-heavy-metal-acdc-iron-maiden-rainbow-queen-666.

Buckland, Peter. "When All is Lost: Thrash Metal, Dystopia, Ecopedagogy." *International Journal of Ethics Education* 1 (2016) 145–54.

Carey, Greg. "The Book of Revelation as Counter-Imperial Script." In *In the Shadow of Empire: Reclaiming the Bible as a History of Faithful Resistance*, edited by Richard Horsley et al., 157–76. Louisville: Westminster John Knox, 2008.

DeMaio, Joey. "Revelation (Death's Angel)." Track 6 on *Into Glory Ride*, recorded by Manowar. London: Music for Nations, 1983. https://genius.com/Manowar-revelation-deaths-angel-lyrics.

Forshaw, Juliet. "Metal in Three Modes of Enmity: Political, Musical, Comic." *Current Musicology* 91 (2011) 44.

Froese, Brian. "'Is It the End, My Friend?' Black Sabbath's Apocalypse of Horror." In *Black Sabbath and Philosophy: Mastering Reality*, edited by William Irwin et al., 20–30. Oxford, UK: Wiley and Sons, 2013.

Heavy Metal and Religion. "Let Us Bow Our Heads and Rock: An Examination of the Relationship between Heavy Metal and Religion." Heavy Metal and Religion, n.d. http://heavymetalandreligion.weebly.com.

Lamb of God. "Reclamation." Track 11 on *Wrath*, recorded by Lamb of God. New York: Roadrunner, 2009. https://genius.com/Lamb-of-god-reclamation-lyrics.

Maier, Harry O. *Apocalypse Recalled: The Book of Revelation After Christendom*. Minneapolis: Augsburg Fortress, 2002.

Nekola, Anna. "'More Than Just a Music': Conservative Christian Anti-Rock Discourse and the U.S. Culture Wars." *Popular Music* 32 (2013) 407–26.

O'Hear, Natasha, and Anthony O'Hear, eds. *Picturing the Apocalypse: The Book of Revelation in the Arts over Two Millennia*. Oxford, UK: Oxford University Press, 2015.

Osbourne, Ozzy, et al. "Children of the Grave." Side A, track 4 on *Master of Reality*, recorded by Black Sabbath. London: Vertigo, 1971. https://genius.com/Black-sabbath-children-of-the-grave-lyrics.

Portier-Young, Anathea. "Jewish Apocalyptic Literature as Resistance Literature." In *The Oxford Handbook of Apocalyptic Literature*, edited by John J Collins et al., 145–62. Oxford, UK: Oxford University Press, 2014.

Saracen. "Horsemen of the Apocalypse." Side A, track 4 on *Heroes*, recorded by Saracen. London: Nucleus, 1981. http://www.songlyrics.com/saracen/horsemen-of-the-apocalypse-lyrics/.

Taylor, Laura W. "Images of Human-Wrought Despair and Destruction: Social Critique in British Apocalyptic and Dystopian Metal." In *Heavy Metal Music in Britain*, edited by Gerd Bayer et al., 89–110. Farnham, UK: Ashgate, 2013.

Tipton, Glenn, et al. "Blood Red Skies." Track 6 on *Ram It Down*, recorded by Judas Priest. New York: Columbia, 1988. https://genius.com/Judas-priest-blood-red-skies-lyrics.

Weinstein, Deena. *Heavy Metal: The Music and Its Culture*. Cambridge, MA: Da Capo, 2000.

Wylde, Zakk. "Doomsday Jesus." Track 2 on *The Blessed Hellride*, recorded by The Black Label Society. Hollywood: Paramount, 2003. https://genius.com/Black-label-society-doomsday-jesus-lyrics.

My Way or the Highway to Hell

Patricia Gruben

The book of Revelation, the final book of the Bible, is constructed as a warning to the seven churches of Asia Minor from its presumed author, the obscure prophet John of Patmos. With its pale horse of death, its seven-headed beast, its great harlot of Babylon, its earthquakes, seas of blood, and flaming mountains falling from the sky, Revelation's apocalyptic nightmares have inspired poets, historians, literary theorists, and religious scholars alike. Opportunistically, it has been taken up by the fundamentalist end times movement as a political tract and guide to a cataclysm known as the rapture, in which the chosen few will be elevated to heaven, while a flood of terrors will be visited on unbelievers below.

This chapter will explore the social and psychological functions of the apocalyptic model and the power of its narrative. The chronicle of the end times, with its promise of election and punishment, offers rewards based on a sense of inclusion while threatening to undermine the psychical integrity of believers through a set of unresolvable contradictions.

THE POWER OF MYTH

The American novelist Mary Gaitskill describes her response to the book of Revelation after becoming a born-again Christian at age twenty-one. As she walked the streets of Toronto,

> The air would crackle with the unacknowledged brutality of life. . . . The angels with their seven stars and their lamps, the beast with his seven heads and ten horns—the static imagery was sinister and senseless to me, and yet all the more convincing for it. I could imagine angels and beasts looming all about us, incomprehensible and invisible to our senses. . . . Their stars and lamps and horns seemed like peculiar metaphors on the page, but, I feared, when the divine horses came down, with their fire and teeth and snake tails, their reality would be all too clear.[1]

Even as a believer, Gaitskill was put off by what she perceived as the Bible's mechanical, prescriptive quality, suggesting "a vast schema in which human ambivalence was simply not a factor." Long after forsaking her evangelical vows, she remained troubled by the Bible's evocation of an "inexorable, ridiculous order that is unknowable by us, in which our earthly concerns matter very little."[2]

My own attachment to fundamentalist Christianity is equally conflicted. I grew up in a second-generation evangelical family in Texas, but my father broke with the church before I was born. On trips to visit family in Dallas, when I met someone who would offer me a blessed day, or a pharmacist who told me that Jesus had stopped her from giving me the wrong prescription, I wondered about their state of mind. Could they live each mundane moment in the genuine belief that every detail of their lives was part of God's plan? Could their faith carry them past the doubts that dissuaded Gaitskill and me? Were they chronically anxious, or had they found a kind of blissful euphoria? What was the psychic cost of living with the anticipation that they might be transported to eternity, but the world they knew would be destroyed in the chaos of the apocalypse? Would their faith prepare them for such a shocking and painful end?

As a filmmaker and screenwriting professor, I study narrative, including Joseph Campbell's models of myth and its influence on popular media. Julius Heuscher, Bruno Bettelheim, and other therapists have explored the way narrative and metaphor have the power to bring deep meaning to our lives and help us overcome trauma—for instance, the way children process fairy tales, in which the hero encounters a challenge, overcomes it, and is transformed by the ordeal.[3] These stories are surrogates for our own psychic emergencies; the destruction of a witch or a wicked stepmother empowers

---

1. Gaitskill, "Lot of Exploding Heads," 5–6.
2. Gaitskill, "Lot of Exploding Heads," 6.
3. Heuscher, *Psychiatric Study*; Bettelheim, *Uses of Enchantment*.

a child to process her rage toward her own mother, which would be too terrifying to acknowledge consciously.

Films, even popular action movies, can take their audiences on profound journeys of conflict and resolution. Apocalyptic films like *Last Night*, *Children of Men*, *On the Beach*, *The Sacrifice*, and even *Mad Max: Fury Road* guide us to question the purpose and even the possibility of survival. The 1957 sci-fi film *The Incredible Shrinking Man* ends with an epiphany for its rapidly diminishing hero, now small enough to stand inside the mesh of a window screen, gazing out at the stars:

> I looked up, as if somehow I would grasp the heavens, the universe, worlds beyond number, God's silver tapestry spread across the night. And in that moment, I knew the answer to the riddle of the Infinite. I had thought in terms of Man's own limited dimension. I had presumed upon Nature. That existence begins and ends in Man's conception, not Nature's. And I felt my body dwindling, melting, becoming nothing. My fears melted away. And in their place came acceptance. All this vast majesty of creation, it had to mean something. And then I meant something, too! Yes, smaller than the smallest—I meant something, too! To God there is no zero. I still exist![4]

As adults, we use stories, myths, and religious parables to help us grapple with existential crises; but if the resolution is too simple, it teaches us nothing. In the Old Testament, God's cruelty toward Job; in the New Testament, Jesus's moment of agonizing doubt on the cross; in the Ramayana, Rama's renunciation of Sita *after* she has walked through fire to prove her fidelity—these moral ambiguities challenge the faith of believers. As Campbell notes, the metaphors of myth and folk tales are statements that point beyond themselves. "These are dangerous because they threaten the fabric of the security into which we have built ourselves and our family. But they are fiendishly fascinating too, for they carry keys that open the whole realm of the desired and feared adventure of the discovery of the self."[5] The complex mysteries of these sacred texts continue to challenge us at a deeper level than the simple binaries of good and evil.

York University film professor Amnon Buchbinder defines a "living story" as an organic work of fiction that leads us to a deeper truth: a story in which the reader or listener creates the text by engaging with its poetics

---

4. Matheson and Simmons, *Incredible Shrinking Man*. See the finale at www.youtube.com/watch?v=YawNw7fdgOg.

5. Campbell, *Hero with Thousand Faces*, 8.

and its subtextual meaning.[6] Buchbinder contrasts his living stories with false narratives that have a similar outward form but lack resonance. He defines two types of what he calls anti-story: *formulaic* and *fundamentalist* narratives. Formulaic narratives are "cobbled together from tropes," using cliché and convention to create drama without depth: predictable romantic comedies, "disease of the week," or "woman in jeopardy" TV movies, which are superficially engaging but quickly fade from memory. Fundamentalist narratives deny that they *are* stories at all. They claim to be literal truth and turn myth-inflected belief into rigid doctrine. Buchbinder writes, "Formula narratives drain away meaning, turning the listener into a passive consumer; fundamentalist narratives . . . have an excessive meaning, a lack of aesthetic distance."[7] "Excessive meaning" delivers all the answers to us on a platter; the viewer has no part in creating a story with personal significance.

The Bible provides us with rich and complex myths which bewilder and frighten and sustain and uplift us through poetic license. It has inspired not only philosophers and saints but also artists as diverse as Michelangelo, T. S. Eliot, Pier Paolo Pasolini, and Margaret Atwood. The book of Revelation is the Bible at its most mystical and fantastic. It is this book that has generated an industry of prophetic eschatology, projecting every image as a sign of things to come.

FUNDAMENTALIST NARRATIVE

Do contemporary evangelical narratives of the end times offer us the psychic tools to make sense of our lives, the metaphors that point beyond themselves into the transcendent?

One version of this narrative is promoted by the End Time Ministries, based in the Dallas suburb of Plano, Texas. Its leader, Irvin Baxter, until his death in 2020 from COVID-19, had a weekly television show on Trinity Broadcasting Network along with podcasts, a radio show, an active website,[8] and a weekly study group at the Plano headquarters, usually conducted by his son-in-law Dave Robbins and simulcast on YouTube. Baxter delivered his message in person nearly every weekend at churches throughout small-town and suburban America. In all these venues he preached dire warnings about the end of days, showing clips from disaster movies and his own DVDs with heavy-metal graphics and titles like *Master Plan of the Dragon* and *World War III: Entrance Ramp for the Antichrist*. He

---

6. Buchbinder, "Biology of Story," 3.
7. Buchbinder, "Biology of Story," 3.
8. See End Time Ministries at www.endtime.com.

also wrote two apocalyptic thriller novels. He led regular tours to Israel, where he hoped to establish a Bible college. Baxter was not a charismatic preacher like popular televangelists Joel Osteen or Paula White; he came across as an earnest, literal-minded high school history teacher. He devoted no time to moral lessons or spiritual guidance; he was completely focused on the minutiae of the apocalypse and on studying world events for signs that it has already begun.

As Matthew Avery Sutton notes in his history of modern evangelism,[9] the primary evangelical framework for the end of days originated with Irish preacher John Nelson Darby, who toured North America in the 1860s quoting this passage from First Thessalonians:

> For the Lord himself shall descend from heaven with a shout, with the voice of the archangel, and with the trump of God: and the dead in Christ shall rise first; then we which are alive and remain shall be caught up together with them in the clouds, to meet the Lord in the air; and so shall we ever be with the Lord (1 Thess 4:15–17 KJV)

Darby believed that the mass ascendance of true believers to heaven would happen at the start of a seven-year tribulation. After the blessed were lifted up, a new leader would take control of those left behind in Europe; this leader would eventually be revealed as the antichrist and the final battle would begin. Thus, from the start of the American apocalyptic movement, religion and global politics were intertwined.

Many evangelists have elaborated on Darby's mash-up of the miraculous and the mundane, especially during times of social and political unrest. In the 1950s, Billy Graham found portents of the apocalypse in communism, the population explosion, the atom bomb, and the decline in church attendance. The omens piled on in the 1960s with the civil rights movement, feminism, drugs, and free love.[10] Graham and others comforted their followers with the notion that this chaos was all part of God's divine plan and that it would be their path to salvation.

In Darby's chronology, known as the pre-tribulation model, believers will ascend to heaven *before* the emergence of the antichrist and the ensuing global catastrophe.[11] Irvin Baxter disagreed; he believed the rapture will happen post-trib, at the *end* of the end of days. This means that even the blessed will need to endure unimaginable horrors. Baxter preached relentlessly about the coming battle on his website, his weekly television show, his

---

9. Sutton, *American Apocalypse*, 16–17.
10. Sutton, *American Apocalypse*, 330.
11. Sutton, *American Apocalypse*, 330.

DVDs, and his live sermons, often with a projected backdrop of wild beasts and monsters inspired by the book of Revelation.

NINE STEPS TO RAPTURE

Baxter's End Time Ministries listed nine events leading to the second coming of Christ:[12]

1. **World War III**: The countdown begins with global war, which may have already started in Syria. The four evil angels of Satan will be unleashed from their prison in the Euphrates River. Russia, Iran, and Libya will attack Israel. A third of Earth's population, or 2.2 billion people, will die. To kill that many in such a short time, the US as the dominant nuclear nation will have to be involved, but at the end of the war the Americans will withdraw as the action continues in Europe and the Middle East.

2. **Palestinian/Israeli Peace Agreement**: Israel and Palestine will be so exhausted by the war that they will sign an armistice; this will mark the start of the final seven years until the Battle of Armageddon.

3. **Palestinian State in West Bank/Building of Third Temple**: Over the next three and a half years, the Jews will build the Third Temple under the supervision of the United Nations.

4. **New Leader**: A charismatic ruler will rise to power in Europe and quickly extend his territory under the One World Order with the support of the UN, the International Monetary Fund, and the World Bank.

5. **Animal Sacrifice in the Temple**: The Jews will return to their ancient practice of animal sacrifice, arousing the animal rights activists and leading to renewed conflict.

6. **False Messiah**: Pressure will build on the leader to put down these protests. He will declare that he is the messiah of the Jews, the second coming of Christ, the Mahdi for the Muslims, and the fifth Buddha all at once, but he will be revealed as the antichrist.

7. **Abomination of Desolation**: This begins the final three and a half years until Armageddon. The antichrist will rule along with his partner, the false prophet. They will fortify the New World Order under the authority of Satan, controlling governments, banking, and media, and suppressing the witnesses who speak for God.

12. Robbins, "Weekly Talk."

8. **Mark of the Beast**: The antichrist will introduce a universal identification number, the mark of the beast, which everyone will be required to wear. Anyone who resists will be excluded from the world economy, unable to buy or sell anything. Some of Baxter's colleagues believe that everyone will be tattooed with a bar code; Baxter himself was equivocal on this question.

9. **Final Battle**: At the end of the seven years, Russia, Iran, and other adversaries will gather against Israel in order to force it to share control of Jerusalem. The Israelites will rush to the Mount of Olives and cry out to God. Christ will reappear, and this time the Jews will crown him as the King of kings. The dead in Christ will be drawn up to heaven, and the living Christians will join them. The rest will fry in hell forever.[13]

THE LOGIC OF PROPHECY

The scientific achievements and rational philosophy of the nineteenth century gave Evangelicals both the means and the necessity to "prove" things that had previously been accepted as matters of faith. The religious historian Matthew Avery Sutton identifies a set of "radical white evangelicals" of the late nineteenth century who countered their perceived enemies in universities, liberal Protestant sects, and the world of science by co-opting their methodology:

> Radical evangelicals ... treated the Bible like a series of propositions that when properly arranged and classified unveiled the plan of the ages. Their emphasis on scientific accuracy, quantification, classification, and interpretive rigor reflected their own dependence on the same modes of thinking that defined theological modernism.[14]

Like his nineteenth-century predecessors, Baxter applied a veneer of rational analysis to his eschatology. He and his followers, like many Fundamentalists, take a book that is written as allegory and map it onto their own agenda, reframing the mysteries as facts in order to justify their conclusions. Baxter said the Old Testament contained a hundred prophecies about the birth of Jesus and they all came true; therefore, its thousand prophecies about the second coming must also be true.[15] He saw current political crises as signs that apocalypse is near or has already begun. Based on deductions

---

13. Robbins, "Weekly Talk."
14. Sutton, *American Apocalypse*, 15–16.
15. See www.endtime.com for a sample of Baxter's assertions.

from his idiosyncratic reading of Scripture, he could prove that World War III is imminent, that it will be started by "the Islamic world," that it will be a nuclear holocaust. He interpreted the various beasts found in Revelation as signifiers of particular countries: the bear is Russia, the four-headed leopard is Germany, the lion is England, the ten-headed beast is the European Union, and the eagle is America. Eagles are rarely mentioned in the Bible, but this turns out to be a virtue. In Rev 12:14, a woman is given the wings of an eagle and flies to the promised land. For Baxter, this meant that the United States will protect Israel but will probably not be a key player in the final battle; it will defy the one world government and become a center for Christian resistance.[16] Thus the US is carefully positioned to be a sympathetic but distant observer of the catastrophe until needed to save the day (much like its policy during the first two world wars).

This isolationism conforms to a conservative orthodoxy opposed to big government as a rival to God's power; sees conflict in the world as foretold and thus part of the divine plan; and manages to put America into a detached, independent but heroic role that evokes the classic loner hero of Hollywood Westerns like *High Noon* and *Shane*.

FATHER KNOWS BEST

Hegelian philosopher Walter A. Davis writes about the role of fundamentalist eschatology in soothing the anxieties of believers about global politics as well as about their personal lives:

> Mapped onto history, the Bible offers us an absolute certitude . . . vanquishing the greatest contingency. In dealing with the Middle East . . . a fundamentalist presidency need not confuse itself with the . . . details of political history or develop a nuanced appreciation of Islam. . . . All one need do is literally match a prophecy to a contingency and . . . literal certitude is attained, or what amounts to the same thing, the fantasmatic imposition upon reality of what one wants to believe.[17]

Baxter was emphatic that any global peace initiatives are dangerous, as are any aspirations to find common cause in world religions. Sustainable development goals, the United Nations Declaration on Human Rights, and international programs for women's empowerment are all seen as efforts to identify, register, and control everyone on earth.[18] The most perilous threat from the

---

16. Robbins, "Weekly Talk."
17. Davis, "Bible Says," 273.
18. See www.endtime.com for a sample of Baxter's critiques.

antichrist is his ambition to unite all people, whatever their origins or beliefs. To be saved, we must follow the narrow path. All other faiths and practices are false and must be shunned. As in the *Left Behind* films, humanist or uncommitted Christians are as vulnerable to annihilation as are atheists and pagans; they were among the primary targets of Baxter's disdain.

Baxter's rhetorical style, expressed primarily through media, affirmed his paternal authority. He lectured from behind a desk, backed by constantly morphing disaster-film images, never more animated than when describing the carnage that will take place during the Apocalypse. There is almost no mention of what heaven might be like, or the virtues required to get there; Baxter saved his enthusiasm for the most devastatingly gory details of the tribulation.

A weekly study group at the Plano headquarters of the End Time Ministries is designed for minimum interaction with participants. At the session I attended, twenty-four people sat in chairs facing Baxter's son-in-law Dave Robbins, who spent the first hour screening a packaged lecture for a live-streaming YouTube session. When that ended, he handed out a printed quiz and spent the next half hour dictating the answers for participants to fill in, leaving no opportunity for questions or discussion. At the end, he turned away to pack up his projector without farewell, and we drifted off quietly into the night. The End Time Ministries' blog page does provide room for comments; here, followers argue over fine points of doctrine and ask theological questions—sometimes arrogant, sometimes heartbreakingly poignant: *How do I know this will happen? How can I stop being afraid?*

Baxter's End Time Ministries provides what Buchbinder would call a fundamentalist narrative, a story that denies it is a story, rather than an allegory that would guide believers through the challenges of mortality and the imagined life beyond. The canned lectures, the disaster-movie graphics, the mute study groups all remind us of how the aura of not only Buchbinder's 'living story" but lived experience itself is denied and suppressed in service of a prescribed doctrine.

The subtext that we do find in Baxter's eschatology reveals the toxic and paranoid underbelly of American "exceptionalism." The deeper myth that he exploited is the myth of the frontier—the outsider, beholden to no one but his own inner voice, following a moral code that grants him privileged status. Baxter inverted the goals of international humanitarianism and religious inclusivity into a paranoia over global control by the One World Order. What a paradox it is that he denied his followers the freedom to question, to imagine, and to practice Christian charity. His preoccupation with chaos and destruction points to a death drive that is perhaps the Fundamentalist's only solution to a denial of death itself.

BIBLIOGRAPHY

Bettelheim, Bruno. *The Uses of Enchantment: The Meaning and Importance of Fairy Tales*. London: Thames & Hudson, 1976.

Buchbinder, Amnon. "Biology of Story." Unpublished paper delivered at "Probing the Boundaries: Global Reflections on Narrative," conference, n.p., Lisbon, May 11, 2014.

Campbell, Joseph. *The Hero with a Thousand Faces*. Bollingen. Princeton, NJ: Princeton University Press, 1972.

Davis, Walter A. "The Bible Says: The Psychology of Christian Fundamentalism." *Psychoanalytic Review* 93 (2006) 268–300.

Gaitskill, Mary. "A Lot of Exploding Heads: On Reading the Book of Revelation." In *Somebody with a Little Hammer: Essays*, 3–9. New York: Pantheon, 2017.

Heuscher, Julius. *A Psychiatric Study of Fairy Tales: Their Origin, Meaning and Usefulness*. Springfield, IL: Thomas, 1974.

Matheson, Richard, and Richard Alan Simmons. *The Incredible Shrinking Man*. Universal City, CA: Universal-International, 1957.

Robbins, Dave. "Weekly Talk." End Time Ministries, Plano, TX, Mar. 29, 2017.

Sutton, Matthew Avery. *American Apocalypse: A History of Modern Evangelicalism*. Cambridge, MA: Harvard University Press, 2014.

The "Evil Child" and the Age/Agency of Cinema's Young Antichrists

Damien's Legacies from
The Omen to *Good Omens*[1]

James Magee Jr.

"DAMIEN, I LOVE YOU! Look at me, Damien! It's all for you!" With these words and a noose around her neck, the nanny to the son of the American ambassador to Great Britain steps off the roof of the diplomat's estate, her suspended body crashing into the second-story window as guests to the boy's lavish fifth birthday party look on aghast. A photographer at the event had only moments earlier speculated whether young Damien Thorn was heir to his father's millions or Jesus Christ himself. Ironically, the boy is believed to be not the Son of God, but the son of his evil adversary, eliciting the adoration of satanic followers willing to die and even kill for him, as well as the loathing of opponents who seek his death. Damien survives the violence that surrounds him and attends his parents' double funeral in the company of the American president, the boy's smile fading into an ancient riddle: "Here is wisdom. Let him that hath understanding count the number of the beast: for it is the number of a man; and his number is 666."

The Omen (1976) continued centuries of exposition on Jewish and Christian traditions about an ultimate agent of evil that came to be known

---

[1]. I am grateful to John Martens for taking the time to read the version of this essay I wrote for the "Visions of the End Times" conference and for offering feedback that helped me focus the discussion in this published revision.

as the antichrist,[2] drawing particularly from the vision of a beast rising out of the sea in the biblical book of Revelation.[3] The eschatological hope of this text and other examples of ancient apocalypse[4] is absent from *Omen*, which also reflects the notion popular in contemporary cinema of the apocalypse as a threat to human existence that must be averted.[5] As a presumed menace to human survival, Damien is targeted for eradication, one of several plot points the movie bequeathed to its sequel, a remake, and various imitations. Indeed, *Omen* has influenced depictions of young antichrists in film for over four decades; the recent release of *Good Omens* (2019), a six-part miniseries featuring a juvenile son of Satan, makes for a timely exploration of Damien's influence at the movies.

As "one of cinema's most iconic child villains,"[6] Damien has received top billing in several recent monographs on the "evil child" in film.[7] He leads off Dominic Lennard's chapter on the challenge of young miscreants to patriarchy,[8] concludes Andrew Scahill's section on the paternal gothic,[9] and serves as the prototype in Karen Renner's exploration of monstrous paternity.[10] Each author offers valuable insights into this malevolent figure's place in popular culture, but the interrelated concepts of *age* and *agency* receive insufficient attention given their importance in society and contemporary scholarship on childhood. After introducing these two concepts

---

2. McGinn, *Antichrist*, 9–56.

3. Rev 13:1–18. Other key biblical images are the "little horn" of Daniel's visions (chs. 7–8), the false messiahs of the "little apocalypse" (Matt 24:24; Mark 13:22), and the "lawless one" (2 Thess 2:1–12). Explicit references to an "antichrist" are confined to two of the Johannine letters (1 John 2:18, 22; 4:3; 2 John 7) and point to individuals who have denied core tenets of the Christian faith.

4. As defined in Collins, "A genre of revelatory literature with a narrative framework, in which a revelation is mediated by an otherworldly being to a human recipient, disclosing a transcendent reality which is both temporal, insofar as it envisages eschatological salvation, and spatial insofar as it involves another, supernatural world" (Collins, *Apocalyptic Imagination*, 5). This definition of apocalypse was originally proposed by a collaboration of scholars involved in the Society of Biblical Literature Genres Project (Collins, "Introduction," 9) and is acknowledged as an important and oft-cited one (DiTommaso, "Apocalypses," 239–40).

5. The film blends elements of Ostwalt's "traditional" and "secular" apocalypses (Ostwalt, "Apocalyptic," 375–76), pointing to the insufficiency of a bifurcated scheme to adequately account for the diversity of apocalyptic movies.

6. Lennard, *Bad Seeds*, 99.

7. Kord is an exception, purposely avoiding in-depth analyses of "famous" films (Kord, *Little Horrors*, 12).

8. Lennard, *Bad Seeds*, 97–107.

9. Scahill, *Revolting Child*, 103–11.

10. Renner, *Evil Children*, 28–37.

alongside myths of children's intrinsic evil and innocence, I will sketch the emergence of the "evil child" in cinema of the 1950s through 1970s. This will provide the background for my analyses of young antichrists in film. I will show that Damien, a more ambiguous character than as he is typically remembered, has spawned competing legacies of malevolence and virtue, both influenced by a developmental framework that ascribes higher levels of agency to older characters. The insights drawn from this exploration of cinema's young antichrists can hopefully benefit future in-depth studies of how "evil kids" are constructed in their respective narratives.

EVIL AND INNOCENCE, AGE AND AGENCY

The idea that young humans inhabit a temporal space that varies according to historical, cultural, and social location is a central tenet of current studies on childhood.[11] This variability is reflected in competing *discourses* on childhood,[12] which draw from two dominant mythological types. The first is the Dionysian child, who harbors "an initial evil or corruption within," which, if "mobilized," leads to widespread destruction.[13] The discourse that depends most on this type is the Puritan, whose namesakes emphasized the doctrine of "original sin"[14] and thus constructed the child as inherently wicked.[15] The second type is the Apollonian child who has "a natural goodness and . . . clarity of vision," being "the source of all that is best in human nature."[16] The Romantic discourse with its construction of the child as pure and innocent is most reliant on this myth.[17] While diametrically opposed, these mythic types and the discourses derived from them can work in tandem,[18] which is particularly true of how cinema's "evil kids" are constructed.

---

11. Montgomery, "Childhood in Time," 46.

12. As noted in Montgomery, according to social constructivists, a *discourse* refers to "a whole set of interconnected ideas that work together in a self-contained way, ideas that are held together by a particular ideology or view of the world" (Montgomery, "Childhood in Time," 47).

13. Jenks, *Childhood*, 62–63.

14. This may be defined as "the whole of humanity . . . in a condition or state of captivity to sin" and "caught in a web of despoilment, corruption, pollution, and disintegration" (Migliore, *Faith Seeking Understanding*, 159).

15. Montgomery, "Childhood in Time," 62.

16. Jenks, *Childhood*, 65.

17. Montgomery, "Childhood in Time," 65–66.

18. Jenks, *Childhood*, 62.

Focusing on these dominant discourses about childhood, Lennard "observe[s no] strict criteria based on age or physiological development" in defining the child at the center of his book.[19] Yet most filmmakers and moviegoers embrace an essentialist rather than constructivist model of childhood, and therefore attach "natural" (though, in reality, culturally relative) meaning to young characters' chronological ages.[20] Renner, alternatively, defines children in her monograph as those under the age of eighteen, quickly acknowledging that "evil kids" nonetheless constitute "a pretty narrow bunch."[21] While attentive to the predominant race, socioeconomic class, and gender of these characters,[22] she overlooks an age-based stratification of her focus group and thus neglects to identify the overwhelming majority of them as *preteens* rather than as toddlers, preschoolers, or teenagers. Expectations of these various subgroups differ,[23] with concomitant responsibilities and rights typically accruing over time,[24] rather than being granted en masse at eighteen as Renner implies.[25]

The "twist ending" to Renner's exploration of "evil kids" in the popular imagination is that they do not exist because, she assumes, children are "[in]capable of mature intention and responsible decision-making."[26] This denial that agency, which may be defined as "the capacity of individuals to act independently,"[27] can be exercised by children, even by cinema's "evil kids" whom Renner claims "know not what they do,"[28] conflicts with Lennard's claim that these young villains "*always* possess a degree of shocking autonomy that fantastically illustrates the agency and power that children are denied in our society."[29] While Lennard views children as deprived of agency, Renner sees them as incapable of it.[30] This disagreement over whether or not "evil kids" exercise agency mirrors the contemporary debate

19. Lennard, *Bad Seeds*, 3.

20. Chudacoff, *How Old Are You*, 3–8; Hockey and James, *Social Identities*, 3–5; James and James, *Key Concepts*, 1–3.

21. Renner, *Evil Children*, 6.

22. Renner correctly identifies "white, middle- to upper-class boys" as constituting "the majority of evil child characters" (Renner, *Evil Children*, 6).

23. Chudacoff, *How Old Are You*, 4–5.

24. Wells, *Childhood in Global Perspective*, 3.

25. Renner, *Evil Children*, 7.

26. Renner, *Evil Children*, 7.

27. James and James, *Key Concepts*, 3.

28. Renner, *Evil Children*, 8.

29. Lennard, *Bad Seeds*, 11 (emphasis mine).

30. While Lennard and Renner both raise the issue of agency in their respective introductions, the concept is rarely discussed in the chapters following.

over children's agency[31] and presents as an area ripe for further exploration, using cinema's brood of young antichrists as subjects. First, however, the originating film must be contextualized. *Omen* did not appear in a vacuum but after two decades of the "evil child" appearing with increasing regularity on movie screens. While Renner reduces evil in these narratives to corrupting influences upon young characters,[32] a more complex framework is needed to account for the diversity of "evil kids" encountered.

BEASTS, BAD SEEDS, AND CUCKOOS: CINEMA'S "EVIL KIDS"

The "evil child" first appeared regularly in literature and on screens in the 1950s amid broader philosophical discussions about evil.[33] James Berger refers to some writers' perceptions of the Holocaust as an apocalyptic event, a "historical rupture [that] shattered certain ideas and hopes regarding social, technological, and aesthetic progress."[34] William Golding was among these authors, and his 1954 dystopian novel *Lord of the Flies* explored evil's origin in the wake of Nazi atrocities.[35] In the 1963 film adaptation, a group of stranded English schoolboys devolve into "savagery,"[36] their violence emanating from the "beast" within and mirroring adults' own devastation away from the island. Humans in the story are universally depraved, reflecting Golding's belief in "original sin."[37]

While Peter Hollindale identifies Golding's thesis as "a vision of humankind . . . tragically vindicated in many parts of the world,"[38] aversion to a universal inclination toward evil is reflected in the dominance of two alternative models: evil restricted to certain individuals and evil external to

---

31. James and James, *Key Concepts*, 4–6; Valentine, "Accounting for Agency"; Wyness, *Childhood*, 7–8.

32. Renner, *Evil Children*, 7–8. Here she appears to have modified her earlier bifurcation of environmental-based and natural-based origins of evil (Renner, "Evil Children," 5–6), viewing it instead as effect rather than cause with "realms of influence that radiate ever farther outward from the child" (Renner, *Evil Children*, 8).

33. Renner, "Evil Children," 1, 5–6.

34. Berger, "Introduction," 391.

35. Golding, *Hot Gates*, 86–87.

36. Golding's use of patronizing colonial discourses that equate "blackness, childishness and savagery" has been exposed (Hawlin, "Savages in the Forest," 130), but the marginalization of children that this and similar examples of paternalism rely on (Alderson, *Introduction to Critical Realism*, 92) should also be challenged.

37. Golding, *Hot Gates*, 86, 88.

38. Hollindale, "*Lord of the Flies*," 2.

humans.[39] *The Bad Seed* (1956) is an example of the first: Rhoda Penmark, an eight-year-old serial killer, inherits murderous impulses from her grandmother.[40] *Village of the Damned* (1960), an adaptation of John Wyndham's novel *The Midwich Cuckoos*, illustrates the second, its supernaturally-empowered "evil kids" being alien in origin and a threat to humanity.[41] These three films reflect different ideas about evil's origin—universal, restricted, external—but all view that evil as an *inherent* attribute of the children featured; they are evil by nature and inevitably behave so.

There was a shift in focus during the 1960s from innately "evil kids" to those *made so*.[42] Alongside stories of inborn malevolence, the 1970s saw examples of children acquiring evil tendencies that can be mapped onto the same three coordinates. The most popular external invasion children face in the movies is demonic possession, the most famous such narrative being *The Exorcist* (1973). In *The Other* (1972), psychosis following the death of his twin brother is the catalyst for a boy's murder spree.[43] Universal yet onset evil—an almost impossible combination—features in the 1976 movie *Who Can Kill a Child?* All the children on a remote island kill their parents; several of the malefactors then sail away to "infect" their compatriots throughout the world. The film opens with seven minutes of footage documenting atrocities committed against children, a lens that allows their violence to be (re)interpreted as revenge or even self-defense.[44]

Other films of the period explored the *apparent* evilness of young characters, eventually overturning these expectations. A boy is believed responsible for drowning his little sister and poisoning his mother in *The Nanny* (1965), only to be exonerated when the deranged family nanny is unmasked as the true culprit.[45] A year earlier, *Children of the Damned*

39. This tripartite scheme is adapted from an analysis of the novel by Gregor and Kinkead-Weekes, *William Golding*, 29, expanding the island community to the whole of humanity.

40. The film was adapted from a successful stage play (Pomerance, "Introduction," 5), itself based on the same-titled novel by William March.

41. The cuckoo's practice of laying eggs in other birds' nests and threatening the survival of the hosts' own offspring is an image that stands behind both book and film (Haberman, "Commentary"). Only implied in the film, the global threat posed by the aliens was explicit in advertising (Clark and Senn, *Sixties Shockers*, 410).

42. Renner, "Evil Children," 3. As Renner subsequently jettisoned any notion of children's evil essence, this claim is unsurprisingly lacking in the parallel section of her later historical introduction (Renner, *Evil Children*, 3).

43. Both films were adaptations of same-titled novels, those of William Peter Blatty and Thomas Tryon, respectively.

44. Serrador, "Child Director"; Lázaro-Reboll, *Spanish Horror Film*, 116–24.

45. This movie was also based on a book, a same-titled novel by Evelyn Piper.

featured six international prodigies whose powers resembled those of *Village*'s aliens,[46] yet their violence may also be interpreted as self-defense. Feared as a different and superior species, the children are perhaps humans evolved a million years, electing for pacifism and perishing in a barrage of bullets and debris.[47]

Renner's assertion that "the history of evil child narratives has largely been a series of efforts to confirm the essential innocence of children"[48] is defensible, not because the central characters are unable to exercise agency, but because those who are not exorcised or absolved are ejected altogether from the category of "child."[49] As the preceding survey has shown, films of the 1950s through 1970s display a variety of approaches to the topic of evil and childhood (summarized in fig. 1), drawing upon both the Dionysian and Apollonian myths of childhood in constructing their central figure. Popular usage of "bad seed" in reference to *any* "evil child"[50] or the characterization of nonsupernatural malefactors as "demonic"[51] reflect an uncritical homogeneity that is often imposed upon this complex corpus. It was into this diverse and paradoxical cinematic milieu that *Omen* appeared. Instead of occupying the margins of the apocalyptic genre as did *Flies* and *Village*,[52] the movie focused on an end times scenario and moved the "evil child" to the center of that drama.

---

46. The opening credits present the film as a sequel to Wyndham's novel rather than its cinematic adaptation.

47. My interpretation is based on the pro-pacifist views of the scriptwriter, who later penned the screenplay for *Gandhi* (Briley, "Commentary"). Kord claims instead that the film is "unequivocal in its denunciation of the human race" and, setting up a binary of killing or being killed, proposes that "the horror of *Children of the Damned* is . . . neither humanity now nor humanity in a million years . . . will be able to consider [the] third alternative" of living (Kord, *Little Horrors*, 79, 81).

48. Renner, *Evil Children*, 7.

49. Lennard, *Bad Seeds*, 4. This same process is used when extreme acts of violence are perpetrated by real children (Jenks, *Childhood*, 129).

50. Showalter, "Introduction," v.

51. Derry, *Dark Dreams 2.0*, 101; Heffernan, *Ghouls, Gimmicks, and Gold*, 187.

52. Derry, *Dark Dreams 2.0*, 80–81.

The "Evil Child" in Cinema (1950s to 1970s)

	Inborn Evil	Acquired Evil	Apparent Evil
Universal	Lord of the Flies (1963)	Who Can Kill a Child? (1976)	Who Can Kill a Child? Children of the Damned
Restricted	The Bad Seed (1956)	The Other (1972)	The Nanny (1965)
External	Village of the Damned (1960)	The Exorcist (1973)	Children of the Damned (1964)

Figure 1

DAMIEN THORN: DEVILISH BEAST OR INNOCENT VICTIM?

Hoping to capitalize on Warner Brothers' success with *Exorcist* to create their own "evil child" flick, producers at Twentieth Century Fox plugged into the apocalyptic fervor sparked by Hal Lindsey's book *The Late Great Planet Earth* (1970), a best-seller that neatly packaged dispensationalism for popular audiences.[53] Dispensationalism is a view of history unfolding in seven "dispensations,"[54] with the transition between the final two marked by global tribulations and the reign of the antichrist.[55] The idea for a film revolving around this evil being as a child was that of Robert Munger, a born-again Christian who in 1974 pitched the concept to his friend and movie producer, Harvey Bernhard. By autumn of the following year, a screenplay by David Seltzer was in production with Richard Donner as director and Munger as religious advisor.[56] The result of this collaboration was *The Omen*, released theatrically in June 1976.

---

53. Shuck, *Marks of the Beast*, 37–41. Co-written with C. C. Carlson, the book was adapted into a documentary-style film narrated by Orson Welles in 1976.

54. These epochs are innocency, conscience, human government, promise, law, grace, and kingdom.

55. Shuck, *Marks of the Beast*, 34, 41–52.

56. Palance, "Omen Legacy."

The film focuses on the character of Robert Thorn and his inquiry into the identity of his "adopted" son Damien. He comes to believe the boy is the antichrist ostensibly prophesied in the book of Revelation[57] and drags the alleged son of the devil[58] writhing and screaming into a church to extinguish his life on holy ground. The man is thwarted in his efforts when the police shoot him dead, but he had succeeded in killing Damien just as the bullet was fired in the first cut of the film shown to Twentieth Century Fox executives.[59] The corporation's insistence the boy survive introduced ambiguity into Seltzer's story about the *delusion* of the devil[60] and members of the Catholic clergy concocting a murderous scheme to usher in a satanic apocalypse. Donner claims that Robert goes insane and characterizes one ex-conspirator who urges him to kill Damien as a religious zealot out of touch with reality.[61] Viewing *Omen* through the lens suggested by its scriptwriter and director sees a human boy caught in the middle of and victimized by religious factions that want to hasten or avert an *imagined* apocalypse.

Critical viewings that take Damien's identity as the antichrist for granted are nonetheless ubiquitous.[62] Attempts to ascribe evil to the boy, however, are problematic. Lennard's claims that Damien has "a remarkably subdued presence," is "curiously neutral in the conflict," and possesses an "agency [that] recedes into insignificance"[63] create tension with his position that young villains *always* display some form of autonomy. Agency is *not* something the character exercises to any degree that would justify an attribution of villainy. A tricycle collision that ends with his mother miscarrying is described by Lennard as Damien's "most serious misdemeanor," yet he

---

57. The poetic prophecy "cited" in the movie is, as Martens quips, from "a new and improved edition [of Revelation], containing quotes missing from the Greek original," a rewriting of the biblical text that contains "a mishmash of ancient and modern apocalyptic themes" (Martens, *End of the World*, 105).

58. The idea of the antichrist as the literal son of the devil was introduced into the popular imagination through Ira Levin's 1967 novel *Rosemary's Baby*, which was adapted to film the following year.

59. Donner and Helgeland, "Commentary."

60. Seltzer, "666."

61. Donner and Helgeland, "Commentary." *Omen* is thus an example of what Berlinerblau refers to as secular art "produced in . . . contentious dialogue with religion" (Berlinerblau, *Secular Bible*, 137).

62. Martens, *End of the World*, 104–9; Dixon, *History of Horror*, 151–52; Gerlach, "Antichrist as Anti-Monomyth"; Winstead, "Devil Made Me Do"; Lennard, *Bad Seeds*, 98–107; Scahill, *Revolting Child*, 103–11; Renner, *Evil Children*, 30; Lewis, "Voting Horrors," 306.

63. Lennard, *Bad Seeds*, 99.

immediately attributes this to the boy's satanic nanny.[64] Several pages later, however, he indicts Damien directly for this offence[65] *and* for killing the Thorns' biological child years earlier, a rather more serious charge and an incredible achievement, being a newborn himself at the time!

Lennard is not alone in trying to pin heinous yet far-fetched deeds on Damien. In addition to the tricycle incident, Renner accuses the boy of willing his first nanny to commit suicide and then remarks how "at the end of the film [he] smiles coyly into the camera to show us just how much he's enjoying himself."[66] This grin was unscripted; the actor Harvey Stephens attempted to restrain a laugh when asked by Donner to look mean.[67] A sinister interpretation of the final gesture rests on an assumption of guilt, and blame for the film's casualties rests on an assumption of satanic identity. Wheeler Dixon articulates this latter supposition explicitly when he writes how "Damien's mere physical presence serves as an instantly comprehensible symbol of destruction," thus he becomes "*responsible* for a decapitation, a hanging, an impalement, and a fatal fall down a flight of stairs."[68] The last of these is most remarkable for *Omen*'s supposed villain, since it is a description of Father Karras's demise in *Exorcist*!

When attempts to persuasively implicate Damien in violent acts fail, there remains evil embodiment; John Martens is representative of this position.[69] Assumed to be the devil's son, he is an "evil child" *by nature*, irrespective of present innocuous behavior. As prophesied harbinger to the apocalypse, destiny looms ominously over the boy[70] and provides justification for those who seek his death. Far from the supernatural being wielding "the supreme power of Satanic DNA" that Renner imagines him to be,[71] Damien is presented as genuinely vulnerable, a "master identity" for

---

64. Lennard, *Bad Seeds*, 99. Lennard writes that Damien "coast[s] his tricycle into the railing on which she is somewhat foolishly perched." However, the woman is not standing on the railing itself but on a small end table into which the boy crashes, knocking her off balance and over the nearby railing.

65. Lennard, *Bad Seeds*, 103. This time he claims that Damien "pushes pregnant Katherine Thorn over a balcony," an even further departure from what is depicted in the film.

66. Renner, "Evil Children," 5. She joins Lennard in imagining that Damien "pushes his adopted mother over a high balcony." Lewis similarly ascribes intentionality to Damien for this and claims he uses supernatural powers to control the behavior of others (Lewis, "Voting Horrors," 306, 314).

67. Donner and Helgeland, "Commentary."

68. Dixon, *History of Horror*, 152 (emphasis mine).

69. Martens, *End of the World*, 104.

70. Winstead, "Devil Made Me Do," 37, 42.

71. Renner, *Evil Children*, 30.

contemporary children,⁷² which attracts the protectionist impulses of the nanny persuaded of his satanic genesis. Given the boy's helplessness and passivity, Scahill refers to him as a child "imbued with evil *potential*."⁷³ Indeed, Scahill comes closest among recent interpreters in entertaining an absolution for Damien, writing how he "retains something almost approaching innocence through his seeming ignorance of his destiny."⁷⁴

While Renner thinks Damien "fit[s] the bill of 'evil child' pretty straightforwardly,"⁷⁵ the preceding analysis calls that evaluation into question. The five-year-old's satanic genesis was uncertain, allowing multiple interpretations. Rejecting supernatural origins based on the intentions of Seltzer and Donner, Damien fits best into the category of inborn evil that is only apparent. According to this interpretation, the closing text from Revelation is not confirmation of Damien's identity as the antichrist, but a cynical evocation of ancient "Scripture" as a lens to distort understandings of present reality. Even if the satanic genesis of Munger's imagination is assumed, the boy's limited exercise of agency and lack of overt malevolence still render him unsuitable for categorization at the external inborn evil coordinate. This Damien's potential for evil, however, was not only activated in a sequel, but the trigger for his first and dominant cinematic legacy.

DAMIEN'S FIRST LEGACY: MALEVOLENT YOUNG ANTICHRISTS

The success of *Omen* led quickly to the sequel *Damien: Omen II* (1978). Neither Seltzer, who was disinterested in the project,⁷⁶ nor Donner, who was then directing *Superman* (1978),⁷⁷ worked on the film. This allowed Bernhard to steer the story unambiguously in the direction of Munger's originating idea and the supernatural,⁷⁸ a decision that Seltzer criticized.⁷⁹ *Damien* narrates the "coming of age" of its eponymous twelve-year-old military cadet,⁸⁰ who is adjured by a secret devotee "to put aside childish things"⁸¹ and face up to

---

72. Christensen, "Childhood and Cultural Constitution," 40.
73. Scahill, "It's All for You," 98 (emphasis mine).
74. Scahill, *Revolting Child*, 106.
75. Renner, "Evil Children," 5.
76. Seltzer, "Omen Legacy."
77. Palance, "Omen Legacy."
78. Bernhard, "Omen Legacy."
79. Seltzer, "Omen Legacy."
80. Scahill, *Revolting Child*, 107.
81. An allusion to 1 Cor 13:11.

who he is. Directed by another follower to the book of Revelation,[82] Damien finds reference to the infamous "mark of the beast."[83] The boy's initial reaction to finding a trio of sixes on his scalp is shock and sorrow, tearfully protesting, "Why me?!" After this woeful response that Scahill likens to Jesus's anguish in Gethsemane,[84] the young antichrist subjects his will to that of his father, the archetypal murderer (John 8:44), and uses his burgeoning supernatural power to systematically eliminate opponents; each gruesome death designed to appear as coincidence.[85] The boy's initial recoil from and subsequent embrace of a satanic persona undercuts a fatalistic interpretation of the character. It is Damien's belief in fate, rather than fate itself, that seems determinant in his crucial moment of choice.

While not as successful at the box office as its predecessor, *Damien* was nonetheless responsible for cementing the supernatural interpretation of *Omen* into the public imagination.[86] There is thus no question that five-year-old Damien is the antichrist in the 2006 remake, his iconic smile at the end construed menacingly by the filmmakers.[87] In accord with Lennard's thesis, the character exerts a *degree* of autonomy, glaring at his mother with malicious intent[88] and intentionally colliding with her. The boy uses his budding supernatural power when his mother is subsequently murdered,[89] but in a role supportive of the satanic nanny to whom he is subordinate. The boy's thrashing about and protests in the climactic church scene are, however, incredulous given his access to at least *some* satanic power as a defense.

666: The Child, released the same year direct to video, suffers similarly with its own uncritical recycling of this and other original *Omen* plot points. Nine-year-old Donald is fully aware of his identity as the antichrist and murders telepathically, yet cowers inexplicably when his adopted father seeks to kill him. The satanic nanny who kneels before Donald as a servant

---

82. Martens's claim that this biblical book functions in *Omen* as "a guidebook for the Devil" (Martens, *End of the World*, 109) is equally applicable to the sequel.

83. Rev 13:16–18; the boy's voice-over also includes Rev 13:3b–4; 19:19; and even part of Dan 8:25! This "mark" has fascinated many over the past two millennia. For a review of the various interpretive approaches to the riddle, both ancient and modern, see Lupieri, *Commentary on the Apocalypse*, 212–18.

84. Scahill, *Revolting Child*, 107. Cf. Mark 14:32–36.

85. Bernhard and Kenny, "Commentary."

86. Neither the third nor fourth installments in the original series of *Omen* movies—*The Final Conflict* (1981) and *Omen IV: The Awakening* (1991)—bear directly on an exploration of the antichrist as a child in film.

87. Moore et al., "Commentary."

88. Moore et al., "Commentary."

89. Moore et al., "Commentary."

and declares she is his sword and shield is a superfluous character in light of the boy's well-honed paranormal abilities. Film narratives that include a supernatural and malevolent young antichrist are compelling only insofar as they effectively negotiate the innocent and vulnerable ideals of childhood with which they are inextricably bound up. While 666 fails at this, several other pertinent movies are more successful.

In *Servants of Twilight* (1991),[90] six-year-old Joey Scavello is pursued by members of the fringe "Church of the Twilight" as the antichrist who must die to avert the apocalypse. Only after the boy appears to summon a swarm of bats to kill the cult's leader and to resurrect his mother does the fanatics' proposal begin to seem credible. Joey's satanic identity is confirmed when he telepathically chokes to death a potential stepdad who refuses to play along with the boy's ruse of innocent childhood. Conversely, eight-year-old Dylan St. Clair in *The Calling* (2000) assumes lethal supernatural abilities only after his induction into a satanic order. The young antichrist is genuinely scared of being crucified upside down as part of the Christmas Eve initiation and of later being drowned by his mother in an inversion of the holy sacrament of baptism on his ninth birthday, but he submits to both rituals as part of the devil's apocalyptic plans. Dylan is miraculously revivified,[91] just as seven-year-old David Gabriel appears to be in *Devil's Angel* (2010)[92] after being struck by a vehicle.[93] Cloned from DNA taken from the Shroud of Turin,[94] this young antichrist inherits Jesus's healing abilities, but not his compassion. Under the influence of a nefarious "invisible friend,"[95] David toys with life and death, whimsically extending or withholding his curative powers.

90. The movie, which premiered on Showtime, is an adaptation of Dean Koontz's 1984 novel *The Servants of Twilight*, originally published under his pen name, Leigh Nichols.

91. This occurs on Easter Sunday in another appropriation of a Christian holiday. Renner claims that none of the young antichrists she has seen on film are killed (Renner, "Apocalypse Begins at Home," 56). It is unclear whether she overlooked Dylan in *Calling* (a movie she does mention) or thought the boy's resurrection disqualified his death from consideration as an example.

92. This is the film's DVD rerelease title; Renner's engagement with the movie is under the original title *I'm Not Jesus Mommy* (Renner, *Evil Children*, 33).

93. It is unclear whether the boy is dead or just unconscious; Renner may be excused for overlooking another example of the young antichrist killed by having embraced the latter interpretation.

94. The scientist who clones David works to the song *Ave Maria* and imagines himself as co-creator of a new savior; the film participates in the same critique of reproductive cloning that is seen in the 2004 "evil child" movie *Godsend* (O'Riordan, "Human Cloning in Film," 149).

95. This elusive character finally appears in a black suit in the final shot of the film, his voice credited in closed captioning as none other than "The Devil."

The first wave of young antichrists that emanated from *Damien* ranged in ages from five to nine and were "portrayed simply *as* evil rather than as free moral agents who have made choices that lead to evil consequences."[96] Agency is often restricted and exercised in degrees. Damien of the remake and Dylan, both sons of Satan, are subordinated to and influenced by evil adults; David, while not an offspring of the devil, is under his power. Donald and Joey act more independently, but their satanic paternity seems determinative of their wicked behavior. These characters' prepubescent age *is* a factor, since the adolescent Damien is the singular exception among this brood; he *chooses* to embrace this evil disposition. Other antichrists close in age, however, do not; it is to this virtuous group, the second of Damien's legacies, I now turn.

DAMIEN'S SECOND LEGACY: VIRTUOUS YOUNG ANTICHRISTS

11/11/11, released direct to video in 2011,[97] is an "evil child" apocalyptic film, but not one that features its juvenile character in the role of the antichrist. The movie nonetheless borrows plot elements from *Omen* such as an evil nanny and a satanic conspiracy. The child at the center of this apocalyptic drama, Nat Vales, is the vessel through which the devil will come when he turns 11 on 11/11/11. As the date approaches, the boy is invaded by evil spirits that drive him to murder and thus to be a worthy receptacle for Satan to inhabit. When an eleventh-hour exorcism fails,[98] Nat's father plunges a sword into his levitating son,[99] killing the boy and averting the apocalypse. While not an antichrist-as-child film,[100] *11/11/11* contains two ideas—boy as vessel for the devil and potential redemption—that appear in more pertinent movies.

---

96. Stone, "Evil on Film," 316 (emphasis original). Stone's observation concerns the majority of evil characters generally, not just "evil kids."

97. The film was produced by the Asylum, which was also responsible for *666*.

98. Wilbur, "*11/11/11*."

99. The movie thus also relies on *The Exorcist* and is a straightforward example of an "evil child" of the external acquired variety.

100. Renner includes the movie in this category, claiming that "Satanists . . . eagerly work to ensure [the child] assumes his satanic powers on his eleventh birthday" (Renner, "Apocalypse Begins at Home," 53). Not only is Nat never referred to as the antichrist, but the devil's invasion of his body would wipe out his personality. Having then included the film, Renner curiously overlooks it as an example of the young antichrist killed in cinema!

The following year saw the release of *Ghost Rider: Spirit of Vengeance*, a hybrid of the superhero and apocalyptic genres.[101] Roarke, the devil's latest manifestation in human form, has sired Danny Ketch[102] to have a superior vessel into which to transfer his soul before his present body deteriorates. According to prophecy, the transference rite must take place in the boy's thirteenth year. Danny allies with Roarke's nemesis, the Ghost Rider, who mentors the boy and urges him to use his dark power for good. Faced with a choice much like the twelve-year-old Damien, Danny elects *not* to embrace evil and thus does not *become*—in the Rider's estimation—the antichrist; satanic DNA is *not* determinative.

A parody of the "evil child" film corpus was inevitable.[103] It was the streaming service Netflix that did so in its original production *Little Evil* (2017), a spoof primarily of *Omen* (at least of its dominant interpretation), which reflects Damien's status as the "evil child" *par excellence* in the public imagination.[104] The movie's son of Satan is five-year-old Lucas, unable to resist his father's evil influence but wanting to be a good boy. His stepfather Gary learns from *The Definitive Book on Devil Children* that Lucas's body will become a portal for Satan on his sixth birthday and averts the apocalypse by *saving* his stepson from the doomsday cult eager to kill him and provide the devil his gateway. Antichrist-as-child movies typically end with their villains unchecked and parental figures dead, banished, or subordinated, but *Little Evil* subverts these conventions with Lucas redeemed and bonding with his stepfather.

Omen was also a source for the satirical treatment of apocalypticism in the six-part Amazon Prime miniseries *Good Omens* (2019).[105] The first working title of the source novel[106] was *William the Antichrist*, a reference to the

---

101. The movie revolves around the Marvel Comics' character of Johnny Blaze/Ghost Rider.

102. In the comics, Danny is not a child but an adult who assumes the powers of the Ghost Rider and who is later revealed to be Johnny's brother (Outlaw, "Ghost Rider").

103. Parody presupposes an identifiable set of conventions associated with a genre, subgenre, or film cycle (Moine, *Cinema Genre*, 126).

104. In line with other movies of the 2010s that evoke nostalgia for pop culture of the 1980s (McFadzean, *Suburban Fantastic Cinema*, 117–18), the filmmakers also poke fun at classic "evil kid" films of this particular decade, as well as at its other horror movies featuring children: *The Shining* (1980), *Poltergeist* (1982), *Children of the Corn* (1984), and *Child's Play* (1988).

105. Whyman, *Nice and Accurate*, 9. Acknowledging the permeable boundaries between types, parody mainly subverts film forms and conventions, whereas satire pokes fun at social and political targets (King, *Film Comedy*, 18).

106. Pratchett and Gaiman, *Good Omens*.

titular character of Richmal Crompton's *Just William* book series.[107] Adam Young, *Omens*' son of Satan, is modeled after the literary William, the British equivalent of the American good-natured "bad boy."[108] Because of a botched baby swap, the young antichrist is raised in the village of Tadfield; neither hell incarnate nor heaven incarnate, Adam is referred to as "human incarnate" despite satanic paternity. The boy and his friends play in Hogback Wood, an "idyllic rural hideaway" styled as their Eden;[109] a wholesome environment thus trumps devilish DNA, allowing Adam to be coded as innocent.

On his eleventh birthday, Adam unconsciously assumes satanic power, which includes the ability to change reality. Incited by demonic voices to end it all, the boy initiates Armageddon with the rationalization that adults have ruined the world, so he must obliterate it and start over.[110] Adam's mostly ignorant alignment with the forces of destruction is fleeting; coming to his senses, the boy leads his friends in vanquishing the embodiments of war, pollution, and famine.[111] Gabriel chides the redeemed young antichrist as a disobedient brat for his role in averting the apocalypse. When the devil confronts his "rebellious son," Adam's potent declaration that Satan is not his dad *and never was* alters reality, reversing the death and devastation the boy instigated and leaving him without satanic identity; he is not the antichrist *and never was*. Adam is grounded by his (now and always earthly) father, but in conformity with his "bad boy" persona, he leaves the backyard to pinch an apple from a neighbor's tree—naughty but by no means evil. *Omens*' denouement for Adam brings the exploration full circle to the interpretation of an innocent Damien in *Omen*; in the final analysis, neither character is the antichrist.

AGE, AGENCY, AND THE "EVIL CHILD" REPRISED

The preceding exploration into *Omen*'s character Damien and his two legacies in over forty years of antichrist-as-child movies has uncovered far more complex engagements with the figure of the "evil child" than the boy's

---

107. Whyman, *Nice and Accurate*, 7, 9, 135. There were over forty books in the series, written between 1919 and 1969, with numerous film and television adaptations (Cadogan, "Multimedia *William*," 105–6).

108. Greenway, "William Forever," 104–5.

109. Whyman, *Nice and Accurate*, 125, 127.

110. Sam Taylor Buck, the actor for Adam, played his character as having a split personality (Whyman, *Nice and Accurate*, 138).

111. Together with death, these constitute the series' "Four Horsepersons of the Apocalypse," with pollution taking the place of pestilence; cf. Rev 6:1–8.

stereotyped image in contemporary pop culture would suggest. Each film examined may be situated along the external evil axis, but the three categories of inborn, acquired, and apparent require fine-tuning to accommodate the range of characters encountered (see fig. 2). Damien of the remake, Donald, Joey, Dylan, and David all behave badly because of their satanic or (in David's case) manipulated genes. While the same may be said of Damien in the sequel, his supernatural power emerges only in his twelfth year *and* he makes a conscious choice at this time to indulge in wicked behavior, which suggests a form of acquired evil, a predisposition *embraced*. Adam and Danny become similarly empowered, but they choose the opposite; theirs is a predisposition to evil *rejected*. Lucas's malevolent actions owe to heredity, but also to an inability to resist his satanic father's bad influence; like Damien in *Omen*, he lacks culpability and is further redeemed from evil through the counteracting good influence of his stepfather.

"Evil" in Antichrist-as-Child Films

Inborn	Acquired	Apparent
Damien [12yo] (*Damien*)	Embraced ← → Rejected	Danny [13yo] (*Vengeance*) Adam [11yo] (*Omens*)
Donald [9yo] (*666*) Joey [6yo] (*Twilight*)	HIGH AGENCY	
Damien [5yo] (*Omen* 2006) Dylan [8/9yo] (*Calling*) David [7yo] (*Angel*)	Evil Disposition ?	Damien [5yo] (*Omen*)
BAD INFLUENCE	LOW AGENCY	Lucas [5/6yo] (*Evil*)
	REDEEMED	
Lucas [5/6yo] (*Evil*)		GOOD INFLUENCE

Figure 2

Significantly, the age of each antichrist is conveyed in his respective movie and may be correlated to the level of agency he displays. Under the influence of developmental psychology and Piaget's scheme of cognition, in particular,[112] young children are often thought incapable of exercising responsible agency.[113] The alleged transition to abstract reasoning around age

---

112. Jean Piaget (1896–1980) proposed four stages of children's cognitive development: sensorimotor (age 0–2), pre-operational (age 2–7), concrete operational (age 7–12), and formal operational (age 12+) (Smith et al., *Understanding Children's Development*, 445).

113. Wyness, *Childhood*, 56–57; see, however, the critiques of Piaget's methods and

twelve within a Piagetian framework[114] coincides here in the West with the average onset of puberty between the ages of ten and fourteen,[115] an acquisition of years that is often accompanied by an increase in participation and concomitant responsibility.[116] The antichrist-as-child film corpus reflects this influential developmental framework. Those characters within the older age range all display higher levels of agency than their under-ten counterparts. Agency, however, is no simple binary of having it or not.[117] Indeed, even the youngest antichrists exercise varying levels of autonomy vis-à-vis their protagonist parental figures, but most are at the same time subordinate to any evil adults present in the story. Similarly, virtuous antichrists submit to and are mentored by good adults even when they are otherwise powerful agents against movie antagonists.[118] Attention to age and agency in these films has proved useful in teasing out subtleties of interpretation, a process that may be fruitfully applied to cinema's other "evil kids."

If the tendency in recent antichrist-as-child cinema has been to explore Damien's alternative legacy, subverting the conventions of the dominant one by narrating the boy's redemption or championing his capacity as an agent of good, other "evil child" movies continue to proffer fatalistic approaches to inborn external malevolence. The recent films *Brightburn* and *Eli* (both 2019) aptly demonstrate this, the latter significantly so since its eponymous character is one of the devil's many children.[119] Attempts to heal the "sick" boy, who is ignorant of his true "condition" throughout most of the movie, fail; even tampering with his satanic genes cannot alter his abrupt transition from innocent victim to murderous beast.[120]

---

conclusions by Alderson, *Young Children's Rights*, 122 and Smith et al., *Understanding Children's Development*, 453–55.

114. Smith et al., *Understanding Children's Development*, 463–64.

115. Stainton-Rogers, "Gendered Childhoods," 191. While also acknowledging cultural and historical variation (Smith et al., *Understanding Children's Development*, 655–57; Lancy, *Anthropology of Childhood*, 294), my own definition of child corresponds with biological juvenility, which terminates with the onset of puberty (Magee, "Cinematic Childhood(s)," 33–34).

116. Butler, "Children's Rights," 16.

117. Oswell, *Agency of Children*, 269.

118. Antichrist-as-child films thus bolster present social hierarchies in which adults exercise authority over children (James and James, *Constructing Childhood*, 3).

119. Because the antichrist has been traditionally understood as a *unique* wicked being, neither Eli nor any of his satanic siblings are referred to as such.

120. After learning of his satanic paternity, Eli's eyes turn red and he snarls like an animal. This dehumanization of supernatural "evil kids" is found elsewhere (Magee, "Is This Your God," 93) and provides the rhetorical justification for those who seek to kill these characters. Damien of the remake is specifically called a beast, and Donald is referred to as "the vilest of serpents."

The Apollonian and Dionysian myths thus continue to flourish in contemporary "evil child" cinema, interacting with each other in complex ways that reinforce contemporary discourses of the innocent and vulnerable child. While films featuring apparently evil antichrists fall outside the horror genre,[121] the dread of pertinent movies within it is the unleashing of the Dionysian child's destructive potential in an apocalyptic scenario. Contrary, however, to what is imagined in Damien's dominant cinematic legacy, increasing children's access to agency and helping them to exercise it responsibly will not bring about the end of the world!

BIBLIOGRAPHY

Alderson, Priscilla. *An Introduction to Critical Realism and Childhood Studies*. Vol. 1 of *Childhoods Real and Imagined*. New York: Routledge, 2013.

———. *Young Children's Rights: Exploring Beliefs, Principles and Practice*. 2nd ed. London: Kingsley, 2008.

Allan, Keith, dir. *11/11/11*. DVD. Burbank, CA: Asylum Home Entertainment, 2011.

Amram, Robert, dir. *The Late Great Planet Earth*. DVD. N.p.: Scorpion Releasing, 2018.

Attenborough, Richard, dir. *Gandhi*. DVD. Culver City, CA: Sony Pictures Home Entertainment, 2007.

Baker, Graham, dir. *The Final Conflict*. DVD. Beverly Hills, CA: Twentieth Century Fox Home Entertainment, 2006.

Berger, James. "Introduction: Twentieth-Century Apocalypse: Forecasts and Aftermaths." *Twentieth-Century Literature* 46 (2000) 387–95.

Berlinerblau, Jacques. *The Secular Bible: Why Nonbelievers Must Take Religion Seriously*. New York: Cambridge University Press, 2005.

Bernhard, Harvey. "The Omen Legacy." *The Omen*. DVD. Beverly Hills, CA: Twentieth Century Fox Home Entertainment, 2006.

———, and J. M. Kenny. "Commentary." *Damien: Omen II*. DVD. Beverly Hills, CA: Twentieth Century Fox Home Entertainment, 2006.

Blatty, William Peter. *The Exorcist*. New York: HarperCollins, 2011.

Briley, John. "Commentary." *Children of the Damned*. DVD. Burbank, CA: Warner Home Video, 2004.

Brook, Peter, dir. *Lord of the Flies*. DVD. New York: Criterion Collection, 2008.

Butler, Clark. "Children's Rights: An Historical and Conceptual Analysis." In *Child Rights: The Movement, International Law, and Opposition*, edited by Clark Butler, 13–36. West Lafayette, IN: Purdue University Press, 2012.

Cadogan, Mary. "Multimedia *William*." In *Turning the Page: Children's Literature in Performance and the Media*, edited by Fiona M. Collins and Jeremy Ridgman, 105–14. Bern: Lang, 2006.

Caesar, Richard, dir. *The Calling*. DVD. Summit Entertainment, 2001.

Christensen, Pia Haudrup. "Childhood and the Cultural Constitution of Vulnerable Bodies." In *The Body, Childhood and Society*, edited by Alan Prout, 38–59. Basingstoke, UK: Macmillan, 2000.

---

121. While *Omen* is typically classified as a horror, the director resisted the label and considered the film a mystery/suspense/thriller (Donner, "666").

Chudacoff, Howard P. *How Old Are You? Age Consciousness in American Culture.* Princeton, NJ: Princeton University Press, 1989.
Clark, Mark, and Bryan Senn. *Sixties Shockers: A Critical Filmography of Horror Cinema, 1960–1969.* Jefferson, NC: McFarland, 2011.
Collins, John J. *The Apocalyptic Imagination: An Introduction to Jewish Apocalyptic Literature.* 3rd ed. Grand Rapids: Eerdmans, 2016.
———. "Introduction: Towards the Morphology of a Genre." In *Apocalypse: The Morphology of a Genre,* edited by John J. Collins, 1–20. Missoula, MT: Scholars, 1979.
Craig, Eli, dir. *Little Evil.* Netflix, 2017. Online. netflix.com/watch/80139506.
Derry, Charles. *Dark Dreams 2.0: A Psychological History of the Modern Horror Film from the 1950s to the 21st Century.* Jefferson, NC: McFarland, 2009.
DiTommaso, Lorenzo. "Apocalypses and Apocalypticism in Antiquity (Part I)." *Currents in Biblical Research* 5 (2007) 235–86.
Dixon, Wheeler Winston. *A History of Horror.* New Brunswick, NJ: Rutgers University Press, 2010.
Donner, Richard. "666: *The Omen* Revealed." *The Omen.* DVD. Beverly Hills, CA: Twentieth Century Fox Home Entertainment, 2006.
———, dir. *The Omen.* DVD. Beverly Hills, CA: Twentieth Century Fox Home Entertainment, 2006.
———, dir. *Superman: The Movie.* DVD. Burbank, CA: Warner Home Video, 2006.
———, and Brian Helgeland. "Commentary." *The Omen.* DVD. Beverly Hills, CA: Twentieth Century Fox Home Entertainment, 2006.
Foy, Ciarán, dir. *Eli.* Netflix, 2019. Online. netflix.com/watch/80206910.
Friedkin, William, dir. *The Exorcist.* DVD. Burbank, CA: Warner Home Video, 2000.
Gerlach, Neil. "The Antichrist as Anti-Monomyth: The *Omen* Films as Social Critique." *Journal of Popular Culture* 44 (2011) 1027–46.
Golding, William. *The Hot Gates and Other Occasional Pieces.* New York: Harcourt, Brace & World, 1966.
———. *Lord of the Flies.* London; Boston: Faber and Faber, 1954.
Greenway, Betty. "William Forever: Richmal Crompton's Unusual Achievement." *Lion and the Unicorn* 26 (2002) 98–111.
Gregor, Ian, and Mark Kinkead-Weekes. *William Golding: A Critical Study of the Novels.* 3rd ed. London: Faber and Faber, 2002.
Haberman, Steve. "Commentary." *Village of the Damned.* DVD. Burbank, CA: Warner Home Video, 2004.
Hamm, Nick, dir. *Godsend.* DVD. Santa Monica, CA: Lions Gate Home Entertainment, 2004.
Hawlin, Stefan. "The Savages in the Forest: Decolonising William Golding." *Critical Survey* 7 (1995) 125–35.
Heffernan, Kevin. *Ghouls, Gimmicks, and Gold: Horror Films and the American Movie Business, 1953–1968.* Durham, NC: Duke University Press, 2004.
Hockey, Jenny, and Allison James. *Social Identities across the Life Course.* Basingstoke, UK: Palgrave Macmillan, 2003.
Holland, Tom, dir. *Child's Play.* DVD. Beverly Hills, CA: Twentieth Century Fox Home Entertainment, 2015.
Hollindale, Peter. "*Lord of the Flies* in the Twenty-First Century." *The Use of English* 53 (2001) 1–12.

Holt, Seth, dir. *The Nanny*. DVD. Beverly Hills, CA: Twentieth Century Fox Home Entertainment, 2008.
Hooper, Tobe, dir. *Poltergeist*. DVD. Burbank, CA: Warner Home Video, 2007.
Jackson, Jake, dir. *666: The Child*. DVD. Burbank, CA: Asylum Home Entertainment, 2006.
James, Allison, and Adrian James. *Constructing Childhood: Theory, Policy and Social Practice*. New York: Palgrave Macmillan, 2004.
———. *Key Concepts in Childhood Studies*. 2nd ed. Thousand Oaks, CA: Sage, 2012.
Jenks, Chris. *Childhood*. 2nd ed. New York: Routledge, 2005.
Juares, Vaughn, dir. *Devil's Angel*. DVD. Deerfield Beach, FL: Maverick Entertainment Group, 2012.
Kiersch, Fritz, dir. *Children of the Corn*. DVD. Chatsworth, CA: Image Entertainment, 2011.
King, Geoff. *Film Comedy*. New York: Wallflower, 2002.
Koontz, Dean. *The Servants of Twilight*. New York: Berkley, 2011.
Kord, T. S. *Little Horrors: How Cinema's Evil Children Play on Our Guilt*. Jefferson, NC: McFarland & Company, 2016.
Kubrick, Stanley, dir. *The Shining*. DVD. Burbank, CA: Warner Home Video, 2007.
Lancy, David F. *The Anthropology of Childhood: Cherubs, Chattel, Changelings*. 2nd ed. Cambridge: Cambridge University Press, 2015.
Lázaro-Reboll, Antonio. *Spanish Horror Film*. Edinburgh: Edinburgh University Press, 2012.
Leader, Anton M., dir. *Children of the Damned*. DVD. Burbank, CA: Warner Home Video, 2004.
Lennard, Dominic. *Bad Seeds and Holy Terrors: The Child Villains of Horror Film*. Albany: State University of New York Press, 2014.
LeRoy, Mervyn, dir. *The Bad Seed*. DVD. Burbank, CA: Warner Home Video, 2004.
Levin, Ira. *Rosemary's Baby*. New York: Signet, 1997.
Lewis, Derek. "Voting Horrors: Youthful, Monstrous, and Worrying Agency in American Films." *Popular Culture Studies Journal* 6 (2018) 306–25.
Lindsey, Hal, with C. C. Carlson. *The Late Great Planet Earth*. Grand Rapids: Zondervan, 1970.
Lupieri, Edmondo F. *A Commentary on the Apocalypse of John*. Translated by Maria Poggi Johnson and Adam Kamesar. Grand Rapids: Eerdmans, 2006.
Mackinnon, Douglas, dir. *Good Omens*. DVD. London: BBC, 2019.
Magee, James. "Cinematic Childhoods(s) and Imag(in)ing the Boy Jesus: Adaptations of Luke 2:41–52 in Late Twentieth-Century Film." MA thesis, Trinity Western University, 2019. https://twu.arcabc.ca/islandora/object/twu%3A523.
———. "'Is This Your God . . . Killer of Children?' Israel's 'Childish' Deity and the Other(s) in *Exodus: Gods and Kings*." In *Encountering the Other: Christian and Multifaith Perspectives*, edited by Laura Duhan-Kaplan and Harry O. Maier, 82–103. Eugene, OR: Pickwick, 2020.
March, William. *The Bad Seed*. New York: HarperCollins, 1997.
Martens, John W. *The End of the World: The Apocalyptic Imagination in Film and Television*. Winnipeg: Shillingford, 2003.
McFadzean, Angus. *Suburban Fantastic Cinema: Growing Up in the Late Twentieth Century*. New York: Wallflower, 2019.

McGinn, Bernard. *Antichrist: Two Thousand Years of the Human Fascination with Evil*. San Francisco: HarperCollins, 1994.
Migliore, Daniel L. *Faith Seeking Understanding: An Introduction to Christian Theology*. 3rd ed. Grand Rapids: Eerdmans, 2014.
Moine, Raphaëlle. *Cinema Genre*. Translated by Alistair Fox and Hilary Radner. Malden, MA: Blackwell, 2008.
Montesi, Jorge, and Dominique Othenin-Gerard, dirs. *Omen IV: The Awakening*. DVD. Beverly Hills, CA: Twentieth Century Fox Home Entertainment, 2006.
Montgomery, Heather. "Childhood in Time and Place." In *Understanding Childhood: An Interdisciplinary Approach*, edited by Martin Woodhead and Heather Montgomery, 45–74. Chichester: John Wiley & Sons, 2003.
Moore, John, dir. *The Omen*. DVD. Beverly Hills, CA: Twentieth Century Fox Home Entertainment, 2006.
———, et al. "Commentary." *The Omen*. DVD. Beverly Hills, CA: Twentieth Century Fox Home Entertainment, 2006.
Mulligan, Robert, dir. *The Other*. DVD. Beverly Hills, CA: Twentieth Century Fox Home Entertainment, 2006.
Obrow, Jeffrey, dir. *Servants of Twilight*. DVD. Santa Monica, CA: Trimark Home Video, 2002.
O'Riordan, Kate. "Human Cloning in Film: Horror, Ambivalence, Hope." *Science as Culture* 17 (2008) 145–62.
Ostwalt, Conrad. "Apocalyptic." In *The Routledge Companion to Religion and Film*, edited by John Lyden, 368–83. New York: Routledge, 2009.
Oswell, David. *The Agency of Children: From Family to Global Human Rights*. New York: Cambridge University Press, 2013.
Outlaw, Kofi. "*Ghost Rider: Spirit of Vengeance*: Will Dan Ketch Replace Johnny Blaze?" *Screen Rant*, Jan. 6, 2012. https://screenrant.com/ghost-rider-spirit-vengeance-danny-ketch/.
Neveldine, Mark, and Brian Taylor, dirs. *Ghost Rider: Spirit of Vengeance*. DVD. Culver City, CA: Sony Pictures Home Entertainment, 2012.
Palance, Jack. "The Omen Legacy." *The Omen*. DVD. Beverly Hills, CA: Twentieth Century Fox Home Entertainment, 2006.
Piper, Evelyn. *The Nanny*. New York: Open Road, 2016.
Polanski, Roman, dir. *Rosemary's Baby*. DVD. Hollywood, CA: Paramount Home Entertainment, 2006.
Pomerance, Murray. "Introduction: Movies and the 1950s." In *American Cinema of the 1950s: Themes and Variations*, edited by Murray Pomerance, 1–20. New Brunswick, NJ: Rutgers University Press, 2005.
Pratchett, Terry, and Neil Gaiman. *Good Omens: The Nice and Accurate Prophecies of Agnes Nutter, Witch*. London: Transworld, 2014.
Renner, Karen J. "The Apocalypse Begins at Home: The Antichrist-as-Child Film." *Frame* 26 (2013) 47–59.
———. "Evil Children in Film and Literature." In *The 'Evil Child' in Literature, Film and Popular Culture*, edited by Karen J. Renner, 1–27. New York: Routledge, 2013.
———. *Evil Children in the Popular Imagination*. New York: Palgrave Macmillan, 2016.
Rilla, Wolf, dir. *Village of the Damned*. DVD. Burbank, CA: Warner Home Video, 2004.

Scahill, Andrew. "'It's All for You, Damien!' Oedipal Horror and Racial Privilege in *The Omen* Series." In *Lost and Othered Children in Contemporary Cinema*, edited by Debbie C. Olson and Andrew Scahill, 95–105. Plymouth, MA: Lexington, 2014.

———. *The Revolting Child in Horror Cinema: Youth Rebellion and Queer Spectatorship*. New York: Palgrave Macmillan, 2015.

Seltzer, David. "666: The Omen Revealed." *The Omen*. DVD. Beverly Hills, CA: Twentieth Century Fox Home Entertainment, 2006.

———. "The Omen Legacy." *The Omen*. DVD. Beverly Hills, CA: Twentieth Century Fox Home Entertainment, 2006.

Serrador, Narciso Ibáñez. "Child Director." *Who Can Kill a Child?* DVD. Orland Park, IL: MPI Media Group, 2007.

———, dir. *Who Can Kill a Child?* DVD. Orland Park, IL: MPI Media Group, 2007.

Showalter, Elaine. "Introduction." In *The Bad Seed*, v–xiii. New York: HarperCollins, 1997.

Shuck, Glenn W. *Marks of the Beast: The "Left Behind" Novels and the Struggle for Evangelical Identity*. New York: New York University Press, 2005.

Smith, Peter K., et al. *Understanding Children's Development*. 5th ed. Chichester, UK: Wiley & Sons, 2011.

Stainton-Rogers, Wendy. "Gendered Childhoods." In *Understanding Childhood: An Interdisciplinary Approach*, edited by Martin Woodhead and Heather Montgomery, 179–220. Chichester, UK: Wiley & Sons, 2003.

Stone, Bryan. "Evil on Film." In *The Bloomsbury Companion to Religion and Film*, edited by William L. Blizek, 310–21. London: Bloomsbury, 2013.

Taylor, Don, dir. *Damien: Omen II*. DVD. Twentieth Century Fox Home Entertainment, 2006.

Tryon, Thomas. *The Other*. New York: New York Review, 2012.

Valentine, Kylie. "Accounting for Agency." *Children & Society* 25 (2011) 347–58.

Wells, Karen. *Childhood in a Global Perspective*. Cambridge, UK: Polity, 2009.

Whyman, Matt. *The Nice and Accurate Good Omens TV Companion*. New York: HarperCollins, 2019.

Wilbur, Keith. "*11/11/11*: Behind the Scenes." *11/11/11*. DVD. Burbank, CA: Asylum Home Entertainment, 2011.

Winstead, Antoinette F. "The Devil Made Me Do It! The Devil in 1960s–1970s Horror Film." In *Vader, Voldemort and Other Villains: Essays on Evil in Popular Media*, edited by Jamey Heit, 28–45. Jefferson, NC: McFarland, 2011.

Wyndham, John. *The Midwich Cuckoos*. London: Michael Joseph, 1957.

Wyness, Michael. *Childhood*. Cambridge: Polity, 2015.

Yarovesky, David, dir. *Brightburn*. DVD. Culver City, CA: Sony Pictures Home Entertainment, 2019.

Apocalypsis: With Love for This World and the Next

Jack Marsh

VARIETIES OF IMMORTALITY

"Unthinkable as it may be, humanity, every last person, could someday be wiped from the face of the Earth."[1] So declares the director of Oxford's Future of Humanity Institute, Dr. Nick Bostrom. His concerns are not new; ancient writers also worried about the end times. Nor is Bostrom's response to the possibility of an end new. Like ancient apocalyptic writers, he also envisions a renewed life/afterlife. In this chapter, I will argue for the power of envisioning an afterlife, as long as we take responsibility for co-creating it.

Bostrom is best known for his 2003 paper proposing what has come to be called the "Simulation Argument." His carefully argued and empirically informed piece leads to the following, somewhat surprising conclusion:

On pain of incoherence, *at least one* of the following propositions must be true:

1. The human species is very likely to go extinct before reaching a "posthuman" stage of technological advancement.

2. Any posthuman civilization is extremely unlikely to run a significant number of simulations of their evolutionary history (or variations thereof).

3. We are almost certainly living in a computer simulation.[2]

1. Anderson, "We're Underestimating the Risk."
2. Bostrom, "Are You Living."

Notice that he doesn't specify which proposition is true, only that at least one is true. Ultimately, Bostrom suggests we ought to distribute our epistemic credence roughly equally over each of the above propositions.

More surprising still, perhaps: a widening contingent of physicists and ethicists seem to take the simulation hypothesis seriously. For example, Neil deGrasse Tyson

> puts the odds at 50–50 that our entire existence is a program on someone else's hard drive. "I think the likelihood may be very high," he said. . . . Somewhere out there could be a being whose intelligence is that much greater than our own. "We would be drooling, blithering idiots in their presence," he said. "If that's the case, it is easy for me to imagine that everything in our lives is just a creation of some other entity for their entertainment."[3]

Of course, arguments of this type are not new. Scholars of religion can be forgiven a slight smile at the crudity of Tyson's formulation. But unlike its mystical and theological predecessors, the simulation hypothesis admits of fairly specific empirical tests, and the "creator" in question may be none other than our own future selves.[4]

All of this is interesting for at least two reasons. First, the future of our species is looking more and more bleak. Bostrom elsewhere argues that we poorly understand and "severely underestimate" human extinction risks.[5] Climate change, overpopulation, ecological collapse, nuclear war, increasing probability of global pandemic, coupled with apparent lack of political will to address these issues, has led to growing pessimism.[6] Stephen Hawking recently updated his so-called "apocalyptic predictions," adding his voice to a growing number of scientists who prophesy humanity's imminent doom:[7]

> [Hawking] warns that humanity needs to become a multi-planetary species within the *next century* if we don't want to go extinct. Last year, he prophesied that we had maybe 1,000 years left on Earth, and the inspiration for this newly urgent timeline is unclear.[8]

In this light, Bostrom's argument supplies a nontrivial probability, and hence, a psychological reason to hope, that the extinction of our species—in

3. Moskowitz, "Are We Living."
4. Moskowitz, "Are We Living."
5. Anderson, "We're Underestimating the Risk."
6. Torres, "It's the End."
7. Torres, "It's the End."
8. Fecht, "Stephen Hawking."

our modest "matrix," at least—may not be the end after all. This amounts to a kind of "afterlife for atheists," as it were. We live in a time where one need not be of a particularly spiritual or religious bent to enjoy the psychological benefits of a belief in an afterlife, or at least an afterlife of a sort.

Second, Bostrom supplies interesting grounds for questioning some of the truisms we've inherited in the philosophy of religion today. Under the pressure of modernity, and of trying to find credible ways to talk about religious meaning in general, we've probably ceded too much ground to reflexive, and in some cases, cynical, skeptics. For example, Nietzsche asserted that belief in an afterlife necessarily devalues this life. Marx asserted that afterlife is a ruling-class tool used to trick the oppressed into embracing their oppression. Freud asserted that religion was illusory wish fulfillment, a symbolic response traceable to a child's need for a sense of protection. Armchair biologists propound Darwinian "explanations" of the belief as an expression of our survival drive. And finally, Heidegger asserted that belief in an afterlife was a way we disburden ourselves of responsibility for our own singular existence, occluding the absurdity and contingency—the *nullity*—at the basis of finite life.[9] With the weight of so much literary, philosophical, and "scientific" authority, it is not surprising that we've looked for other ways to talk about religious meaning in general, ways that can't be mistaken for mere wishful thinking. Those familiar with the above arguments know they have some critical value, but at the end of the day, most of us *hope* for an afterlife because *we love and affirm life* and don't want it to end. Beliefs in afterlife become problematic only in moral and political contexts, it seems to me.

With millenarianism, the belief in an imminent apocalypse and reign of blessedness for the elect, too much reliance on the afterlife can be deadly. In the Muslim world, millenarianism can be seen in the deviant promise of paradise for the suicide bomber. In Israel, new radicalized forms of ultraorthodox Zionism bring to mind false messiahs of the medieval past. In the US, Protestant fundamentalists seem determined to actually bring about the apocalypse by continually voting their supporters into the White House.[10] But the *absence* of belief in a morally meaningful afterlife itself can also potentially motivate pathological forms of social engagement, as the chiliastic violence of twentieth-century fascism and Stalinism made painfully plain.[11] After all, if the present is all we have, we may be tempted

---

9. Nietzsche, *On the Genealogy of Morals*; Marx, "Contribution to the Critique"; Freud, *Future of an Illusion* and *Civilization and Its Discontents*; Dow, "Is Religion Evolutionary Adaptation?"; Heidegger, *Being and Time* and *Identity and Difference*.

10. See Segal, *Life after Death*, 2.

11. Angel, "Afterlife in Jewish Thought."

to purchase social glory at too high of an ethical cost. Indeed, as Rabbi Hayyim Angel rightly notes, it seems "we live in a world where billions overemphasize afterlife, and billions underemphasize it."[12]

Perhaps the best way to deal with this two-sided problem is to grab it by the horns. Isn't the Eternal precisely that which doesn't wholly depend on context to be assessed as thus and so? That Hitler was a terrible artist and beaten by his father leaves our moral assessment of the man unaltered. That Gandhi or Martin Luther King Jr. affirmed an afterlife doesn't render their service and sacrifice null or self-oriented. Indeed, doing right *because it's right* is worthy of reward, if only the reward of our recognition of its worthiness, in general and as such. Faith perhaps is nothing more than free commitment to a superlative *worth*, to a meaning that *ought* to be. In this light, the simulation argument is simply the latest in a very ancient, variegated, and global human tradition that finds goodness and value in life. I think we scholars of religion should once more take the possibility of an afterlife seriously in our lives and work.

For this, early traditions of Jewish and Christian apocalyptic offer helpful resources that emphasize both ethics and cosmology. I want to suggest that the two prongs of Biblical apocalyptic—*prophetic eschatology* and *otherworldly journey*—present two necessary moments of theistic *apocalypsis*—or "revelation"—in general.[13] In the cases where there is an *otherworldly journey*, the journey provides a logical clarification of the meanings that orient religious practice for the relevant community. *Prophetic eschatology* brings those meanings to bear on the current constellation of worldly power in ways that guide the community's expectations and practices. Or, in different words, following A. J. Heschel, what classical Judaism termed *halakah* and *aggadah*—or ethics and theology—are two necessary and interpenetrating moments of authentic *apocalypsis* in general.[14]

CHRISTIAN APOCALYPTIC

As Segal has masterfully demonstrated, popular belief in a morally meaningful life after death was widespread throughout the Roman world in the first century CE.[15] Virgil's poetry—what perhaps amounted to oral scripture for your common Roman of the day—had already moralized the Homeric epic, incorporating long-standing Platonic and other myths of posthumous

---

12. Angel, "Afterlife in Jewish Thought."
13. See Collins, *Apocalyptic Imagination* and "Apocalypse."
14. Heschel, *Between God and Man.*
15. See Ferguson, "Stoics and Cynics."

punishment and reward within its ode to filial and civic piety.[16] Moreover, popular religious cultures of Second Temple Judaism were totally suffused with moralized beliefs in resurrection, immortality, and the coming "kingdom of God."[17] Jewish apocalyptic, exemplified by the Essenes, had already given birth to what would later be known as "Merkabah" mysticism, forms of eschatological spirituality gathered around visionary experiences described in Isaiah, Ezekiel, Daniel, and Enoch. The "chariot" was a central trope precisely because the canon told of Elijah and Enoch being "taken" by God—"ascending" to the throne, to God's heavenly abode—on a fiery chariot. Segal argues that the apostle Paul's writings demonstrate that ascent "traditions existed in Pharisaism as early as the first century." He writes,

> Paul's visionary life allowed him to develop a concept of the divinity of the Christ or Messiah in a way that was both a unique development within the Jewish mystical tradition, and at the same time, characteristically Christian.[18]

In the New Testament, there are at least three distinct apocalyptic traditions present that differ in detail, but which seem to agree in certain crucial respects:

First, a tradition behind 2 Pet 3:10–13, that understands the "the day of the Lord" to involve catastrophic destruction:

> The heavens will pass away with a roar and the elements will be destroyed with intense heat, and the earth and its works will be burned up. . . . But according to His promise we are looking to a new heavens and a new earth, in which righteousness dwells.[19]

The focus of the epistle is not on the gothic details of the foretold troubles, but on exhorting the church to *remain faithful through them*, and specifically to avoid stupid speculations and those who peddle them. The covenant *faithfulness* of God and trust in his messianic promise, joined to the *faithfulness* of the believer in the church's everyday practices, was what mattered for this author.

Next, there is the Pauline tradition of salvation for gentile churches. Paul had much to say about Jesus's return, specifically in his earliest known letters. But his most interesting and neglected views occur at the heart of his theological masterpiece: the book of Romans. Written to address controversies between Jewish and gentile Christ followers in the church of Rome,

---

16. Segal, *Life after Death*.
17. See Sigvartsen, "Afterlife Views"; Levenson, *Resurrection and Restoration*.
18. Segal, *Life after Death*, 408, 399, 438.
19. Scripture quotations in this chapter are from the NASB.

the text gives a relatively systematic presentation of Paul's mature views on the messiahship of Jesus and its legal, ritual, cosmic, and eschatological significance. The extension of God's covenant promise to the gentiles reaches beyond humankind, to the whole of creation:

> For the creation waits in eager expectation for the children of God to be revealed. For the creation was subjected to frustration, not by its own choice, but by the will of the one who subjected it, in hope that the creation itself will be liberated from its bondage to decay and brought into the freedom and glory of the children of God. (Rom 8:19–21)

The apocalyptic return of the Messiah does not erase or discard the old cosmos or the "old covenant," but with a clear nod to the prophet Isaiah, it revivifies, restores, and creatively renews them, delivering them from the rule of war, decay, and death. Paul's formulation is striking here for another reason: assuming it's not merely a literary anthropomorphism, he says *God and creation hope*, as if *God is waiting for us* to get our act together, and as if *creation itself waits* laboriously for humanity to embrace its own election. Here, Paul creatively joins two different Jewish traditions. As Segal has masterfully demonstrated, Paul creatively applies visions of "glorification" from the Jewish mysticism of the day to the *material* resurrection of the dead and the renewal of *material* creation. For Paul, this *deliverance*—or "salvation"—from decay and death was made possible by the life, death, resurrection, and the promised return of Jesus of Nazareth, the Messiah.

Finally, the book of Revelation presents a vision of redemption and restoration. It is the most developed and literary apocalyptic vision among the early writing of nascent Christianity. Its author is a member of a Hebrew community of Christ followers. Probably written in the early eighties during a period of harassment by outsiders, its composition closely follows the book of Daniel in structure. The author takes special care to emphasize that God's judgment will "destroy those who destroy the earth" (Rev 11:18). Interestingly, he interweaves both ascent (4:1) and descent (21) motifs throughout his vision, suggesting that the consummation of the age is the collaborative work of the *mutual faithfulness* of God *and* God's people:

> And I John saw the holy city, new Jerusalem, coming down from God out of heaven, prepared as a bride adorned for her husband. And I heard a great voice out of heaven saying, Behold, the tabernacle of God is with men, and he will dwell with them, and they shall be his people, and God himself shall be with them, and be their God. (Rev 21:2–3)

When God is made to declare, "Behold, I make all things new" (v. 5), the author uses the term *kainos*, not *neos*. *Neos* refers to existence in time; *kainos* refers to the quality or modification of an already existing thing. *Kainos* suggests *renewal* or a qualitative change by comparison to the already extant. As Trent notes, these words are not usually interchangeable, and this is reflected in later patristic literature. John Chrysostom (347–407 CE), for example, considers the distinction important enough to base two different exhortations on each word: "What we do in the case of houses, always restoring them when they become dilapidated, do also in the case of yourself. . . . Do not despair nor lose heart, but renew [*anakainison*] it by repentance."[20] The author of Revelation seems to envision the day of the Lord as involving the redemption and restoration of the existing cosmos, a transformative fulfillment of divine promise that brings forth "new gems as well as old" (Matt 13:52). What passes away is not the earth or the cosmos itself, but the *rule of lawlessness, decay, and death*.

PROPHETIC PRACTICE

There is a contrast at play between 2 Peter and Romans/Revelation, between what we might call *activist* and *quietist* eschatology. The former recognizes some form of dual responsibility in God's grand project of redemption: God's part and humanity's own part in the redemptive consummation of the age. The latter implies God's unilateral action to a passive humanity merely tasked to hold on and behold God's own activity. In our time, more quietist eschatology can propel irresponsible (and biblically illiterate) forms of indifference to ethical and political challenges, e.g., "God will fix climate change, so we need not worry," etc. Part of what it means to be a *faithful community* under chaotic social conditions is resolutely *living out the call*—including the obligation to carefully steward creation— even in the face of uncertainty. In our own day, that might mean vocally criticizing irresponsible forms of climate skepticism, on the one hand, and overly general "scientific" pessimism about our practical ability to counter the challenge of climate change, on the other.[21] Both kinds of skepticism involve potentially paralyzing political effects, as speculation about posthuman or messianic futures can function as compensating hope that saps motivation for mobilizing meaningful and ecologically sound action. We see this, for example, when billionaire industrialist Elon Musk preaches

---

20. Trench's New Testament Synonyms, "New."

21. The issue of "living out the call" provides a good way to distinguish between noble and ignoble forms of skepticism, something we desperately need given the prominence of theatrical skepticism in today's academy.

about an afterlife while wasting resources on vanity projects such as space travel, justified by razor-thin utilitarian justification.

But too hasty an activism might be also problematic. For example, overly panicked calls to authoritarian action could endanger current systems of research aimed at yielding increasingly effective ways to halt climate change. Thus, any such action must calculate potential effects on wider social and economic systems that power public and private research in climate science and relevant technologies. Trying to bring about eschatological justice and peace—all at once and all by ourselves, rather than in collaboration with nature and other communities—is as idolatrous as shirking stewardship obligations by passive indifference. Just as insufficient creation care is a type of biblical infidelity, so is impatience, the product of caring too much about our own individual lives and times.

The proper prophetic practice required for us to do our part to meet the challenges of the day is correlated with a proper apocalyptic attitude. Together, they enable us to act to preserve, maintain, and creatively transform our world with resolute composure in light of both God's call and concrete conditions. Tensive eschatologies that assign responsibility to both humanity and God (or our future selves) present the only responsible way forward. They create a shared ground for political action to responsibly steward our world in light of both historic grievances, such as colonialism and unequal resource consumption, and shared imminent problems, such as climate change. Overconsumption and overpopulation are destroying the world, literally. It is time to call councils, reinterpret understandings, and revise. In this work, world valuing and preserving eschatologies are the ones worth our time. This does not require an exclusive metaphysical commitment to the planet earth as "all there is." Rather, it means that whatever else there might be and wherever it may be, we are committed to planet Earth as one world among others. We owe it our best efforts to preserve, maintain, and perfect it, for future generations, come what may, be it another carbon-based alien species, a messiah, or God in God's self.

BIBLIOGRAPHY

Anderson, Ross. "We're Underestimating the Risk of Human Extinction." *Atlantic Monthly*, Mar. 6, 2017. www.theatlantic.com/technology/archive/2012/03/were-underestimating-the-risk-of-human-extinction/253821.

Angel, Hayyim. "Afterlife in Jewish Thought." *Conversations: The Journal of the Institute for Jewish Ideas and Ideals* 23. https://www.jewishideas.org/article/afterlife-jewish-thought.

Bostrom, Nick. "Are You Living in a Computer Simulation?" *Philosophical Quarterly* 53 (2003) 243–55.

Collins, John J. "Apocalypse: Jewish Apocalypticism to the Rabbinic Period." Encylopedia, 2005. http://www.encyclopedia.com/environment/encyclopedias-almanacs-transcripts-and-maps/apocalypse-jewish-apocalypticism-rabbinic-period.

———. *The Apocalyptic Imagination: An Introduction to Jewish Apocalyptic Literature.* Grand Rapids: Eerdmans, 2016.

Dow, James. "Is Religion an Evolutionary Adaptation?" *Journal of Artificial Societies and Social Simulation* 11 (Mar. 2008). http://jasss.soc.surrey.ac.uk/11/2/2.html.

Fecht, Sarah. "Stephen Hawking Says We Have 100 Years to Colonize a New Planet—or Die. Could We Do It?" *Popular Science*, May 5, 2017. http://www.popsci.com/stephen-hawking-human-extinction-colonize-mars.

Ferguson, R. James. "Stoics and Cynics in the Roman World." In *Essays in History, Politics and Culture*, page numbers unavailable. N.p.: n.p., 1999.

Freud, Sigmund. *Civilization and Its Discontents*. Edited by James Strachey. New York: Norton, 2010.

———. *The Future of an Illusion*. Edited by James Strachey. New York: Norton, 1989.

Heidegger, Martin. *Being and Time*. Translated by John Macquarrie and Edward Robinson. London: SCM, 1962.

———. *Identity and Difference*. Translated by Joan Stambaugh. New York: Harper & Row, 1969.

Heschel, Abraham J. *Between God and Man: An Interpretation of Judaism*. New York: Free, 1997.

Levenson, Jon D. *Resurrection and the Restoration of Israel: The Ultimate Victory of the God of Life*. New Haven, CT: Yale University Press, 2006.

Marx, Karl. "A Contribution to the Critique of Hegel's Philosophy of Right, Introduction." Marxists, 1844. https://www.marxists.org/archive/marx/works/1843/critique-hpr/intro.htm.

Moskowitz, Clara. "Are We Living in a Computer Simulation? High-Profile Physicists and Philosophers Gathered to Debate Whether We Are Real or Virtual—and What It Means Either Way." *Scientific American*, Apr. 7, 2016. www.scientificamerican.com/article/are-we-living-in-a-computer-simulation/.

Nietzsche, Friedrich. *On the Genealogy of Morals, and Other Writings*. Translated by K. Diethe. Cambridge: Cambridge University Press, 2006.

Segal, Alan. *Life after Death: A History of the Afterlife in Western Religion*. New York: Doubleday, 2004.

Sigvartsen, Jan A. "The Afterlife Views and the Use of the Tanakh in Support of the Resurrection Concept in the Literature of Second Temple Period Judaism: The Apocrypha and the Pseudepigrapha." PhD diss., Andrews University, 2016.

Torres, Émile P. "It's the End of the World and We Know It: Scientists in Many Disciplines See Apocalypse, Soon." *Salon*, Apr. 30, 2017. https://www.salon.com/2017/04/30/its-the-end-of-the-world-and-we-know-it-scientists-in-many-disciplines-see-apocalypse-soon/.

Trench's New Testament Synonyms. "New." Study Bible, n.d. http://studybible.info/trench/New.

Skipping to the End
A Look at Messianic Zionism in Modern-Day Israel

Catherine Keene Merchant

While the ongoing Israeli/Palestinian conflict is undoubtedly one of the most entrenched in the region, it is unfortunately not the only societal divide that plagues the young state. The split between religious and secular Jews within Israel has gradually widened over time, as the underlying issues between the two groups have intensified with demographic and political development. Moreover, even among religious Jews, there exist so many different groups with such wildly different lifestyle choices and political perspectives that we cannot possibly address them all at this time. People agree that Israel was established primarily as a secular Zionist state in 1948. Yet, over time, its role as the spiritual center of Jewish life and "the place from which redemption will start and where the Messiah is destined to make his first appearance"[1] has increasingly been embraced by some religious Jews, especially those who have joined the growing band of Messianic Zionists who now believe themselves to be living on the brink of *akharit hayamim* (the end of days).

Those who were alive during the Six Day War had believed the military capture of Jerusalem in 1967 to be the final "end to violence, dereliction, and separation . . . a return to paradise."[2] However, when Israeli officials immediately gave control of the Temple Mount back to Islamic authorities,

---

1. Dan, "Jerusalem in Jewish Spirituality," 64.
2. Armstrong, *Jerusalem*, 400.

some of these groups were emboldened to take violent action to "change the course of history . . . [because] miracles don't just happen."[3] Unfortunately, this shift from a blessed "end to violence" into a more than fifty-year-long violent struggle is not unique to the Middle East or Jewish extremism. Sadly, throughout history there have been innumerable utopian movements that have brutally turned groups against one another in the name of religious ideals or peace. In this chapter, however, I focus on just one example of this pervasive phenomenon. Here I will explore the spiritual beliefs of these far-right sects and their ongoing attempts to spark the redemption.

SPIRITUAL BELIEFS

The land of Israel and Jerusalem fulfill many different roles in Jewish spirituality, both mythologically and historically. They are seen to represent "the glories of the past, the moments in history in which Man and God have become closest."[4] Since midrash teaches that Jerusalem was the very first piece of land that God made, it is "the center of the universe, the meeting point between chaos and creation."[5] In addition, since Torah says God gave "the land of Canaan" to Abraham and his descendants "as an everlasting possession" (Gen 17:8), many religious Jews believe that the land has always belonged to them throughout the ages. As the initial placement of Solomon's Temple and its holy of holies, Jerusalem is seen as the dwelling place of the *Shekhinah* (the divine or feminine presence of God), where God resides and is forever able to communicate with God's people.[6]

Therefore, when Jews lost control of the land after the destruction of their Second Temple and were exiled by the Romans in 73 CE, rabbis postulated that their people must have sinned greatly and needed to be punished.[7] They theorized that the *sinat hinam* (or "unjustified hatred")

---

3. Juergensmeyer, *Terror in the Mind*, 54.
4. Dan, "Jerusalem in Jewish Spirituality," 60.
5. Dan, "Jerusalem in Jewish Spirituality," 60.
6. Buber, *Midrash Lamentations Rabbah*, 20.
7. Goldenberg, "Destruction of Jerusalem Temple," 192. The belief that one's religious group was suffering because of its own sins is not particular to Judaism. This was a common belief among various groups throughout the ancient Near East that is linked to, as Dutcher-Walls states, the "worldview . . . that each state was ultimately governed by a high god who legitimated the ruling house and religious order of that state—[such that] the triumvirate of god, palace and temple was understood to control the world of that state and to be in competition with other god-state formations" (Dutcher-Walls, "Disturbing the Peace," 6). When one god "failed" against another god and a nation was defeated in battle, its inhabitants at that time often blamed themselves for not having been sufficiently pious. Today it is important for everyone—especially non-Jews—to

of the first-century Jews led to their devastation.[8] Yet the exact nature of this "hatred" remains in dispute to this day. Some rabbis think this hatred stemmed from the intense jealousy that everyday Jewish people held for one another in the first century, as they "compete[d] with them in the struggle for existence"[9] under oppressive Roman rule. Others believe that disputes over specific religious practices "brought them to bloodshed under false pretenses and many other evils until the Temple was destroyed."[10] Still others believe it was the inability of the Jewish people to unite as a single force against the Roman occupation that led to their downfall.[11] In any case, there is no widespread agreement on this matter.

Similarly, beliefs about the eventual return of the Jews to the Land of Israel remain wildly diverse. For example, the Sefer Zerubavel, a Hebrew apocalypse written in the seventh century, prophesied: "Jerusalem ... will be destroyed again during the wars of that era, but from one corner of the city the victorious messiah will emerge and overcome the hosts of the devil."[12] Thus, the Jews would be saved by the Messiah and peace would prevail on the homeland only after his coming. But before that the Jewish people could do nothing but atone for their sins "through some combination of suffering and increased piety."[13] Conversely, other rabbis—such as the Vilna Gaon from the late 1700s—argued that *kibbutz galuyot* (the ingathering of the exiles) would be the first step toward redemption.[14] Only after all the Jews had returned and built the Third Temple would the messiah come to earth, as "the redemption of the whole world depends upon the actions of Jews in creating the conditions necessary for messianic salvation."[15]

One's understanding of the role of the Jews in the end of days scenario depends on which school of thought they follow. If one believes that Jews are barred from the land of Israel because of their previous sins, then attempting to return before the messiah liberates them is sacrilege. However, for those who believe it is their responsibility to pave the way for the messiah, inaction is inexcusable, as even "the redemption of God Himself

---

keep this in mind so that we do not mistakenly believe the God of Abraham to be especially bloodthirsty or ancient Jews to be especially sinful.

8. Goldenberg, "Destruction of Jerusalem Temple," 193.
9. Zimmerman, "Sinat Chinnam."
10. Zimmerman, "Sinat Chinnam."
11. Zimmerman, "Sinat Chinnam."
12. Dan, "Jerusalem in Jewish Spirituality," 63.
13. Hertzberg, "Jerusalem and Zionism," 149.
14. Yaniv, "Vilna Gaon."
15. Juergensmeyer, *Terror in the Mind*, 58.

from His mystic exile" depends upon the Third Temple.[16] While many see this latter belief as more empowering for Jewish people and certainly more supportive of Israeli statehood, unfortunately it can also be misused to prove that God supports an ethnic cleansing of Palestinians from the region. For indeed, as with so many other groups in so many different religions and scenarios, "apocalyptic belief has been [or become] an incentive to religious violence."[17]

Even today, this matter deeply divides the Jewish religious community, as rabbis around the world disagree over whether or not the modern state of Israel should be considered the prophesied "ingathering of exiles" that must come before the building of the Third Temple and the Messianic Age.[18] Many religious Jews agree with former Israeli cabinet member, Rabbi Yehudah Amital, that Zionism is "the Lord's vehicle for preparing Israel for its redemption. The habitation of the Land of Israel by a group of its children, transforming wastelands into gardens, and the establishment of independence within its borders, are stages in the process of redemption."[19] This sentiment is perhaps best expressed in the widely used "Prayer for the State of Israel," which asks God to:

> Please bless the state of Israel, first fruit of the flourishing of the fruit of our redemption. . . . Appoint for a blessing all our kindred of the house of Israel in all the lands of their dispersion. Plant in their hearts a love of Zion. And for all our people everywhere, may God be with them, and may they have the opportunity to go up to the land.[20]

Meanwhile, Jews in the Diaspora often "utilize other prayers" because they disagree with the message that all the world's Jews must physically return to Israel if they are to be collectively redeemed as a people.[21] In addition, most Haredim believe that redemption can only come about through the observance of Torah, rather than through political means.[22] Moreover, Hasidic Jews have been even less eager to embrace this view, due to their reliance on the *tsadiqim*, "minor messianic figure[s]" who are "responsible for the spiritual and material welfare" of their communities.[23] According to

16. Scholem, *Kabbalah*, 166.
17. Maier, "Apocalypse of Religious Violence," 1.
18. Ravitzky, *Messianism, Zionism*, 12.
19. Snitkoff, "Praying for the Welfare."
20. *Shabbat Vehagim*, "Prayer for the State."
21. Snitkoff, "Praying for the Welfare."
22. Snitkoff, "Praying for the Welfare."
23. Dan, *Kabbalah*, 98.

Joseph Dan, these teachers somewhat "'neutralized' the messianic drive in Jewish religious activity" for those who followed them,[24] which has resulted in Hasidic Jews being less focused on the redemption than other religious Jews. Some sects even vehemently oppose the state of Israel as "a foreign government established by Jewish heretics."[25]

THE RISE OF MESSIANIC ZIONISM

In the early days of the Zionist movement, secular leaders like Theodor Herzl, Chaim Weizmann, and David Ben-Gurion advocated for the foundation of the state of Israel primarily as a refuge for the world's Jews, not as a return to the spiritual homeland. They believed that "the old religious traditions of Judaism had been superseded and left behind,"[26] and they had little sympathy for the people whom they believed to be "sitting back helplessly waiting for the Messiah."[27] Nevertheless, as their movement grew over time, what began initially as a nationalist cause for Jewish autonomy soon merged with the spiritual longing of many religious Jews for their ancestral homeland in Palestine. Even Herzl himself, who had presented both Palestine and Argentina in his *Der Judenstaat* treatise in 1896 as potential locations for the Jewish state, acknowledged the great importance that a return to Jerusalem would have, as it "is our unforgettable historic homeland. The very name would be a marvelously effective rallying cry."[28] While some religious Jews fully rejected—and, in certain cases, continue to reject—Zionism as a desecration of the land, other "Orthodox believers . . . proposed, on the basis of kabbalistic teaching, that active immediate stirrings toward the redemption would be useful. They ruled that such efforts would be permitted and even a necessary step toward arousing stirrings in heaven."[29] Thus, many of these believers agreed to make *aliyah* (the Jewish return to Israel) and help to rebuild the nation.

Once in Jerusalem, some of these religious Jews fell under the guidance of Rabbi Abraham Isaac Kook, the chief rabbi of the Holy Land from 1921 until his death in 1935. He espoused his belief that "the future of the Holy Land belonged to God"[30] and that even the secular Jews who were

---

24. Dan, *Kabbalah*, 98.
25. Dan, *Kabbalah*, 98.
26. Armstrong, *Jerusalem*, 366.
27. Armstrong, *Jerusalem*, 353.
28. Herzl, "Jewish State," 222.
29. Hertzberg, "Jerusalem and Zionism," 162.
30. Hertzberg, "Jerusalem and Zionism," 162.

largely driving the Zionist movement were unintentional co-creators in God's plan.[31] His followers were assured that the end of days would be near and that God would soon send the Messiah, if only they could reclaim the entire land of Israel for themselves. Thus, many of his disciples joined ultra-nationalist Vladimir Jabotinsky's terrorist group "The National Military Organization" (better known in Israel by its Hebrew acronym "Etzel"), "which engaged in armed struggle with the British authorities to force them to yield all of Palestine, including Jerusalem, to the Jews."[32]

Leading up to 1948, most of those making *aliyah* were Ashkenazim—or Eastern European Jews—who were escaping pogroms in Eastern Europe and eventually the widespread genocide of the Shoah.[33] Yet after the state of Israel declared independence in 1948 and won a decisive victory in the Arab-Israeli War of 1948–49, increased violence and hostility by Muslim Arabs towards the Mizrahim—or Jews from Middle Eastern and North African countries—led to them emigrating to Israel, as well.[34] In fact, as the population of Israel increased by more than one million Jews from 1948–67, nearly half these new immigrants were Mizrahim.[35] Unlike the secular Ashkenazi founders of the Zionist movement, the Mizrahim tended to be more religiously observant and "had a passion for Jerusalem rooted in its living ties to the religion of their ancestors."[36]

The influx of more religious Jews to Israel changed the tenor of the new state in many ways. Yet it was not until 1967 that the religiously observant became more excited about Messianism. The key event in this shift was Israel's seemingly miraculous victory in the 1967 war and the capture of Jerusalem and the historic lands of Judea and Samaria (better known today as the West Bank). The idea that their small Israeli state could win such a decisive military victory against four larger Arab states at once and thereby seize the rest of their religious homeland—all in six days, like the original six days of creation—seemed to the religiously observant Jews like a clear sign of the coming messiah. Many of them believed that their final step before the redemption would be the building of the Third Temple, after which there would be "the ultimate union between humanity and God" when the people would "be united forever."[37]

31. Goodman, "Three Paradoxes."
32. Hertzberg, "Jerusalem and Zionism," 165.
33. Picard, "Building the Country," 4.
34. Picard, "Building the Country," 5.
35. Chetrit, "Mizrahi Politics," 51.
36. Hertzberg, "Jerusalem and Zionism," 175.
37. Dan, "Jerusalem in Jewish Spirituality," 60.

Yet the opportunity to build the temple never arrived. Instead, General Moshe Dayan met with the Islamic religious leaders of the Haram al-Sharif a few days later and promised to return control of it to them as a rightful Muslim holy place, so long as the Jews were able to worship at the Western Wall.[38] This decision sparked widespread criticism from the religious community, who saw it as his betrayal of the entire Jewish people. Their hopes for an imminent redemption were suddenly dashed by a secular leader. Moreover, they were reminded of the many times throughout history—including during the very recent Shoah—when they and their ancestors had done everything imaginable to make peace with their gentile neighbors, only for those neighbors to betray them and later slaughter them en masse. These religious Jews—and, most likely, all Jews around the world—carry intergenerational trauma that is both "learned and lived," according to the designations set out by psychologist Roger Frie.[39] That means that many of them had directly lived through the Shoah, and even those who had not still felt "the indirect experience of that event through inherited memories and the experience of one's elders."[40] Consequently, they were convinced the Arab states would never maintain their end of the peace agreement.[41] They believed the only way to protect Israel and later usher in the redemption would be through their own militarized citizen action.

As a result, soon after the Six Day War, many young rabbis and rabbinical students who were associated with Rabbi Tzvi Yehuda Kook (the son of Chief Rabbi Abraham Isaac Kook) began meeting to discuss plans to settle the West Bank for religious reasons.[42] One of these students, Moshe Levinger, traveled to Hebron for Passover in 1968 and refused to leave.[43] He claimed that he had every right to live there because "the Land of Israel must be in the hands of the Jewish people—not just by having settlements, but that it's under Jewish sovereignty."[44] Levinger's actions were clearly illegal, yet many Israelis sympathized with him and his cause.[45] After more than a year and a half of controversy, the government allowed him and his followers to establish the Israeli town of Kiryat Arba just outside Hebron.

---

38. Armstrong, *Jerusalem*, 407.

39. Frie, *Not in My Family*, 58. This book came to me by way of Buerschaper's paper, "My Grandfather's Hidden History."

40. Frie, *Not in My Family*, 58.

41. Whether or not they were right about this remains hotly contested, even today.

42. Lustick, *For Land and Lord*, 42.

43. Lustick, *For Land and Lord*, 42.

44. Gorenberg, Accidental Empire, 106.

45. Lustick, *For Land and Lord*, 42.

It became the first of the more than 244 subsequent Jewish settlements and illegal outposts that have been erected across the West Bank, Gaza, Golan Heights, and Sinai Peninsula.[46] These legal and illegal dwellings use "the creation of facts in the field" as a "powerful political weapon" to buffer the young state and make it nearly impossible for the Israeli government to withdraw from the seized territory.[47]

Nevertheless, after the 1973 Yom Kippur War and the Israeli government's subsequent disengagement agreement with Egypt, the Sinai Peninsula settlements were removed and this territory was returned to the Egyptians. Advocates of the settler movement resolved to increase Israel's territorial hold on the rest of the occupied land and joined forces into a single larger organization, Gush Emunim, or the "Bloc of the Faithful."[48] Although they were originally a faction within the National Religious Party (NRP), they soon split off into their own political movement, whose purpose was to maintain Jewish control of Jerusalem and the West Bank.[49] Members of this group also became devoted to "making garments for the priests and sacred vessels, according to biblical specifications, for the future service in the Third Temple, which they were sure would soon be built, within divine help, in Jerusalem."[50] In 1984, twenty-five of their members were arrested in conjunction with the larger "Jewish Underground" for conspiring to blow up the Dome of the Rock, in order to make way for the Third Temple. Shortly thereafter, their organization was dissolved.

During this same timeframe, another ultranationalistic religious leader, Rabbi Meir Kahane, began preaching that "insofar as Jews were exalted and their enemies humiliated, God was glorified and the Messiah's coming was more likely."[51] He founded the far right-wing political party Kach, which was banned in 1988 after one term for its "racist" and "undemocratic positions."[52] His extremist views were later studied and embraced by Kiryat Arba resident Baruch Goldstein, who killed more than thirty Muslim worshippers and injured more than a hundred more when he opened fire with an assault rifle in the Ibrahimi Mosque in Hebron during Ramadan prayers on February 25, 1994. Goldstein was beaten to death by the crowd of worshippers who survived his attack. His grave has since

46. BBC, "Israel and the Palestinians."
47. Lustick, *For Land and Lord*, 43.
48. Sprinzak, *Gush Emunim*.
49. Sprinzak, *Gush Emunim*.
50. Hertzberg, "Jerusalem and Zionism," 177.
51. Juergensmeyer, *Terror in the Mind*, 53.
52. Juergensmeyer, *Terror in the Mind*, 52.

become a shrine for Messianic Zionists who believe that Goldstein is a hero because "peace would not come until all biblical lands were redeemed by Jewish occupation and the Arabs had gone."[53]

In 1995, former Israeli Prime Minister Yitzhak Rabin's attempt to make peace with the Palestinians and settle on a two-state solution was stopped short when religious Bar-Ilan University student Yigal Amir shot and killed him with a pistol for being "a mortal danger" to the Jewish state.[54] Amir believed that this "execution . . . would be justified by the 'pursuer's decree' [i.e., allowing one to kill a murderous pursuer in self-defense] of Jewish legal precedence" because there had been a great deal of discussion among "militant rabbis" in the months before Rabin's death about the religious justifications for his political assassination."[55] Since Rabin had intended to return much of the West Bank and Gaza to the Palestinians, these groups saw him as a serious threat to the coming redemption. They believed Rabbi Ya'akov Moshe Harlap's teaching that "the most important point is the land of Israel. From it everything flows, and except for holding tightly to it, there is no way to bring holiness into the world."[56]

Unfortunately, this line of reasoning continues within Messianic Zionism today. Last year alone, 482 "nationalist crimes" were committed by extremist Israeli settlers against West Bank Palestinians.[57] These typically "consisted of painting nationalist and anti-Arab or anti-Muslim slogans, damaging homes and cars, and cutting down trees belonging to Palestinian farmers," although sometimes the attacks are much worse than that.[58] In one particularly disturbing incident from 2015, Israeli settler Amiram Ben-Uliel firebombed a Palestinian home in Duma, killing three members of the Dawabsheh family, including their eighteen-month-old son, Ali. Meir Ettinger—the grandson of Meir Kahane—was later found to be the ringleader of the attack. Moreover, private footage from an Orthodox wedding ceremony that took place weeks later shows guests "dancing with guns and daggers, stabbing a picture of the infant baby that was burned in the attack . . . and singing songs of revenge."[59]

It is certainly true that Palestinians have committed similar crimes against Israelis over the years and have slaughtered thousands. Nevertheless,

---

53. Juergensmeyer, *Terror in the Mind*, 63.
54. Juergensmeyer, *Terror in the Mind*, 60.
55. Juergensmeyer, *Terror in the Mind*, 60.
56. Gorenberg, *Unmaking of Israel*, 100.
57. Harel, "Israeli 'Jewish Terror' Incidents."
58. Harel, "Israeli 'Jewish Terror' Incidents."
59. Juergensmeyer, *Terror in the Mind*, 49.

I do not believe it is difficult to see the connection between these groups' collective obsession with political control, redemption, and revenge and previous Jewish intergenerational trauma. They might say that these acts of violence are necessary for religious and political purposes, but I personally believe they run deeper than that.[60] For, as Irene Policzer writes in her essay "Deconstructing Adam and Eve: A New Theory on the Origins of Violence," "The more traumatic the experience is, the more difficult it is to get rid of it."[61] Sometimes—as in the case of the Shoah—the trauma might even be so great that it manifests later "in forms of behavior in which the traumatic experience is reenacted by our subconscious mind" so that we can attempt to address it.[62] While that makes a lot of sense psychologically, it is unfortunately all too tragic in the case of extreme Messianic Zionism. Their members' desperate, often violent actions to bring about redemption and eternal peace have—thus far—only inflamed violence against them.

CONCLUSION

From this brief analysis, we are better able to understand some of the spiritual motivations and violent actions of the extreme religious Jews who believe that their union with God and final redemption cannot occur until the entire land of Israel is within Jewish control and all the Arabs have been driven out. This is not a view held by all, or even most, Jews. Indeed, Jewish law decrees that "Thou shalt not kill" and "thou shalt not steal" (Exod 20:13 and 15). Moreover, the writers of Leviticus tell us that landowners must "share their wealth. With everyone. Native and immigrant. Male and female. Family and strangers. Sighted and blind. No one is 'othered.' No one is left out."[63] Yet, as is unfortunately the case with at least some members of every religion, these sects have latched on to the biblical verses that serve them and have entirely ignored all those that encourage compassion and ethics. Sadly, their religiosity has become much more focused on the land of Israel than on the people of Israel. As a result, these groups pose a significant threat to resident Palestinians and other Israelis, both of whom they perceive as standing between them and final redemption.

---

60. To be clear, this is often thought to be the case in acts of violence, period. I do not think this is particular to Israelis.
61. Policzer, "Deconstructing Adam and Eve," 7.
62. Policzer, "Deconstructing Adam and Eve," 7.
63. Duhan-Kaplan, "Violence of Othering," 3.

BIBLIOGRAPHY

Armstrong, Karen. *Jerusalem: One City, Three Faiths.* London: HarperCollins, 1996.

BBC. "Israel and the Palestinians: Can the Settlement Issue Be Solved?" *BBC*, Nov. 18, 2019. https://www.bbc.com/news/world-middle-east-38458884.

Buber, Solomon. *Midrash Lamentations Rabbah.* Vilna, 1899.

Buerschaper, Leslie. "My Grandfather's Hidden History: Exploring Memory and Intergenerational Trauma after WWII." Paper given at Religion and Violence Conference, Vancouver School of Theology, Vancouver, Can., 2019.

Chetrit, Sami Shalom. "Mizrahi Politics in Israel: Between Integration and Alternative." *Journal of Palestine Studies* 29 (2000) 51–65.

Dan, Joseph. "Jerusalem in Jewish Spirituality." In *City of the Great King*, edited by Nitza Rosovsky, 60–73. London: Harvard University Press, 1996.

———. *Kabbalah: A Very Short Introduction.* New York: Oxford University Press, 2006.

Duhan-Kaplan, Laura. "The Violence of Othering: Hate Your Neighbor as Yourself." Paper given at Religion and Violence Conference, Vancouver School of Theology, Vancouver, Can., 2019.

Dutcher-Walls, Pat. "Disturbing the Peace . . . Preaching When God Is the Source of Violence." Paper given at Lester Randall Preaching Festival, Yorkminster Park Baptist Church, Toronto, 2018.

Frie, Roger. *Not in My Family: German Memory and Responsibility after the Holocaust.* New York: Oxford University Press, 2017.

Goldenberg, Robert. "The Destruction of the Jerusalem Temple: Its Meaning and Its Consequences." In *The Late Roman Period*, edited by Steven T. Katz, vol. 4 of *The Cambridge History of Judaism*, 191–205. Cambridge: Cambridge University Press, 2006.

Goodman, Micah. "Three Paradoxes of Religious Zionism." *Haaretz*, Sept. 11, 2015. https://www.haaretz.com/2015-09-11/ty-article/.premium/three-paradoxes-of-religious-zionism/0000017f-db23-db22-a17f-ffb304150000.

Gorenberg, Gershom. *The Accidental Empire: Israel and the Birth of the Settlements, 1967–1977.* New York: Times, 2006.

———. *The Unmaking of Israel.* New York: Harper, 2011.

Harel, Amos. "Israeli 'Jewish Terror' Incidents Targeting Palestinians Tripled in 2018." *Haaretz*, Jan. 6, 2019. https://www.haaretz.com/israel-news/2019-01-06/ty-article/.premium/israeli-jewish-terror-incidents-targeting-palestinians-tripled-in-2018/0000017f-f550-d887-a7ff-fdf4ebfc0000.

Hertzberg, Arthur. "Jerusalem and Zionism." In *City of the Great King*, edited by Nitza Rosovsky, 149–77. London: Harvard University Press, 1996.

Herzl, Theodor. "The Jewish State." In *The Zionist Idea: A Historical Analysis and Reader*, edited by Arthur Hertzberg, 204–25. Garden City, NY: Doubleday, 1959.

Juergensmeyer, Mark. *Terror in the Mind of God.* 4th ed. Oakland: University of California Press, 2017.

Lustick, Ian S. *For the Land and the Lord: Jewish Fundamentalism in Israel.* New York: Council on Foreign Relations, 1988.

Maier, Harry. "The Apocalypse of Religious Violence." Paper given at Religion and Violence Conference, Vancouver School of Theology, Vancouver, Can., 2019.

Picard, Avi. "Building the Country or Rescuing the People: Ben-Gurion's Attitude Towards Mass Jewish Immigration to Israel in the mid-1950s." *Middle Eastern Studies* (2017) 382–99.

Policzer, Irene. "Deconstructing Adam and Eve: A New Theory on the Origins of Human Violence." Paper given at Religion and Violence Conference, Vancouver School of Theology, Vancouver, Can., 2019.

Ravitzky, Aviezer. *Messianism, Zionism, and Jewish Religious Radicalism.* London: University of Chicago Press, 1996.

Scholem, Gershom. *Kabbalah.* New York: Quadrangle, 1974.

Shabbat Vehagim. "Prayer for the State of Israel." Reconstructing Judaism, Apr. 15, 2016. https://www.reconstructingjudaism.org/article/prayer-state-israel/.

Snitkoff, Ed. "Praying for the Welfare of the State of Israel." My Jewish Learning, n.d. https://www.myjewishlearning.com/article/praying-for-the-welfare-of-the-state-of-israel/.

Sprinzak, Ehud. *Gush Emunim: The Politics of Zionist Fundamentalism in Israel.* New York: American Jewish Committee, Institute of Human Relations, 1986. http://eagle.orgfree.com/alabasters_archive/zionist_fundamentalism.html.

Yaniv, Samuel. "The Vilna Gaon and His Vision of Redemption." Lecture at Bar-Ilan University, Ramat Gan, Isr., Apr. 17, 2010. https://www.biu.ac.il/JH/Parasha/eng/yomatz/yani.html.

Zimmerman, Binyamin. "Shinat Chinnam and the Destruction of the Temple." Israel Koschitzky Torat Har Etzion, Jan. 17, 2016. https://www.etzion.org.il/en/philosophy/issues-jewish-thought/issues-mussar-and-faith/sinat-chinnam-and-destruction-temple.

A Spiritual Ecology of Apocalypse

Jason M. Brown

BEGINNING THE END

Dear Ancestors,

I, Srexix Local, The Temporary Leader of EarthWon, write to you from the year 2519. I hope to provide peace of mind, as all of the turmoil you face in 2019 will be resolved, I assure you. Please know that your generation is not held in a bad light by our people. Although you have many limitations, we now know that no pain endured in the history of humanity is worse than that you currently experience. We are eternally grateful for the bravery and strength you show in surviving your coming century.

—MAX GROSS, 2019[1]

IN MY ENVIRONMENTAL HUMANITIES classes, I ask my students to speculate about the future of a world on the brink of cataclysmic anthropogenic climate change. The assignment evokes everything from nightmarish oppressive totalitarian secular states to blissful animistic earth-religions. Most of the students opt for some version of the former. I do not know what

---

1. Max's entire short story is published at my student writing blog. See Brown, "Environmental Humanities Hub."

this says about the rising generation, except that we do not know what the future holds, and it most certainly will be very different from our current reality. This growing uncertainty is increasingly expressed as "apocalyptic" worry. Although the biblical motif of apocalypse has more to do with its Greek etymology, to "uncover" or "reveal," popularly the word *apocalypse* is understood as a sort of calamitous final judgment or end of days.[2] Many scientists, journalists, and activists frame the Anthropocene Age, the age of human domination, as either a great promise or a terrible threat.

In the hands of the media, quantitative climate science has appeared as a series of apocalyptic markers. Past these points, environmental reporting suggests, climate change could be unstoppable, and thus spell the end of human civilization and many other lifeforms as well. For example, climate activist Bill McKibben's threshold of 350 parts per million of carbon dioxide in the atmosphere was a kind of climate-based numerological slogan, until in 2015, we blew past 400 parts per million. The Intergovernmental Panel on Climate Change (IPCC) warned in 2018 that we have twelve years to sufficiently cut anthropogenic carbon emissions and prevent the worst effects of a "climate catastrophe." The Breakthrough National Centre for Climate Restoration, a think tank in Melbourne, Australia, published a recent report warning of the very real possibility that human civilization could expire around the year 2050.[3] The Bulletin of the Atomic Scientists began a Doomsday Clock in 1947 to symbolically warn humanity of the threat of nuclear war. Today the clock is closer to midnight than it has ever been (one hundred seconds), thanks not only to the ongoing threat of nuclear weapons but to the massive threat climate change poses to global civilization.[4] Most recently, New York City has collaborated with artists and activists to unveil a digital countdown clock near Union Square. The clock highlights the shrinking window world leaders have to rein in carbon emissions and work toward global drawdown before 2050.

Journalist David Wallace-Wells thinks these thresholds should terrify us. Wallace-Wells wants us to look at what is at stake if we continue on a business-as-usual trajectory. In good prophetic fashion, his writing often emphasizes the worst-case scenarios.[5] For example, he writes, in 2016 melting permafrost in Siberia released an ancient strain of anthrax, a highly infectious bacteria which killed several people. Going forward, rising temperatures and continued deforestation could increase the incidents of

2. Keller and Thatamanil, "Is This an Apocalypse?"
3. Spratt and Dunlop, *Existential Climate-Related Security Risk*.
4. Mecklin, "At Doom's Doorstep."
5. Wallace-Wells, *Uninhabitable Earth*.

pandemics and epidemics such as COVID-19 or Ebola. In addition, climate-induced food scarcities could cause up to fifty thousand deaths by 2050.[6] Destructive flooding, drought, and hurricanes will become more extreme and more frequent. In the possible scenario of five- to six-degree warming, we would see a massive increase in incidences of heat stress and heat death, even causing many places on earth to be permanently uninhabitable. New York City could become as hot as present-day Bahrain, and the Hajj, the pilgrimage carried out by faithful Muslims in Mecca, Saudi Arabia, could become impossible in fewer than two decades.[7] Ocean levels could rise from between two to ten meters, and the ocean currents that contribute to regional climates could drastically shift or even stop all together. In addition to surges in carbon dioxide, hydrogen sulfide and methane could also be released from the global north's permafrost regions and ocean floor, further warming the atmosphere in a tail-spinning negative feedback loop. Hydrogen sulfide has an additional impact; it is toxic and can strip away layers of ozone which protect us from harmful levels of UV radiation.[8]

None of these worst-case scenario outcomes are inevitable, though there is certainly much work to do to prevent them. However, there remains within the environmental community little agreement about our strategy for overcoming this monumental existential threat. Where might we look for inspiration? In this chapter, I look to an unlikely place: first-century Judea. During that time, there were at least five Jewish political movements of consequence: the Sadducees, the Pharisees, the Essences, the Zealots, and the Jesus movement. Below, I will draw an open-ended analogy between the different ways these sects approached Judaism and the various ways environmental groups at the dawn of the Anthropocene address the climate crisis. Then, going beyond the framework of my own analogy, I will hold up present day Indigenous activists, well acquainted with apocalypses of their own, as a model for contemporary approaches to environmental issues.

FIRST-CENTURY JUDEA:
AN ECOLOGICAL ALLEGORY

During a seminar at Yale Divinity School, I had a strange thought. I was enrolled in the joint-degree program between the department of Forestry and Environmental Studies and the Divinity School, so the relationship between religion and ecology was on my mind. It occurred to me that the sects of

---

6. Harvey, "Food Scarcity."
7. Wallace-Wells, "Uninhabitable Earth."
8. Wallace-Wells, "Uninhabitable Earth."

first-century Judaea as identified by the Jewish historian Josephus could be viewed as an analogy for contemporary environmental discourses.

Yosef ben Matityahu, or Titus Flavius Josephus in Latin, often referred to as simply Josephus, was a first-century Jewish historian. According to Josephus, there were four main social movements in Judea: Pharisees, Sadducees, Zealots, and Essenes. The most prominent of the social movements was the Pharisees, of which Josephus himself became a member. The word *Pharisee*, as understood through its Aramaic and Greek cognates, means "to set apart or separate." Pharisees were a broad Second Temple social movement which, after the destruction of the temple by the Romans in 70 CE, became the foundation for Rabbinic Judaism. Pharisees, according to Josephus, believed in a strict obedience to the Law of Moses, interpreted through the Oral Torah, and affirmed a post-mortal reward for those who obeyed. Josephus began to observe the rules of the Pharisees at an early age, which he compared to the Stoics.[9]

The Sadducees took their name from Zadok, the first high priest of the First Temple. During the Second Temple period, whne the temple was central to Jewish society, Sadducees were an elite class of temple priests, concerned primarily with the duties outlined in the Torah for temple clergy. The Sadducees were also the official contacts with Roman officials, and they administered the Jewish governing body, the Sanhedrin. They were responsible for collecting taxes and governing internal affairs of the Roman province of Judea. According to Josephus, the Sadducees believed in free will but did not affirm the Pharisaic view of the immortality and judgment of the soul after death.[10]

The name of the Essenes, called *Isiyim* by Josephus, may be connected with a Greek word for "holiness." However, a clear etymology and delineated group identity is contested among scholars. Many scholars accept that the community at Qumran, the location of the Dead Sea Scrolls, was Essenian; however, others suggest that the Qumran group was closer to the Pharisees.[11] Scholars believe that those communities which we can identify as Essenian were quasi-monastic, often celibate ascetics, who may have broken away from the Sadducees in disgust over the running of the temple in Jerusalem. Motivated by their close reading of Isaiah, they fled to the desert to prepare the way of the Lord, believing that the world was about to radically change. They saw themselves as the true believers. The War Scroll text, found in Cave 1 of the Dead Sea Scrolls, imagined the unfolding of

9. Josephus, *Life of Flavius Josephus*, Kindle loc. 87.
10. Josephus, *Jewish War*, Kindle loc. 27534.
11. See for example, Collins, *Dead Sea Scrolls*; Lim, *Oxford Handbook*.

final events before the current evil age. The sons of light would defeat the sons of darkness. God would come and restore the kingdom of God on earth to the status of the kingdoms of David and Solomon. Various iterations of this timeline predicted no messiah, one messiah, or even two: a warrior savior and a priestly messiah.[12]

The Zealots, according to Josephus, were Jewish freedom fighters, a militant anti-imperial movement that sought to expel the pagan Romans by force. Zealot is a translation of the Hebrew *kanai*, meaning someone who is zealous for God. The Zealots were founded in 6 CE by Judas of Galilee as a reaction against the census of Quirinius. The Zealots attempted to expel the Romans during the first Jewish-Roman wars of 66–70 CE. One result of the war was the destruction of the temple in Jerusalem. Scholars do not describe a clearly delineated ideology for these radicals. Politically, they were most likely aligned with the Pharisees, but they advocated violence against Romans and Greeks. A splinter group, the Sicarii, even advocated killing fellow Jews who collaborated with the empire.[13]

While Josephus mentions Jesus of Nazareth in passing, Jesus was not in the fore of Josephus's historical writings. Only with the rise of gentile Christianity did the Jesus movement became a major player in world history. Our best sources on Jesus are the books of the New Testament, but these are, of course, biased toward his wonder-working messiahship. Jesus was in many ways a Pharisee in outlook, though he was quick to point out hypocritical motives among some of the Pharisees. He was not a Sadducee, as he had little interest in entering the ranks of the temple priesthood. Still, he spent much of his time within the temple precincts preaching and worshipping. He was not a Zealot, but he was not afraid of overturning the tables of the money lenders to point out their corruption. There is no evidence that he knew of the Essenes, but there is speculation that he perhaps visited them at some stage before his ministry, or during his forty days in the desert.[14]

ANALOGY TO THE ENVIRONMENTAL MOVEMENT

Now certainly there is complexity in every era and within every movement. Yet I cannot help seeing some parallels between the scene in first-century Judea and today's environmental movement. The different religious and

12. Livius, "Messiah."
13. Smith, "Zealots and Sicarii."
14. This theory was popular with nineteenth-century esotericists such as Rudolf Steiner and theosophist Helena Blavatsky in her work *Isis Unveiled*, 144. See also Szekely, *Essene Origins of Christianity*, 184–205.

political perspectives of these early Jewish groups offer a helpful lens for understanding differences between environmental perspectives today.

The "Pharisees" of the environmental movement are continually focused on the power of individual actions. Environmental Pharisees religiously turn off light switches. They promote green lifestyles and filling out online carbon footprint calculators. Environmental Pharisees often adhere to a strict dietary code, such as being vegetarian or vegan. And they believe that a zero-waste lifestyle is the highest ecological virtue. They emphasize the importance of personal purity in relation to environmental crises by purchasing fair trade. They eschew support for large corporations by buying local and organic. They strive to live car-free or ride a bike. If they can afford it, they invest in solar panels for their homes, even going off grid, if possible. Theirs is a confidence in individual actions that add up to a broad shift in consciousness, and an eagerness to do their part for the environment. This shift, they hope, will bring about the changes we hope to see in the political system and the economy.

The "Sadducees" of the environmental movement, analogous to the elite Judean priests, are the captains of the nonprofit environmental and conservation industries. They are the middle managers and campaign organizers of mainstream organizations like the Nature Conservancy, Sierra Club, and Greenpeace. They are interested in real and substantive change, but not at the cost of a seat at the table with the powers that be. They are open to corporate sponsorship and advocate a way forward that balances business and environment. They are always seeking to scale up, build coalitions, and pass legislation, even if that means watering down the outcomes of a campaign. They are renewable energy boosters and often admit that nuclear energy should be on the table, at least while we transition to a green economy. They advocate for the proposed Green New Deal, which promises massive government investment in renewable energy and green jobs. The Sadducees of the environmental movement see gradual, within-the-system actions as the key to environmental change.

The "Essenes" of the environmental movement, like the ancient Essenes, have become disillusioned with the mainstream environmental movement. They often see mainstream environmentalism as a sell-out to industrial capitalism and empire. They are skeptical of corporate renewable energy projects that require vast tracts of land to operate and continued mining of precious metals to get going. Many of them believe that the most important thing one can do is to live as though the world has already gone through an ecological apocalypse. They believe it is too late for broad-scale change and have perhaps moved to rural or wild places to await the great conflagrations that are inevitably coming. While they eschew the possibility of changing the system from within, they seek to model the reality they wish to live in by embodying ecological sustainability. As civilization as we know it inevitably collapses under its own weight, they strive to tell new stories about the human places in the world that connect us to our distant past. These are the back-to-the-landers, the primitivists, the permaculturalists, and the dark ecologists.[15] Like some of the Essenes, they believe there is no messiah coming to save us from a mounting conflict between the forces of light and dark.

The environmental "Zealots" are the radicals. For them, the only way to permanently solve the ecological crisis would be to overthrow the entire system and start over. Capitalism is the problem, not the solution. We cannot compromise with empire. Radical environmentalist groups such as Earth Liberation Front (ELF) or Earth First!—who have advocated violence against property—belong to this camp. Environmental Zealots are critical of lifestylism, in-the-system-careerism, and even back-to-the-landers.

Today, the Zealot environmentalists—the radicals—have by and large faded from mainstream concern. Groups like ELF or Earth First! are no longer making headlines as they did in the 1980s and 1990s. The allure of personal lifestylism, practiced by my so-called environmental Pharisees, is alive and well but does not by itself present a serious solution to the larger concerns of climate breakdown and species extinction. In contemporary conversations about avoiding our potentially apocalyptic future, two other schools of environmental discourse stand out, the "neo-Sadducees" and the "neo-Essenes."

THE NEO-SADDUCEES

What I am calling the "Neo-Sadducees" would be those environmentalist organizations and activists who more or less believe that through the proper application of technology, we could usher in a kind of techno-utopian heaven on earth. They believe we need to think more creatively about land use, biodiversity, and energy. In recent years, the Neo-Sadducee side of post-environmental discourse has begun to self-identify as ecomodernist or pragmatist environmentalism. They do not want a piecemeal approach, for example, worrying about personal recycling like the Pharisees do. Nor do they want to fight an entire ideological battle against the dominant political-economic system as the Zealots wish to do. Instead, they are optimistic about integrating ecological principles into the system itself.

---

15. I describe what I mean by Dark Ecologists in the section on Neo-Essenes.

One example of Neo-Sadducee rejection of traditional conservation is their criticism of the idea of Nature. For them, setting aside nature preserves and wilderness areas does little to address the environmental crisis. Michelle Marvier, Peter Kareiva, and Robert Lalasz of the Breakthrough Institute argue that these traditional conservation approaches are more about preserving "islands of the Holocene" than about offering practical ways into the Anthropocene.[16] This "fortress" approach to conservation is simply not sufficient in an era of complex economics and even more complex global ecologies that now include massive cities, commerce, and novel ecosystems.

Neo-Sadducee, ecomodernist approaches to the ecological crisis are characterized by a strong belief in the application of technology through human reason. (This humanism may not have a direct parallel in ancient thought.) For example, the authors of the *Ecomodernist Manifesto* write:

> As scholars, scientists, campaigners, and citizens, we write with the conviction that knowledge and technology, applied with wisdom, might allow for a good, or even great, Anthropocene. A good Anthropocene demands that humans use their growing social, economic, and technological powers to make life better for people, stabilize the climate, and protect the natural world.[17]

These Anthropocene boosters have great confidence in human genius. They say we need to embrace technology, state-centered decision making, and a human-values-centric approach to ecological sustainability. Their ecomodernist mythos celebrates the idea that despite our converging crises, human beings have reached the status of gods with our substantial knowledge and control over the earth.[18] The future, including the management of the planet's climate and ecological systems, is more and more in our hands. They embrace nuclear energy, seek to intensify agriculture, densify cities, and decouple human technology from nature. They are also often serious advocates for at least some form of geo-engineering of the climate if it comes to that. Geo-engineering, more controversial even than nuclear energy, would use technology to manipulate the sun's radiation or the climate. Like good temple priests, they feel confident that we have mastered the earth's liturgical cycles and interacting components; that our dominion over the earth was foreordained.

---

16. Marvier et al., "Conservation in the Anthropocene."

17. Asafu-Adjaye et al., "Ecomodernist Manifesto."

18. This is, in fact, precisely what historian Yuval Noah Harari argues in his book *Homo Deus*.

THE NEO-ESSENES

From a Neo-Essene perspective, this confidence in technology is misplaced. For example, Norwegian philosopher Arne Naess advocates for what has become known as an ecocentric ethic, which establishes the living biosphere as the locus of value. By identifying the small individual self with the larger ecological self, we would be more likely to protect the earth's ecosystems. Naess argues that we need a broader philosophical shift in our understanding of our relationship to the planet, not just better technology or policy. Human beings are not the center of the world; thus, Naess and others like him advocate for massive humane reductions in global human population, a stronger commitment to protecting large swaths of wild nature, and sustainable small-scale agriculture.[19] To express this view, Naess coined the term "deep ecology," in opposition to what he called "shallow ecology."[20]

English writer Paul Kingsnorth, whom I would characterize as a Neo-Essene, left the mainstream environmental movement in disgust. He calls himself a recovering environmentalist and has moved to a small farm in Northern Ireland. He has also recently converted to Orthodox Christianity. Echoing his deep ecology foreparents, he believes that much of Neo-Sadducee environmentalism has traded one technological solution for another:

> Now it seemed that environmentalism was not about wildness or ecocentrism or the other-than-human world and our relationship to it. Instead it was about (human) social justice and (human) equality and (human) progress and ensuring that all these things could be realized without degrading the (human) resource base that we used to call nature back when we were being naïve and problematic.[21]

These are direct hits at an ecomodernist humanism that elevates human reason and value, and that has deconstructed nature as a romantic trope. Kingsnorth has, of course, been roundly condemned as a romantic, as naïve, a Luddite, and as getting in the way of progress toward substantive policy shifts in line with international agreements, targets, and projections. Yet, for Kingsnorth, the mainstream environmental movement would be willing to kill nature to save it. Kingsnorth responds to criticism that he is an escapist by echoing the words of artist Ian Hamilton Finlay, who was also accused of escapism when he moved to a small rural property. Finlay said, "Certain

---

19. Deval and Sessions, *Deep Ecology*, 66–67.
20. Naess, "Shallow and Deep."
21. Kingsnorth, *Confessions of Recovering Environmentalist*, 76.

gardens are described as retreats when they are really attacks . . . you can change a bit of the actual world by taking out a spade."[22]

Kingsnorth was a founding voice for the emerging journal *Dark Mountain*, which seems quite open to the possibility of civilizational collapse. The Dark Mountain Project elevates and organizes artists who have become disillusioned with the direction of civilization and the environmental movement's response to it. They seek to begin to retell the human story from whatever enclaves remain. The *Dark Mountain Manifesto* articulates eight principles rejecting the idea that environmental problems can be solved primarily through technical solutions.[23] Taking broad swipes at ecomodernist humanism, it says, "Onto the root stock of Western Christianity, the Enlightenment at its most optimistic grafted a vision of an Earthly paradise, towards which human effort guided by calculative reason could take us." The manifesto affirms with Ralph Waldo Emerson that "the end of the human race will be that it will eventually die of civilization." Kingsnorth has elsewhere used the label of a "dark ecologist," echoing his distrust of civilization. Perhaps, however, it is ironic that the Dark Mountain Project denounces human importance by centering their own kind, human artists!

A BETTER WAY INTO THE DARK

There are, of course, many more threads to the contemporary environmental movement. But I am seeing these two poles gaining increasing magnetism among contemporary environmentalists. The environmental movement seems quite divided when it comes to our common fate. We need to work harder to build broad consensus among the branches and streams of contemporary environmentalism. We need prophetic and visionary leaders to lead us into the dark, so that we do not retreat into enclaves of deprecating self-loathing or hubristic optimism.

Where can we look for guidance in a time of both upheaval and tribalistic political posturing? Looking back at the first-century scene I have sketched out above, I see both cautions and opportunities. The Talmudic rationale for the destruction of the Jerusalem temple points to the importance of unity. And the life of Jesus offers an example of a middle way. However, as I will show in greater detail below, my greatest hope is inspired by the voices of contemporary Indigenous activists whose peoples have suffered enormous trauma at the hands of global civilization, yet who remain deeply committed to human goodness and ecological healing.

---

22. Kingsnorth, *Confessions of Recovering Environmentalist*, 102–3.
23. Kingsnorth and Hine, "Manifesto."

After the year 70 CE, the Jewish people were devastated by the loss of their beloved temple. Yet the resilience of the Jewish people enabled them to adapt, grieve, heal, and express their devotion in new ways. In subsequent centuries, rabbinic commentators sought to understand the tragic destruction of the temple by the Romans. Why had God allowed this to happen? Because, said the rabbis of the Talmud, people engaged in *sinat chinam*, Hebrew for "baseless hatred." These rabbis saw that the factionalism between groups led to the destruction of the temple. Because the various Jewish sects could not come together, they were not able to mount an effective strategic defense. Thus, the Romans were eventually able to overtake the city and destroy the temple.[24] I worry that the environmental movement will fail if the various "sects" do not come together.

The life of Jesus offers an example of a middle way. In his Jewish context, Jesus was a prophetic teacher rooted in the pedagogy of the Pharisees. Yet, Jesus often critiqued the Pharisees for their narrow focus on the letter of the law over the broader spirit of intimacy with God. While we cannot paint all Pharisees with the same brush—and early fractures in the Christian community often stereotyped the Pharisees—in Jesus we see a rabbinic teacher who warns against too narrow a focus on the minutiae of procedure (see Luke 11:37–54; Matt 23:1–39; Mark 12:35–40). In contemporary environmentalism, a sustainable Neo-Pharisee lifestyle is laudable, but it does not elevate practitioners above those who may not be able to devote as much time and resources to a green lifestyle.

Jesus was not afraid of civil disobedience and even destroyed some property to protect the temple from commercialization (see Matt 21:12–13; John 2:13–16). Yet he was not a Zealot, who would spill the blood of Roman soldiers or Jewish tax collectors accused of collaboration with pagans. In fact, Jesus spent a lot of his time with tax collectors. Jesus loved the temple and observed the Jewish holy days. He worshipped, prayed, and taught in the temple, without becoming a temple worker or cozying up to Rome in order to keep the temple institution afloat. Jesus did not shy away from criticizing empire, even though it could cost him his life. He spent plenty of time in the silence of wild place, but he did not reject the world outright and retreat permanently to the desert.

---

24. I am indebted to Rabbi Laura Duhan-Kaplan for this insightful reading of first-century Judea from a Jewish perspective. The Talmudic commentaries come from Yismach Yisrael on Pesach Haggadah Magid, Ha Lachma Anya, 3:3, p. 42a–b.

INDIGENOUS HOPES

Indigenous peoples in North America, and many other parts of the world, have already experienced an apocalypse. Professor Kyle White, a Citizen Potawatomi Nation Indigenous philosopher at Michigan State University, shows how Indigenous peoples and the dominant settler societies of North America live on divergent timelines. The dominant society sees apocalypse as posing a threat in the future. For Indigenous peoples, it is something that has been here already. The long arc of Indigenous cultural memory goes back before colonization to time immemorial. This interim period of genocide and ecocide will also eventually come to an end.[25] Whyte writes,

> It would have been an act of imagining dystopia for our ancestors to consider the erasures we live through today, in which some Anishinaabek are finding it harder to obtain supplies of birch bark, or seeing algal blooms add to factors threatening whitefish populations, or fighting to ensure the legality in the eyes of the industrial settler state of protecting wild rice for harvest.[26]

Indigenous peoples' tenacity in surviving the waves of attempts at eradication and assimilation is astounding. And as Indigenous peoples collectively heal from this cultural trauma, they are revitalizing, resurging, and reclaiming their traditions and restoring their traditional territories.

Despite their collective trauma, many Indigenous activists I have interacted with remain deeply compassionate toward humanity. Lyla June, a Diné activist who was active during the Dakota Access Pipeline protests from 2016–17, is a fierce critic of the deep damages that colonial structures have inflicted on Indigenous peoples. Yet as someone of both Navajo and European ancestry, she acknowledges that many of the peoples who fled Europe were also traumatized by imperial forces. Far from seeing humans as gods who rule the earth as the ecomodernists, or as a cancer that kills, like certain strands of the Neo-Essenes might, June writes, "Human beings are meant to be a keystone species." Human beings are meant to hold a sacred place in the ecology of earth. We are, in fact, "gifts to the land."[27] For June, human beings have inherited a unique role *among* the creatures of this planet. Her view is neither techno-utopian nor misanthropic but *relational*. Human beings are to sink deep roots into the land. Every being has intrinsic value, *including* human beings. We don't have to justify our existence by some scale of ecological merit or denigrate it on some scale of ecological sin.

---

25. Whyte, "Indigenous Science."
26. Whyte, "Our Ancestors' Dystopia," 208.
27. Johnston, "Lyla June."

ENDING THE BEGINNING

Apocalypse may not actually be about endings. It may be about beginnings, about opening a new vision of what is possible. Or, at the very least, it may be about recovering tried and true resources from viable or forgotten visions of human flourishing and incorporating them into our present context. The way forward is neither a path that presumes to solve every problem through new gadgets and engineered solutions, nor one that requires giving up and retreating to the countryside or the wilderness (forever). Rather, the way forward, as difficult and painful as it may be, is a way that relies on the resilience and grace of the world which is always offering abundance and fecundity to those who will not take it for granted. We will need a comprehensive and all-hands-on-deck sort of strategy moving forward. While there are many pathways, ultimately, it is my hope that we can avoid further costly factionalism and defeatism and work toward systemic, coordinated efforts that integrate policy, technology, and the depths of the human heart.

BIBLIOGRAPHY

Asafu-Adjaye, John, et al. "An Ecomodernist Manifesto." Ecomodernism, 2015. http://www.ecomodernism.org/manifesto-english/.

Blavatsky, Helena P. *Isis Unveiled: A Mastery-Key to the Mysteries of Ancient and Modern Science and Theology.* 2 vols. Pasadena, CA: Theosophical University Press, 1976. First published 1877.

Brown, Jason, ed. Environmental Humanities Hub. www.envhub.wordpress.com.

Collins, John J. *The Dead Sea Scrolls: A Biography.* Oxford, UK: Oxford University Press, 2012.

Deval, Bill, and George Sessions. *Deep Ecology: Living as if Nature Mattered.* Salt Lake City: Smith, 1985.

Harari, Yuval Noah. *Homo Deus: A Brief History of Tomorrow.* New York: Signal: 2016.

Harvey, Chelsea. "Food Scarcity Caused by Climate Change Could Cause 500,000 Deaths by 2050, Study Suggests." *Washington Post*, Mar. 2, 2016. https://www.washingtonpost.com/news/energy-environment/wp/2016/03/02/food-scarcity-caused-by-climate-change-could-cause-500000-deaths-by-2050-study-suggests/.

Johnston, Lyla June. "Lyla June on the Forest as Farm." Esperanza Project, Nov. 15, 2019. https://www.esperanzaproject.com/2019/native-american-culture/lyla-june-on-the-forest-as-farm/.

Josephus, Flavius. *The Jewish War.* In *The Works of Josephus: Complete and Unabridged.* Harrington, DE: Delmarva, 2016. Kindle.

———. *The Life of Flavius Josephus.* In *The Works of Josephus: Complete and Unabridged.* Harrington, DE: Delmarva, 2016. Kindle.

Keller, Catherine, and John J. Thatamanil. "Is This an Apocalypse? We Certainly Hope So—You Should Too." *ABC*, Apr. 15, 2020; updated Apr. 20, 2020. https://www.abc.net.au/religion/catherine-keller-and-john-thatamanil-why-we-hope-this-is-an-apo/12151922.

Kingsnorth, Paul. *Confessions of a Recovering Environmentalist and Other Essays*. London: Faber and Faber, 2017.

———, and Dougald Hine. "The Manifesto." Dark Mountain Project, 2009. https://dark-mountain.net/about/manifesto/.

Lim, Timothy H., ed. *The Oxford Handbook of the Dead Sea Scrolls*. Oxford Handbooks. Oxford, UK: Oxford University Press, 2010.

Livius. "Messiah." Livius, 2001; last modified Oct. 10, 2020. https://www.livius.org/articles/religion/messiah/.

Marvier, Michelle, et al. "Conservation in the Anthropocene: Beyond Solitude and Fragility." *Breakthrough Journal* 2 (Fall 2011) 29–37. https://thebreakthrough.org/journal/issue-2/conservation-in-the-anthropocene.

Mecklin, John, ed. "At Doom's Doorstep: It Is 100 Seconds to Midnight." Bulletin of the Atomic Scientists, Jan. 20, 2022. https://thebulletin.org/doomsday-clock/.

Naess, Arne. "The Shallow and the Deep, Long-Range Ecology Movement: A Summary." *Inquiry* 16 (1973) 95–100.

Smith, Morton. "Zealots and Sicarii, Their Origins and Relation." *Harvard Theological Review* 64 (Jan. 1971) 1–19. https://doi.org/10.1017/S0017816000018009.

Spratt, David, and Ian Dunlop. *Existential Climate-Related Security Risk: A Scenario Approach*. Melbourne: Breakthrough—National Centre for Climate Restoration, 2019. https://docs.wixstatic.com/ugd/148cb0_90dc2a2637f348edae45943a88da04d4.pdf.

Szekely, Edmund Bordeaux. *The Essene Origins of Christianity*. Nelson, Can.: International Biogenic Society, 1993.

Wallace-Wells, David. "The Uninhabitable Earth." *New York Magazine*, July 10, 2017. https://nymag.com/intelligencer/2017/07/climate-change-earth-too-hot-for-humans.html.

———. *The Uninhabitable Earth: Life after Warming*. New York: Duggan, 2019.

Whyte, Kyle P. "Indigenous Science (Fiction) for the Anthropocene: Ancestral Dystopias and Fantasies of Climate Change Crises." *Environment and Planning E: Nature and Space* 1 (2018) 224–42.

———. "Our Ancestors' Dystopia Now: Indigenous Conservation and the Anthropocene." In *The Routledge Companion to the Environmental Humanities*, edited by Ursula K. Heise et al, 206–15. New York: Routledge, 2017.

"That You Might Stand Here on the Roof of the Clouds"

Finding Hope in a Cauldron of Encounter, War, and Conflict in Nineteenth-Century New Zealand

GRAHAM BIDOIS CAMERON

INTRODUCTION

IN THE NINETEENTH CENTURY, my subtribe of Pirirākau, like all other tribes in New Zealand in this period, faced its greatest existential threat: an encounter with the British Empire that was intent on the colonization of the Māori people and the settlement of the lands of New Zealand. This was more than just a physical threat; colonization includes the active and planned ethnocide of a people.

So, in addition to military resistance, Pirirākau also attempted to adapt their own theological knowledge to respond, react, and then to survive this encounter with the British settlers. This initially saw the Pirirākau embrace Catholicism, but in the mid-1860s an emissary from the first Māori Christian prophetic movement arrived. His arrival saw the near complete conversion of our people from Catholicism to this new faith movement. Within thirty years, our subtribe had moved from a traditional cosmology to French Catholicism and finally to this Indigenous Christian faith. This is the journey of an intelligent and inquiring people in matters of faith and spirituality.

This chapter tracks this nineteenth-century journey by one Māori subtribe to demonstrate their authority over their own theological development, their continued connection to their foundational theological concepts, and a recognition of the possibilities in the rapid faith changes in that century. Within a cauldron of encounter, war and conflict, and confiscation and loss, faith and hope allowed our people to maintain their identity, often despite the intention of the Church itself.

Māori storytelling is not linear; it is a relational and experiential process. I want you to experience something of the weight of the story that we carry in our tribe. So, this is not a linear history of Pai Mārire, the first Māori Christian faith, or even of my tribe and their historical experiences. It is a story, first; as such, I move back and forth between history, theology, and biography, before concluding with insight into the significance of Pai Mārire.

I love stories, rich with truth and wisdom. In the Māori[1] language, story is referred to as a *pūrākau*. "Pū" in this refers to originating or root, and "rākau" a tree. A *pūrākau* then is the taproot of the tree, a rich image that conveys a truth: that the great stories have no end but to grow, develop, and seed further stories, eventually resulting in a forest of stories. Māori today regularly lament how much of our knowledge has been lost. Yet the wisdom of our ancestors was never kept as knowledge, but as narratives, created with a purpose and *whakapapa* (relational, genealogical connections). Just one line of a narrative that is rediscovered acts as a seed from which a narrative can flourish again into its fullest expression with the right nurturing and conditions. The encounter of my ancestors with French Catholicism and their conversion to the first Māori Christian faith Pai Mārire is just such a taproot; a narrative that has the potential to seed anew stories for my *hapū* (subtribe) of Pirirākau and our region of Tauranga Moana.[2]

Pirirākau is a subtribe of the Ngāti Ranginui tribe, one of three main tribes in Tauranga Moana. Our ancestors maintained villages and fortifications in the rugged bush on the foothills of the Kaimai Range and the coast. The bush villages included extensive gardens and were launching stations for trade, tribal alliances, and the gathering of food from the bush, while on the coast the focus was seafood and cropping. Today we have four *marae* (cultural centers of community and familial connection): Poutūterangi, Paparoa, Tūtereinga, and Tawhitinui.

1. Māori are the indigenous Polynesian people of New Zealand whose ancestors journeyed back and forth from the South Pacific islands in approximately 1000 CE to establish hunter-gatherer communities. The basic societal structure is into genealogical groups of close relational connection, the smallest of which are *whānau*, the family unit; then *hapū*, a group of family units (subtribe) connected by one eponymous ancestor; and *iwi*, a tribe of connected *hapū*.

2. Tauranga Moana (commonly referred to as "Tauranga") is on the east coast of the North Island of New Zealand; it is approximately two hundred kilometers southeast of New Zealand's largest city, Auckland.

This narrative contains two stories that miraculously, wonderfully became one. The first is the story of Pirirākau, a people formed by the sea, the rivers, the land, and the mountains; a people whose very language was formed by the sounds, images, and experiences of that land; a people whose *whakapapa* assured them of a connection between the divine and chiefly ancestors and themselves. This first story picks up at the point at which Pirirākau faced its greatest existential threat: an encounter with a people and an empire who were more powerful, more numerous, and who regarded themselves as superior. This first story tells of Pirirākau attempting to adapt their own knowledge of the divine reality and promise to respond, react, and then to survive this encounter. The second is the story of writings from an Indigenous people[3] in the Middle East who made Scripture and law, and who then attached them uncomfortably to power and might. Writings that spoke of grace and love but which arrived in the hands of missionaries who spoke of change and sovereignty. This second story tells of the Scriptures arriving with Catholic missionaries to Tauranga Moana. It tells us how these Scriptures found a way past the bias and prejudice of the missionaries who carried them, such that they spoke to the hearts of the Māori and inspired new thoughts in them. These Scriptures guided the Māori during their time of suffering to an entirely new Māori Christian faith, Pai Mārire, that embraced a new millenarian vision of divine power that would overcome empire. Unlike other regions, in Tauranga Moana, a fervent millenarianism meant that our ancestors awaited a miraculous outworking of that divine judgment.

A BRIEF HISTORY OF CONFLICT IN TAURANGA MOANA

Māori suffered enormous land loss in New Zealand in the nineteenth century, losing five sixths of the entire country within sixty years because of unjust and rapacious land sales, racist legislation, and war. In addition, the Māori population plunged from over 100,000 to 42,000 in the same period.

This was also the experience of Pirirākau. Choosing to defend our land and to not acknowledge the authority of the British, Pirirākau were regarded as being "in rebellion against her Majesty's authority"[4] and were subject to the full force of the New Zealand Settlements Act 1863. Consequently, our ancestors were caught up in the 290,000 acres of Tauranga Moana that was

---

3. The prevailing contemporary academic opinion is that the Israelites are an offshoot of a mix of predominantly Indigenous peoples in Canaan. See Gottwald, *Tribes of Yahweh*, 455–56.

4. Adds, "Te Āti Awa."

confiscated by the then New Zealand Parliament's Order-in-Council following a Pacification Meeting[5] in August 1864. Close to the entirety of Pirirākau land—93,188 acres—was taken by way of a forced sale.

The two most significant military engagements of this period in Tauranga Moana were at Pukehinahina (Gate Pā) and Te Ranga (Pyes Pā). The battle at Pukehinahina (Gate Pā) is regarded as one of our greatest victories of that period, with 110 British soldiers either dead, wounded, or left behind after the rout. This victory led to plans for a larger attack in June 1864. The British Colonel Greer had received intelligence about the planned attack[6] and, consequently, preemptively engaged and defeated local Māori at partially built fortifications at Te Ranga on June 21, 1864. Though it is denied by Pākehā (New Zealanders of European ancestry) military historians, our history is that women and children were in the fortifications at that time, as the construction was not complete, and that they were among the dead. The defeat at Te Ranga led to the signing of a surrender on July 25, 1864. Another tribe, Ngāi Te Rangi, signed the surrender on behalf of our Ngāti Ranginui tribe, leading to the confiscation of our land. The confiscation was enforced by military action some three years later. The British troops who were supported by Māori mercenaries from another region attacked the villages in our tribal area in a scorched earth campaign known as "Te Weranga." The loss of homes and supplies led some Pirirākau to depart the region.

This was a great setback for Pirirākau, and people looked for an explanation in the Pai Mārire faith that had promised so much. The Māori King Tāwhiao attributed failure to the fulfilment of his vision that "an angel would be sent with precise directions as to the conduct of the war."[7] To his disappointment and despair, the angel failed to appear as promised in the midst of the war, and his followers were greatly grieved, some declaring that "the whole thing was a humbug."[8] However, in Tauranga Moana, failure was attributed to the people, not the gods. When our chief Penetaka Tuaia was challenged that the Pai Mārire god was a false god, he responded, "We have not seen that our god is wrong . . . the error has been with the men."[9]

5. Following the British victory at the Tauranga Moana battle of Te Ranga, on Aug. 5 and 6, 1864, Governor Grey and officials held a pacification meeting at Te Papa in Tauranga to facilitate the confiscation of land from local Māori.

6. Nicholas, Ngāti Ranginui tribal historian, personal communication (type unspecifed) with author, 2014.

7. *Daily Southern Cross*, May 7, 1867, 5.

8. *Daily Southern Cross*, May 7, 1867, 5.

9. *Daily Southern Cross*, May 7, 1867, 5.

MĀORI UNDERSTANDINGS OF CHRISTIANITY

Before we can examine the specific faith journey of Pirirākau that led us to Pai Mārire, we need to explore Māori understandings of the Christian message, that is something of Māori theology. Broadly speaking, theology tends towards one of two unifying elements: a creation or a redemption-centered theme. Creation-centered theology posits that "grace builds on nature, but only because nature is *capable* of being built on, of being perfected in a supernatural relationship with God."[10] Māori contextual theology, indeed all Indigenous contextual theology, is creation-centered theology.

Divine revelation builds off a creation foundation; in Māori society, that foundation is expressed in two key terms: *tapu* and *mana*. Dominican priest and scholar Michael Shirres[11] identified two elements of *tapu*: the "element from reason . . . 'being with potentiality for power.' The element from faith sees *tapu* as the 'mana of the spiritual powers.'"[12] The first element, which he regarded as the primary one, "begins with existence. Everything that is, has its own intrinsic *tapu*, a *tapu* which begins with its existence and which is sourced in the *mana* of the spiritual powers."[13] As tapu is potentiality, then the point is not "what it is, but . . . what it can become."[14] As with Shirres, Catholic scholar and priest Henare Tate asserted that the potentiality of *tapu* is enacted in *mana*. Anglican scholar and minister Māori Marsden explains *mana* as "lawful permission delegated by the gods to their human agents and accompanied by the endowment of spiritual power to act on their behalf and in accordance with their revealed will."[15] Marsden's concept of *mana* as spiritual power is central to both Shirres's and Tate's views. For both, *mana* is *tapu* in action, as in "its operation, it acts either to create, or to produce (from existing material), further beings with their own tapu. Each of these beings has, and exercises, its own mana, deriving from its own tapu, or from the tapu of others."[16] *Mana* is, then, *tapu*-centered and therefore acts to enhance *tapu* in relationships for

---

10. Bevans, *Models of Contextual Theology*, 21.

11. Father Michael Shirres is a controversial figure in New Zealand. He was a self-confessed pedophile whose abuse damaged many children in the communities in which he served over decades. While his work is significant and important for those seeking to understand Māori theological concepts, I want to acknowledge the grief and hurt experienced by the people he abused and the triggering impact of reading his name and seeing his theological work honored.

12. Shirres, *Tapu*, 5.

13. Shirres, *Tapu*, 5.

14. Shirres, *Tapu*, 10.

15. Marsden, "God, Man, Universe," 119.

16. Tate, "Foundations," 84.

both or all parties. The enhancement of *tapu* further enhances *mana*, and thus greatly increases a person's capacity to act.

PIRIRĀKAU AND THE GODS

The Pirirākau understanding of *tapu* and *mana* was derived from a complex precontact cosmology and theology of originating beings and interventionist deities. It is our first story. The expectation of our ancestors was that they could direct, manipulate, and beseech interventionist deities to act in certain ways if appropriate and correct processes were followed. They had no such expectation that human interaction would impact the actions of originating beings but saw the interventionist deities as mediators in the relationships with those beings. The cosmology of originating beings and interventionist deities and how they were utilised functioned as a precontact contextual theology. The day-to-day interaction and relationship with natural environment and historical experience are then translated into theological language and thinking. The first principle is that all beings and objects, created and uncreated, have a *tapu*, a dignity and well-being that is to be enhanced in relationship to the *tapu* of others. All cosmologies exist to exemplify the enhancement and interrelationship of *tapu* between people, originating beings, and interventionist deities and the environment. It is also a dynamic theology; it requires action and reflection to enhance *tapu*. The originating beings and interventionist deities are themselves dynamic actors, and the relationships with these actors is mediated by the complexity and accuracy of the understanding of the *whakapapa* connection to originating beings and interventionist deities, not through the worship of said divinities. This is the bedrock of the first story: Pirirākau's own knowledge of the divine reality and promise.

PIRIRĀKAU AND CATHOLICISM

With the encounter with the British Empire, Pirirākau were introduced to the second story and transformed from members of an insular Pacific society to world citizens alongside the new European settlers. The largest and most significant mission in New Zealand in the nineteenth century was the Anglican Church Missionary Society; however, our encounter with Christianity was with the Roman Catholic mission. Significant Pirirākau women had married French men in the early nineteenth century. Along with their valued trade connections and artisan skills, these men brought their Catholic faith, and so they extended an invitation to Bishop Pompallier[17] to

17. Jean-Baptiste Francois Pompallier was appointed as the first Roman Catholic

found a mission in Tauranga Moana. The French missionaries who arrived were members of a Catholic Church that had an uneasy role in the expansion of French influence. The French Revolution of 1789–99 had created a schism between the later French state and the Catholic Church. Consequently, Catholic missionaries in the early nineteenth century often had little support from the French state (unlike the Anglican missionaries who were at the forefront of the British Empire with their civilising mission). Yet they could not help but be affected by the transformative Enlightenment ideas of the scientific method and positivism.

The Catholic mission encounter with Pirirākau was colored by a complex mix of racial determinism, humanist equality, and paternalistic moral framing. Father Philippe Viard founded a Catholic mission in Tauranga Moana in 1840. That first Catholic Māori Mission in Tauranga Moana lasted a little more than a decade, and by 1860 priests had ceased visiting the area at all. Until the arrival of two priests in 1886,[18] Pirirākau were left to their own devices to follow their Catholic faith as their conscience dictated.

Pirirākau were irrevocably transformed by the story; not so much by the efforts of the missionaries as the conviction of Pirirākau leadership that Catholicism, and more generally Christianity, enhanced their power and authority—their *mana*—to a greater extent than had their first story, their precontact theology. Nineteenth-century Catholic missionary work in New Zealand is notable for the lack of sustained efforts to transform Māori communities socially or politically; the first priority for the Catholic mission was not the integration of Māori into servitude for the benefit of a particular European empire but integration into the Roman Catholic Church, an empire in its own right. In this, they presumed our Pirirākau ancestors already had the capacity to recognize and determine to live life according to the law that was pleasing to God; in this sense, the missionaries intended to interpret what they found rather than arriving with a predetermined motivation to transform or civilize us. Rather than slavish obedience to the law, Pompallier focused on relationship to connect Māori to the Catholic Church. He appealed to the long church history and the relational connectedness of the communion of saints as an equivalent to *whakapapa* and, therefore, a basis for his authority.

---

vicar apostolic of Western Oceania in 1836 and was the central figure in the establishment, development, and struggles of the Roman Catholic mission in New Zealand until his resignation in 1869.

18. St. Joseph's Catholic Church Committee, *St. Joseph's Catholic Church*.

PIRIRĀKAU AND PAI MĀRIRE: A NEW HOPE

The experience of war and loss bought the two stories together. The integration of the pre-encounter divine reality and promise of Pirirākau and the story of the gospel was realized in the 1860s in Pai Mārire (Perfect Peace and Goodness). In this cauldron of grief and loss, Pai Mārire pointed from our darkest days to a divinely realized hope of restoration of *tapu* and *mana*. Pai Mārire has been unfairly maligned in New Zealand for over a century as a violent, bloodthirsty, syncretic, eclectic, polytheistic faith that returned to the worst practices of precontact Māori society. Yet from small beginnings, the founder Te Ua Haumene and his followers in Taranaki on the west coast of the North Island built one of the most significant Māori prophetic movements of the nineteenth century that has continued, in a somewhat different form, to the twenty-first century. The introduction of Pai Mārire to Pirirākau arose out of the terrible injustice of the complete confiscation of all our traditional lands. Despite the losses in 1864, Pirirākau maintained its support of the pan tribal Kīngitanga (Māori King Movement),[19] ensuring we suffered ongoing oppression and injustice. So the Kīngitanga sent a Pai Mārire emissary, Tiu Tamihana,[20] in support of our cause in December 1864.

TE UA HAUMENE, THE PROPHET OF PAI MĀRIRE

Pai Mārire was revealed to Te Ua Haumene in 1862 in Taranaki, a region on the central west coast of the North Island of New Zealand. Te Ua was born in Waiaua, Taranaki, in the early 1820s. At age three, he and his mother Paihaka were enslaved. In slavery he learned to read and write in Māori and was educated in the New Testament. Te Ua later claimed that the book of Revelation had a particular impact on him. Te Ua was about seventeen or eighteen years old when John Whiteley of Nottinghamshire and his wife came to reestablish the Wesleyan mission station in 1839. Whiteley ran a successful mission with a steady growth in baptisms. Te Ua was among those converts and was baptized Horopāpera (Zerubbabel). Shortly afterwards, in 1840 he returned to Waiaua in Taranaki as an assistant monitor for the missionaries Charles Creed and John Skevington. In 1846, a new missionary arrived

---

19. The Māori King Movement was an Indigenous monarchy founded in 1858. It was established to restrict continued land sales and encourage the British Crown to uphold its agreeements in the 1840 Treaty of Waitangi, the founding document for New Zealand society and settlment.

20. Kahotea, "Rebel Discourses," 103.

in the region, Johann Riemenschneider of the North German Missionary Society. He was a Reformed Protestant from Bremen, working alongside the Lutherans. Te Ua became a "second teacher" for Riemenschneider in Waiaua and was indeed married by him in 1850.

By the 1860s, Ngāti Ruanui, Te Ua's tribe, were members of the Kīngitanga. Te Ua himself helped administer a local government and maintained the boundaries of the land under the *mana* of the Māori King. In 1862, a strange series of events occured that coincided with Te Ua's vision. We would do well to remember that Te Ua was about forty years old when he had his visitation. In the mid-nineteenth century, the life expectancy for Māori was around thirty years old.[21] Te Ua had already lived what must have been regarded as a full life in Taranaki among his people and would have occupied a senior position in the life of his village and tribe. He was a Christian for the majority of his life and held church positions for most of his adult years.

In late 1862, the long ship Lord Worsley grounded upright on the Taranaki coast. In the first week of September 1862, the angel Gabriel spoke to Te Ua Haumēne:

> It was on the first day, 1862, that God's message of love was taken to his forgotten and deserted people. Little was known of the people's thinking and feeling and so was coined the term 'tuwareware' (forsaken).... It was on the fifth day of September that the Angel of God appeared to me. He asked me to keep my counsel [or start fasting] on the sins of my people.[22]

He later explained the experience in an interview with a local reporter, commenting: "I was one night seized with an illness (or affliction), and felt as if some one were shaking me. I heard a voice saying, 'Who is this sleeping? Rise up! Rise up!' I then became *porewarewa* (stupefied; crazed; in a vision state)."[23] Te Ua's overriding concern from his vision was tied to the fate of the Lord Worsley: "I urged that the ship and its cargo be guarded so that the news might be taken and reach the councils of the Kingites."[24] A series of miraculous acts persuaded people of Te Ua's prophetic calling. Te Ua claimed that "thrice I was bound in chains and thrice I was freed by the angel."[25] While the details are obtuse, he also seems to have claimed to have resurrected his own child:

21. Pool, "Death Rates."
22. Penfold, "Ua Rongo Pai," 1–4.
23. *Daily Southern Cross*, Mar. 16, 1866, 4–5.
24. Clark, *Hauhau*, appendix 1.
25. Penfold, "Ua Rongo Pai," 4.

> The eleventh [day] was a day of putting to death—the day on which I killed my child as a living payment (redemption) for my people, forgetful, desolate and in doubt.[26]

While this is hyperbolic and the child was not deliberately sacrificed, it is nevertheless true that his child was ill and returned to health, which came to be seen as a miracle healing or a resurrection.

Evidence of these powers was central to the truth of Te Ua's claim; Pai Mārire was after all, an "adjustment cult,"[27] an attempt at an integration of narratives, connecting "the plight of his people with the threatened or homeless condition of the Jews."[28] Te Ua and his growing band of faithful followers had now truly moved beyond the walls of the church; their renegotiation of Christianity was the beating of a narrow new path between the threat of war and a fragile peace. Could they have imagined that within a handful of years, that path would become a broad highway that would capture the attention of an entire nation?

PAI MĀRIRE: THE FIRST MĀORI CHRISTIAN MOVEMENT

Pai Mārire is New Zealand's first contextual Christian theology. There is no sense in which there had been a reversion to older cosmologies and theologies; rather, Te Ua Haumene sifted the traditions of our ancestors for elements that could serve as vehicles to enhance an orthodox Christian message. The Trinity remained central; Rura (Archangel Gabriel) and Riki (Archangel Michael) have been incorrectly identified as deities, whereas the evidence is for an angelic Christology. Rura and Riki are presented as two servants in the hierarchy and structure of the imperial kingdom of God, rather than the Godhead themselves—a view consistent with communicated European Church tradition. Te Ua was a confident interpreter of the Gospels; an orthodox Christian God and an active faith relationship with God were central to his thinking.

Rather than raising the spectre of syncreticism, examining Te Ua's reworking of the Scriptures and church traditions can lead us to conclude that Pai Mārire is a mature, insightful Indigenous development of Christianity that addressed the political, social, and spiritual needs of the people in that time of conflict. This maturity can be traced to prior to Te Ua's revelation. By the 1860s, Christianity had not been subsumed into traditional spirituality,

---

26. *Taranaki Herald*, "Pai Marire."
27. Clark, *Hauhau*, 102.
28. Clark, *Hauhau*, 78.

nor was it used in a cynical ploy to gain technologies and literacy. Instead, traditional concepts of *tapu* and *mana* were couched in terms of the Scriptures and church traditions, as Christianity became the vehicle for the expression of Māori identity and ideas. Pai Mārire was not a rejection of Christianity but a rejection of the cultures and empires of the missionaries. Pai Mārire resembles quite closely contemporary Pentecostalism in the encouragement of personal relationship with God, the sacrament of glossolalia, the socially conservative interpretation of Scripture, the heavy reliance on the apocryphal Scriptures and the Pentateuch, the encouragement of emotional expression in worship, and the rejection of a priestly heirarchy.

THE WRITINGS OF PAI MĀRIRE

Te Ua's theology is handed down to us in the *Ua Gospel Notebook*. The most complete text of the *Ua Gospel Notebook* and the one on which I rely is the notebook that was scribed by Karaitiana Te Korou. While an important source, one must note that the *Ua Gospel Notebook* "predates the public career of the faith, and was not a response to it."[29] Consequently, Pai Mārire was a faith movement that was required to respond to the politics and conflict of the day, rather than a faith movement founded in the politics and conflict of the day.

The word *gospel* is derived from the Greek word *euangellion*. Initially that word was used to describe the Christian message, but by the second century it was used specifically to refer to narratives of Jesus's life, deeds, death and resurrection, and finally the four narratives approved by the church: Matthew, Mark, Luke, and John. As noted above, the first two chapters of *Ua Gospel Notebook* are characterized as the gospel of Te Ua Haumene. However, it is not a gospel as described above. Te Ua Rongopai is more akin to early Christian literature—like Acts—and New Testament apocraphya, such as the Acts of Paul and Thecla and the Acts of Peter.

The *Ua Gospel Notebook* has twelve distinct sections, though the chronology is unclear. It is not laid out by date; it appears likely that Te Korou added the headings of his own accord, and there are pages torn out of the notebook. It abounds with simple yet compelling sketches, predominantly flags and *niu* (ritual ships' riggings), but also tools, animals, and people. The two gospels, or Ūpoko, are most relevant to us here.

---

29. Head, "Gospel," 10.

Ūpoko I

The first ūpoko is the narrative of Te Ua's revelation and trials. Like an epistle, this ūpoko opens with the prophet's greetings and a description of his intent, which is to bring God's love to his people. Te Ua then recounts the suffering and trials he has endured for God following the visitation of an angel. He testifies to thrice having miraculously escaped bondage, to having been badly beaten, and all by his own people. The story serves to emphasize the ignorance and shame of the people to whom he has brought his prophetic message. He closes with a warning against deceit, the pursuit of riches, and the abandonment of God, entreating his readers to follow the example of Abraham and Abel, whose legacy Te Ua is following.

Ūpoko II

The second ūpoko is significantly longer and similar in genre to Revelation. It is rich in imagery and symbolism, and a combination of judgment and encouragement. The first half initially addresses John Whiteley, Rev. H. H. Brown, and potentially Te Kooti Te Rato, all missionaries at that time. In rich symbolism, Te Ua criticises their theological racism, providing an interesting rebuttal with the equality between races being demonstrated in the environment and everyday items. He then addresses again accusations of madness and drunkness against him, and turns to encourage his followers by describing the works of the Atua Mārire (the God of Peace and Goodness) and some of the laws for a faithful follower. In this ūpoko, he makes a clear connection between Pai Mārire, the Kīngitanga, and the challenge of a coming armed conflict. He closes with an apocalyptic vision, a complex interplay of images that includes clouds, trees, potentially flags, and which seems to draw a parallel between Te Ua's work and Christ's return. The second half of the ūpoko is a series of instructions to the faithful. It is reminiscent of the letters to the churches in Revelation, as Te Ua addresses the Pillars, the Dukes, the Seers, the Teachers, the Judges, and then his followers.

What follows the two ūpoko is a service book, nine epistles, and records of rituals. Te Ua was an intelligent and insightful reader of the biblical texts available to him, and he uses both direct and indirect references and quotations to emphasize his teachings. The central biblical texts, that is to say those most often referred to and quoted in the *Ua Gospel Notebooks*, are Psalms, Zechariah, Matthew, Luke, and Revelation. This is significant because the historical and enduring myth is that Pai Mārire is an exodus-derived faith, and an Old Testament/Hebrew Bible-based response, rather than a Christian theology in its own right.

MILLENARIANISM & PAI MĀRIRE

Unlike other regions in New Zealand, a unique feature of Pai Mārire in Tauranga Moana was a fervent millenarianism that saw followers eschew coastal settlements for their bush homes to await the coming judgment. Pai Mārire arrived in Tauranga Moana with a message of peace in the face of sharp conflict. Followers took seriously the instructions of the prophet to be peaceable in their conduct—it would, after all, be the Atua Mārire (the God of Peace and Goodness) who would bring judgment to fulfilment. Unfortunately, the message of peace was unheard by the Crown; in 1867, they launched a scorched earth campaign, Te Weranga, against Pirirākau. The unrealized promise of divine judgment and the continued and unrelenting land sales and enforced confiscations led to doubts about the hope of Pai Mārire among Pirirākau.

The Pai Mārire faith moved Pirirākau away from the model in which Christianity is the storyteller and Pirirākau the listener to privileging Pirirākau as the storyteller. Pai Mārire challenged the church: "Come now, we must speak honestly as equals, face to face, unified by our faith." The contextual theology of Pirirākau is a legitimate expression of Christianity and a legitimate interpreter of the message. It is a praxis, a movement of action and reflection; God is not outside history and humanity but "in the fabric of culture, but also and perhaps principally in the fabric of history."[30] This theology is removed from scholars and "generated in the writing of throwaway leaflets, in unrecorded homilies, group discussions, and in people's hearts."[31] Therefore, it is a practical theology that comes out of the experience of predominantly Indigenous and/or oppressed communities and is focused on justice in this world.

Pai Mārire is a contextual theology tied to contact, colonization, and to the theft of our land, our economy, and our society by a rapacious invading empire. If my ancestors carried and developed a theology on that journey of loss and grief, it is on that journey that they encountered Christ more in the flesh than in the word, and on that journey that they clung to a theology of liberation.

The story of Pirirākau and the story of the Scriptures have come together as one narrative of a God revealed as the true expression of *tapu* and *mana*, who is one with the oppressed, the suffering, and the impoverished within their language, their land, and their culture. In attempting to express their faith and spirituality, Pirirākau were motivated by their desire to maintain their identity while seeking justice. Pai Mārire led us to a God of the

---

30. Bevans, *Models of Contextual Theology*, 70.
31. Bevans, *Models of Contextual Theology*, 74.

powerless. Visions, wisdom, the environment, and the community affirmed a God made flesh in their concrete reality of colonization, conflict, and confiscation; life—under constant threat—was itself sacramental for both the individual and the community. This Pai Mārire contextual theology has never lost track of its connection with the catholicity of the church and the centrality of the Trinity. Like all Māori contextual theologies, the Pai Mārire intention was maintenance of their relationship with God as the source of all *tapu* and *mana* as well as a critique of the theologies of the settler Catholic Church and its support for colonization and confiscation.

PAI MĀRIRE: A HOPE, AS YET UNREALIZED

We see Pirirākau in Pai Mārire indigenizing, replacing, and renewing the symbols of their Christian faith. The journey is all the more remarkable because our ancestors chose to move from their precontact theology to embrace Christianity and yet retained their autonomy to connect it deliberately and firmly with their own world and experience.

Unfortunately, the hope to see the day of deliverance was stillborn. Upon the return of the majority of the exiled Pirirākau to Tauranga Moana and the surrender of the Māori King in the 1880s, many of our ancestors returned to Catholicism as a path to reintegrate back into a now settler-dominated Tauranga Moana. Yet Pai Mārire remains, like a deeply buried taproot. We still tell each other the story that during a time of conflict and loss, the Scriptures spoke in a new way about ancient relationships between the divine and people. We maintain the symbols: the colors on the jerseys of our rugby union club are purported to be the colors of the original flags brought by Pai Mārire emissaries; the prayers and songs we learned can still be heard; and to wish another wellness and success in our community, we say, "Pai mārire!" So that taproot endures and we, the first people of Tauranga Moana, strive to see shoots reach skywards again so as to return our great forests of narrative, giants within whose branches we will again "stand . . . on the roof of the clouds."[32]

BIBLIOGRAPHY

Adds, Peter. "Te Āti Awa of Taranaki: War and a Kind of Peace." *Te Ara: The Encyclopaedia of New Zealand*, Feb. 8, 2005; updated Mar. 1, 2017. https://teara.govt.nz/en/document/3893/the-new-zealand-settlements-act-of-1863.

Bevans, Stephen. *Models of Contextual Theology*. Maryknoll, NY: Orbis, 2004.

Clark, Paul. *"Hauhau": The Pai Marire Search for Maori Identity*. Auckland: Auckland University Press, 1975.

32. Haumene, "He ohaki."

Daily Southern Cross (Auckland), Mar. 16, 1866.
Daily Southern Cross (Auckland), May 7, 1867.
Gottwald, Norman K. *The Tribes of Yahweh: A Sociology of the Religion of Liberated Israel, 1250–1050 B.C.E.* Maryknoll, NY: Orbis, 1979.
Haumene, Te Ua. "He ohaki no te Kīngitanga o Potatau Te Wherowhero o Tāwhiao, 1860–70." Sept. 1, 1863. In Auckland University Library.
Head, Lyndsey. "The Gospel of Te Ua Haumene." *Journal of the Polynesian Society* 101 (1992) 7–44.
Kahotea, D. "Rebel Discourses: Colonial Violence, Pai Mārire Resistance and Land Allocation at Tauranga." PhD thesis, University of Waikato, 2005.
Marsden, Māori. "God, Man, Universe: A Maori View." In *Te ao hurihuri: Aspects of Maoritanga*, edited by Michael King, 117–37. Auckland: Reed, 1992.
Penfold, M. "Ua Rongo Pai" [Gospel according to Te Ua]. With corrections by George Grey. Unpublished manuscript. Auckland Libraries Heritage Collections.
Pool, Ian. "Death Rates and Life Expectancy." *Te Ara—The Encyclopaedia of New Zealand*. 2011. http://www.teara.govt.nz/en/death-rates-and-life-expectancy.
Shirres, Michael. *Tapu: te mana o nga atua; The Mana of the Spiritual Powers: A Maori Theological Understanding of Tapu*. Ponsonby, NZ: Te Hahi Katorika ki Aotearoa, 1993.
St. Joseph's Catholic Church Committee. *St. Joseph's Catholic Church Te Puna Centennial 1900–2000*. Tauranga, NZ: St. Joseph's Catholic Church Committee, 1999.
Taranaki Herald. "Pai Marire." *Taranaki Herald* (New Plymouth, NZ), May 27, 1865.
Tate, H. "The Foundations of a Systematic Māori Theology: He tirohanga anganui ki ētahi kaupapa hōhonu mō te whakapono Māori." PhD thesis, Melbourne College of Divinity, 2010.

Friendship and Apocalyptic Visions
Christian, Jewish, and Māori Teachings

Anne-Marie Ellithorpe

APOCALYPTIC LITERATURE HAS THE potential to positively inform social imaginaries and friendship practices by providing an imaginative counter to contemporary perceptions of the world. Thus, despite contemporary understandings of apocalypse that focus on conflict, violence, and dystopia, this chapter explores the potential for apocalyptic visions of friendship, justice, and peace to enrich social imaginaries and transform relational practices. To this end, I identify friendship as permeating the social imaginary promoted by the twelfth-century Cistercian abbot Aelred of Rievaulx in *De spirituali amicitia*; consider friendship's relevance to the *apocalyptic social imaginary*; acknowledge visions of living side by side emerging from contexts of oppression in eighth-century BCE Judah and in nineteenth-century CE Aotearoa New Zealand; and suggest ways in which apocalyptic visions inform our friendship practices. These visions of living side by side are found within the ancient text of Isaiah and within assertions made by Indigenous leaders promoting nonviolent resistance to oppression.

Living side by side with other peoples provides opportunities to reflect on our social imagination and the social imaginaries we have inherited. The social imagination of any one person is influenced by the *social imaginary* of the broader culture or a subgroup therein. The social imaginary, as described by Canadian philosopher Charles Taylor, refers to ways in which human beings envision their social existence, including how they relate with others, and the deeper normative images and ideas underlying their expectations of others.[1] These imaginaries shape practices and can promote justice or, in a diseased form, perpetuate injustice. Social imaginaries are not static. As the imaginary is transmitted socially, there is potential for collaborative and transformative shifts in vision of the way things are to take place.[2] While the term *imaginary* often refers to culture-wide understandings, it is important to note that not all subgroups within a given culture share all aspects of a particular social imaginary.

FRIENDSHIP, AELRED, AND THE APOCALYPTIC SOCIAL IMAGINARY

The ways in which people imagine their social surroundings are often carried in stories, legends, and images, rather than in theoretical terms.[3] The social imaginary may be shaped by creation stories (including biblical and Indigenous creation narratives) and by eschatological end-time images and narratives. Various peoples, communities, and traditions bring differing interpretive frameworks to shared stories and narratives. For example, some have interpreted the creation stories of Genesis as affirming individualistic understandings.[4] However, within the premodern social world, these stories were not seen as affirming isolation and self-sufficiency or as being antithetical to friendship.

The social imaginary encouraged in *De spirituali amicitia* by Aelred of Rievaulx, the Cistercian abbot of Rievaulx Abbey from 1147 to 1167 CE, is permeated with friendship.[5] Aelred depicts friendship as congruent with both creational and eschatological intent. Friendship is inherent to creation; God placed God's "own love of society in his creatures, so making friendship part of the order of creation."[6] Aelred's culminating vision includes restored universal friendship; he speaks of an eschatological time "when the friendship to which on earth we admit but few will pour out over all and flow back to God from all, for God will be all in all" (3:134). Friendship is portrayed as both the original vocation of the world and its "eschatological realization."[7] As such friendship is the "materialization of

---

1. Taylor, *Modern Social Imaginaries*, 23.
2. Taylor, *Secular Age*, 175.
3. Taylor, *Modern Social Imaginaries*, 23.
4. See Terrell, *Talent for Friendship*, 14, 190.
5. See Aelred of Rievaulx, "Spiritual Friendship."
6. Dutton, "Introduction," 28–29.
7. Pezzini, "Aelred's Doctrine," 244.

both memory and hope, a flash of joy and fulfillment turned towards both a happy past and a happier future."[8]

Aelred's vision may initially appear to be inconsistent with contemporary eschatological visions, and particularly with an apocalyptic social imaginary. As many contributors to this volume note, in popular usage the term *apocalyptic* is currently used to refer negatively to catastrophic, destructive events. But in biblical scholarship, *apocalypse* is a value neutral term used to describe a kind of literature.[9] Apocalypse means "revelation"; apocalyptic is derived from a Greek word meaning "to reveal, uncover, unveil." Within apocalyptic literature, revelation takes place through coded language that communicates clearly to those "in the know" but not to the uninitiated.[10] Aelred's vision is consistent with *this* definition of apocalypse.

What characterizes an apocalyptic social imaginary? Historian Malise Ruthven has written a chapter entitled "The Apocalyptic Social Imaginary" but does not define this term.[11] What appear to be consistent throughout apocalyptic writings and movements are hopes for deliverance from oppression, including from foreign rule. Apocalyptic thinkers portray God as ultimately bringing down all empires.[12] They subvert the view of reality promoted by the dominant empire as they seek to promote an alternative imagination. Things—they imply—are not exactly as they seem, or more precisely, "things are not only as they seem."[13] Apocalyptic texts critique empire and express resistance to strategies of terror, conquest, and colonization.[14] As Leo Perdue and Warren Carter assert, "From the eighth century BCE onward, many of the classical prophets and their editors, including their apocalyptic heirs, sought to move beyond the destructiveness of imperial rule towards a peaceful kingdom that would allow all nations to worship the true God, YHWH, and to cease the making of war."[15]

Thus, apocalyptic writings are an expression of civic friendship (broadly construed)—they are an expression of wanting the best for a

---

8. Pezzini, "Aelred's Doctrine," 244.

9. As described by John J. Collins, this genre is characterized by "a narrative framework, in which a revelation is mediated by an otherworldly being to a human recipient, disclosing a transcendent reality which is both temporal, insofar as it envisages eschatological salvation, and spatial insofar as it involves another, supernatural world" (Collins, "Introduction," 9).

10. Perdue and Carter, *Israel and Empire*, 84, 120.

11. Ruthven, "Apocalyptic Social Imaginary."

12. Perdue and Carter, *Israel and Empire*, 244.

13. Johnson, *Discipleship on the Edge*, 19.

14. Perdue and Carter, *Israel and Empire*, 200.

15. Perdue and Carter, *Israel and Empire*, 68.

dominated people, for a people in crisis. Further, a so-called "apocalyptic social imaginary" that focuses on violence and dystopia is a distortion of the ideals of many biblical apocalyptic texts, with their implicit call for transformation.[16]

Friendship is implicit in the coded language of John's Apocalypse in the New or Second Testament. As biblical scholar Harry Maier asserts, the overall apocalyptic narrative of Revelation is designed "to convince its listeners of the need and demand for faithful witness."[17] Overcoming takes place through "the word of their testimony" (Rev 12:11).[18] Such witness may be seen as an expression or practice of friendship. Along with the use of coded language pointing to communication between friends, the hospitality of Rev 3:20 and the imagery of multiple diverse peoples gathered in worship are also indicative of friendship. In stark contrast with dispensationalist understandings that imply social reform is a waste of time in view of the impending new heaven and new earth, the book of Revelation critiques (albeit obliquely) the economic dominance of Rome (that is, the Roman Empire). My focus here, however, will be on apocalypse within the more ancient text of Isaiah, where, as in Revelation, economic injustice provokes divine judgment, yet images of comfort, transformation, and friendship are also evident.

LIVING SIDE BY SIDE: FRIENDSHIP AND APOCALYPSE IN ANCIENT JUDAH

Isaiah challenges injustice and, through symbolic imagery, advocates for (and promises) the kind of transformation that allows for civic friendship and peaceful coexistence. Some scholars see Isaiah as a compilation of three works, but I will draw on recurring themes throughout. The book's opening (Isa 1:1) dates the prophetic vision of Isaiah, son of Amoz, concerning Judah and Jerusalem, to the reigns of mid-eighth-century BCE Kings. Isaiah accuses the state of excessively exploiting the common people (3:12–15); he identifies the judicial system as corrupt, making "unjust laws" (10:1). Biblical scholar William Domeris notes that as local officials abuse their power, peasants suffer.[19] Domeris identifies violence as endemic to oppression.[20]

---

16. See Rorty, "Philosophy as Science," 13.
17. Maier, "Revelation Matters."
18. Scripture quotations in this chapter are from the NRSV.
19. Domeris, *Touching Heart of God*, 53.
20. Domeris, *Touching Heart of God*, 117.

Corruption in leadership is not Isaiah's only concern; Isaiah also portrays anxiety regarding the threat and impact of Assyrian invasion. The destruction of Israel (the Northern Kingdom) and the incorporation of Judah (the Southern Kingdom) into the Assyrian provincial system "had cataclysmic repercussions for the peasants of Judah."[21] The destruction of the Northern Kingdom contributed to a marked increase in population in Judah, putting "pressure on the fragile ecosystem and on its ability to sustain peasant life."[22]

The book of Isaiah initially proclaims judgment on Israel and Judah. Subsequently, judgment is also passed on the invading empires and their gods. Alongside judgment, we find oracles of comfort, consolation, and hope, including apocalyptic writings that promote visions of transformation, friendship, justice, and peace. In Isa 11:6–8, predatory animals are depicted as living together with non-predatory animals without consuming them:

> The wolf shall live with the lamb, the leopard shall lie down with the kid, the calf and the lion and the fatling together, and a little child shall lead them. The cow and the bear shall graze, their young shall lie down together; and the lion shall eat straw like the ox. The nursing child shall play over the hole of the asp, and the weaned child shall put its hand on the adder's den.

This prophetic oracle, initially written to encourage an oppressed and perhaps despairing community with the hope of transformation, becomes apocalyptic with the anticipation of transformation for all creation.[23] Following the proclamation of a new (renewed and restored) heaven and earth (65:17), Isaiah asserts: "The wolf and the lamb shall feed together, the lion shall eat straw like the ox; but the serpent—its food shall be dust!" (65:25). The serpent, like the adder of 11:8, may represent those whose (corrupt) actions had become deadly for those who are innocent, but who now find sustenance in ways that are harmless to others.[24] The expectation of transformation is also found in Isa 43:18–21:

> Do not remember the former things or consider the things of old. I am about to do a new thing; now it springs forth, do you not perceive it? I will make a way in the wilderness and rivers in the desert. The wild animals will honor me, the jackals and the ostriches; for I give water in the wilderness, rivers in the desert

---

21. Domeris, *Touching Heart of God*, 52.
22. Domeris, *Touching Hart of God*, 53.
23. See also Clements, "Wolf Shall Live," 93.
24. See also Duhan-Kaplan, *Mouth of the Donkey*, 73.

to give drink to my chosen people, the people whom I formed for myself so that they might declare my praise.

One can interpret the hope-filled oracle of Isa 11 (and 65) in several ways. As outlined by Rabbi Laura Duhan-Kaplan in *Mouth of the Donkey: Re-Imagining Biblical Animals*, many interpreters concur that this vision symbolically portrays "an ideal human community" where currently unlikely friendships are made possible.[25] The animals may be interpreted as symbols of empire, implying that the transformation of empires, from predatory to peace seeking, is possible.[26] Unlikely friendships between nations contribute to justice and thus peace. Alternatively, the animals may be symbolic of social classes, portraying the possibility that predatory elite classes can also change, and that just laws and equitable marketplace practices are feasible. Relationships of genuine reciprocity between social classes promote justice and therefore peace. Both symbolic approaches can be supported intertextually and perhaps both are implied—both predatory classes and empires were certainly issues for Judah during the lifetime of Isaiah and his namesakes, and beyond.

The two placements of the oracle close with the declaration: "They shall not hurt or destroy on all my holy mountain." The first adds that "the earth will be full of the knowledge of the LORD as the waters cover the sea" (11:9). Perhaps it is such knowledge that ultimately brings an end to violence, promotes justice, and makes possible unlikely yet life-giving friendships between people, classes, nations, and empires. Knowledge of God promotes the transformation of human nature, character, relationships, and communities.

This oracle is more than a vision *of* divinely inspired civic friendship; it also provides a model *for* creating civic friendships. As Duhan-Kaplan notes in her reflections on this text, analyzing the portrayals of the animals on this model:

> Citizens freed from oppression don't seek revenge. Instead, they turn away from that destructive impulse, and educate youth in peaceful values. Mothers raise their children with a diverse set of friends. Then, the community recognizes the power of pacifism. New generations of children grow up without trauma. And finally, "no evil will be done."[27]

---

25. Duhan-Kaplan, *Mouth of the Donkey*, 69.
26. Duhan-Kaplan, *Mouth of the Donkey*, 69.
27. Duhan-Kaplan, *Mouth of the Donkey*, 70.

Change is possible, as knowledge of (and thus right-relationship with) God overflows into transformed power relationships, the redirection of aggression, a passion for peace, and genuinely wanting the best for and being active on behalf of the other, whether at the personal, community, or nation-state level.

TOWARDS LIVING SIDE BY SIDE: FRIENDSHIP AND APOCALYPSE IN NINETEENTH-CENTURY AOTEAROA

Biblical apocalyptic texts, initially written to speak into specific contexts, have been a source of comfort, motivation, and inspiration for subsequent readers seeking to resist oppression and to promote justice, peace, and friendship. As the following account suggests, such texts resonated with nineteenth-century Indigenous leaders in Aotearoa New Zealand, seeking through peaceful means to resist the violence of colonization.

In 1840, representatives of the British Crown signed a treaty (Te Tiriti o Waitangi, the Treaty of Waitangi) with Māori tribal leaders and subsequently declared sovereignty over the land the colonizers called *New Zealand*. Although the original version of the treaty was written in English, a Māori version translated by missionary Henry Williams and his son Edward was offered to Māori leaders and subsequently translated back into English. There were inconsistencies between the two versions. In the Māori translation of the treaty, Māori gave *kawanatanga* (governance) to the queen; in the English version, Māori gave *rangatiratanga* (sovereignty) to the British crown. Nevertheless, from an Indigenous perspective, this treaty was understood to be one of covenantal friendship. In a paper titled "Early Recollections," missionary Henry Williams wrote:

> In the midst of profound silence I read the treaty to all assembled. I told all to listen with care, explaining clause by clause to the chiefs; giving them caution not to be in a hurry, but telling them that we, the Missionaries, fully approved of the treaty, that it was an act of love towards them on the part of the Queen, who desired to secure to them their property, rights, and privileges. That this treaty was as a fortress for them against any foreign power which might desire to take possession of their country.[28]

Yet the treaty was subsequently dishonored. Māori property, rights, and privileges were not secured. Rather, with the ongoing process of colonization, Māori communities were increasingly displaced, with loss of land

---

28. See Carleton, *Life of Henry Williams*, 2:12.

provoked by racist legislation, unjust land sales, and land wars. In an 1877 court case, Chief Justice James Prendergast asserted that the treaty was a legal nullity, thereby creating a legal precedent for the ongoing appropriation of land and perpetuation of injustice. Many Māori tribes participated in land wars against colonial troops as Māori attempted to protect their land. However, since the Māori were accused of open rebellion against the queen, colonial legislation allowed for the confiscation of their land.

In response to colonial violence, and to the confiscation of land in the Taranaki region, two Māori leaders and prophets—Tohu Kākahi and Te Whiti o Rongomai—established Parihaka, a community committed to peace and friendship, on fertile land that had been declared confiscated in the 1860s.[29] Displaced Māori from elsewhere in Aotearoa were attracted to Parihaka. Within four years of its establishment in 1866, Parihaka had become the largest Māori community in the country.[30]

Subsequently, as government surveyors sought to prepare the land for European settlers, Tohu and Te Whiti called for peaceful resistance. Parihaka Māori ploughed the land, signifying their ongoing ownership through occupation of the land. Having developed a love for the Scriptures, it seems clear that the Parihaka prophets were aware of the religious symbolism of this act, reflecting as it did the exhortation in Isaiah (2:4) to turn "swords into ploughshares." Ploughmen, however, were arrested, fined, deported elsewhere in the country, and imprisoned.

On November 5, 1881, government troops invaded Parihaka. Te Whiti and Tohu were arrested, taken away, and subsequently detained in the South Island. J. P. Ward was appointed by the government as interpreter for Te Whiti and Tohu during this detainment. They requested and were provided with a *Paipera*, that is, a Māori translation of the Bible. (This translation had been completed in 1868). At one point in Ward's account of his wanderings with these prophets, Ward describes the peculiar language of the book of Revelation and the wild imagery of Isaiah as occupying "a great part of Te Whiti and Tohu's time."[31]

We cannot know for sure which imagery from Isaiah particularly resonated with these Māori advocates for nonviolent resistance to oppression. However, they may well have been drawn to and inspired by Isaiah's oracle, describing life in a time of justice and peace through the analogy of interspecies friendships. This is consistent with their commitment to nonviolent

---

29. See Ministry for Culture and Heritage, "Invasion of Pacifist Settlement."
30. Buchanan, "Why Ghandi Doesn't Belong," 1078.
31. Ward, *Wanderings with Maori Prophets*, 129.

resistance and with the vision of coexistence that Te Whiti articulated following his and Tohu's initial arrest.

Ironically, given his commitment to nonviolence, Te Whiti o Rongomai was charged with "wickedly, maliciously and seditiously contriving and intending to disturb the peace, inciting insurrections, riots, tumults, and breaches of the peace, and, to prevent by force and arms the execution of the law did wickedly declare false, wicked, seditious and inflammatory words." These words allegedly included phrases such as "*naku te whenua*" (the land belongs to me) and "*naku nga tangata*" (the people belong to me).[32] As Te Whiti responded to this charge on November 12, 1881, he stated that his vision was for all, both Pākehā (settlers) and Māori, to live "peacefully and happily on the land."[33] His ideal was for non-Indigenous and Indigenous to live side by side in peace, with Māori (as dominant ruler) learning from the white man's wisdom, without becoming "subservient to his immoderate greed."[34] Earlier, Tohu spoke of Māori and Pākehā (settlers) as two tribes "living together quietly."[35]

Isaiah depicts the possibility of learning to live side by side with diverse others, and Te Whiti and Tohu affirm such a vision. Their vision of Māori and Pākehā living in harmony is essentially a vision of *civic friendship*. Resistance to oppression by the Parihaka community was—and is—an expression of civic friendship, of wanting the best for the other and being active on their behalf, inspired at least in part by apocalyptic texts. The Parihaka community suffered greatly from the impact of injustice, poverty, and division within the subsequent decades. Nevertheless, the contemporary Parihaka community continues to pursue practices of nonviolence and seeks to empower those who have been disempowered.[36]

LEARNING TO LIVE SIDE BY SIDE: APOCALYPTIC VISIONS AND CONTEMPORARY FRIENDSHIP PRACTICES

Apocalyptic literature provides an imaginative counter to contemporary perceptions of the world, with potential to positively inform our social imagination and our friendship practices. Biblical apocalyptic visions remind us

32. Waitangi Tribunal, *Taranaki Report*, 239.
33. Saunders, *History of New Zealand*, 2:467. See also Waitangi Tribunal, *Taranaki Report*, 239.
34. *New Zealand Herald*, Nov. 30, 1907, cited in Gadd, "Teachings," 450.
35. Tohu continued, "Till the pakehas came with their evil close to us" (Scott, *Ask That Mountain*, 95).
36. Ruakere Hond, cited in Warne, "Why Wasn't I Told?"

that things are not only as they seem, and that change is possible. Our social reality is relational and holistically spiritual; it does not equal the market, capitalism, or the neoliberalism that undergirds global capitalism, nor is it otherworldly. The apocalyptic vision is one of transforming, empowering, and healing change within the very fabric of society; it points towards witness and worship, not war, and to friendship and justice that overcome oppression and allow diverse others to live side by side.

As friends, teachers, family members, and participants within (and perhaps leaders of) communities (of faith and otherwise), apocalyptic visions of friendship, peace, and justice call us to likewise foster an alternative imagination to that of dominant empires, classes, and corporations. Such apocalyptic visions inspire us to seek nonviolent ways to creatively counter oppression, to foster diverse friendships, and to support one another in overcoming trauma. This includes nurturing communities that can read apocalyptic texts with imagination and that are willing to listen to and learn from the ways in which our oppressed ancestors have read these texts. Engaging with apocalyptic visions of friendship, justice, and peace may well lead our communities to critique unequal power relationships; seek radical social and economic change; address issues of land stewardship; and work to end poverty, powerlessness, and shame. As Domeris acknowledges: "Combating poverty means levelling the playing fields even if this is apparently unjust to those who have for centuries exploited the poor."[37]

Isaiah's apocalyptic oracle portrays a relationship between knowing God and friendship, justice, and peace. To riff off Isaiah's oracle, in a way inspired by but also going beyond Duhan-Kaplan's analysis:

> Just as the waters cover the sea, may the earth be full of the knowledge of the LORD. May such knowledge bring an end to hurt and destruction globally, transform power relationships, and enable peaceful friendship-shaped coexistence. In the face of the crises we currently face, may an apocalyptic social imaginary support us in nurturing diverse friendships, pursuing justice, creatively seeking freedom from oppression, thinking and acting collectively, mentoring our youth in peaceful values, and enabling children to grow up without trauma, as we foster communities shaped by care, compassion, and civic friendship.[38]

May this prayer, desire, and vision inform our practices until we experience the eschatalogical reality of restored universal friendship pointed to by Aelred of Rivaulx. Ultimately, may "the friendship to which on earth we

37. Domeris, *Touching Heart of God*, 177.
38. See Duhan-Kaplan, *Mouth of the Donkey*, 79.

admit but few . . . pour out over all and flow back to God from all, for God will be all in all" (*Spir. Amic.* 3:134).

BIBLIOGRAPHY

Aelred of Rievaulx. *Spiritual Friendship*. Edited by Marsha L. Dutton. Collegeville, MN: Liturgical, 2010.

Buchanan, Rachel. "Why Gandhi Doesn't Belong at Wellington Railway Station." *Journal of Social History* 44 (2011) 1077–93.

Carleton, Hugh. *The Life of Henry Williams, Archdeacon of Waimate*. 2 vols. Auckland: Wilsons & Horton, 1877.

Clements, R. E. "The Wolf Shall Live with the Lamb: Reading Isaiah 11:6–9 Today." In *New Heaven and New Earth: Prophecy and the Millennium; Essays in Honour of Anthony Gelston*, edited by P. J. Harland and Robert Hayward, VTSup 77, 83–99. Boston: Brill, 1999.

Collins, John J. "Introduction: Towards the Morphology of a Genre." *Apocalypse: The Morphology of a Genre* 14 (1979) 1–20.

Domeris, William. *Touching the Heart of God: The Social Construction of Poverty among Biblical Peasants*. New York: T&T Clark, 2007.

Duhan-Kaplan, Laura. *Mouth of the Donkey: Re-Imagining Biblical Animals*. Eugene, OR: Cascade, 2021.

Dutton, Marsha L. "Introduction." In *Spiritual Friendship*, edited by Marsha Dutton, 13–52. Collegeville, MN: Liturgical, 2010.

Ellithorpe, Anne-Marie. *Towards Friendship-Shaped Communities: A Practical Theology of Friendship*. Oxford, UK: Wiley Blackwell, 2022.

Gadd, Bernard. "The Teachings of Te Whiti O Rongomai, 1831–1907." *Journal of the Polynesian Society* 75 (1966) 445–57.

Johnson, Darrell W. *Discipleship on the Edge: An Expository Journey through the Book of Revelation*. Vancouver: Regent College Publishing, 2004.

Maier, Harry O. "Why the Book of Revelation Matters." Paper presented at Visions of the End Times Conference, Vancouver School of Theology, Vancouver, Can., May 23, 2017.

Ministry for Culture and Heritage. "Invasion of Pacifist Settlement at Parihaka." New Zealand History, updated Nov. 5, 2020. https://nzhistory.govt.nz/occupation-pacifist-settlement-at-parihaka.

Perdue, Leo G., and Warren Carter. *Israel and Empire: A Postcolonial History of Israel and Early Judaism*. Edited by Coleman A. Baker. London: Bloomsbury, 2015.

Pezzini, Domenico. "Aelred's Doctrine of Charity and Friendship." In *A Companion to Aelred of Rievaulx (1110–1167)*, edited by Marsha L. Dutton, Brill's Companions to the Christian Tradition 76, 221–45. Boston: Brill, 2017.

Rorty, Richard. "Philosophy as Science, as Metaphor, and as Politics." In *Essays on Heidegger and Others*, 9–26. Cambridge: Cambridge University Press, 1991.

Ruthven, Malise. "The Apocalyptic Social Imaginary." In *Modernism, Christianity and Apocalypse*, edited by Erik Tonning et al., Studies in Religion and the Arts 8, 354–83. Boston: Brill, 2015.

Saunders, Alfred. *History of New Zealand*. 2 vols. Christchurch: Smith, Anthony, Sellars, and Co. Ltd., 1899.

Scott, Dick. *Ask That Mountain: The Story of Parihaka*. Auckland: Heinemann/Southern Cross, 1981.
Taylor, Charles. *Modern Social Imaginaries*. Durham, NC: Duke University Press, 2004.
———. *A Secular Age*. Cambridge, MA: Harvard University Press, 2007.
Terrell, John. *A Talent for Friendship: Rediscovery of a Remarkable Trait*. Oxford, UK: Oxford University Press, 2014.
Waitangi Tribunal. *The Taranaki Report: Kaupapa Tuatahi*. Wellington, NZ: GP, 1996.
Ward, John P. *Wanderings with the Maori Prophets, Te Whiti & Tohu: Being Reminiscences of a Twelve Months' Companionship with Them, from Their Arrival in Christchurch in April, 1882, until Their Return to Parihaka in March, 1883*. Nelson, NZ: Bond, Finney & Company, 1883.
Warne, Kennedy. "Why Wasn't I Told?" *New Zealand Geographic* 142 (2016). https://www.nzgeo.com/stories/parihaka/.

The Transhuman Apocalypse
Utopia or Dystopia?

Kiara Falk

INTRODUCTION

TRANSHUMANISM IS A MOVEMENT that believes the human race, as is, contains serious flaws; it sees emergent technology that transcends our original bodies and minds as the pathway to achieving a utopian society. Fields of research such as cybernetics, nanotechnology, genetic engineering, and medical science have produced tangible improvements in aids for the disabled, medical care and monitoring, and increased food production. These results would seem to lend credence to the transhumanist vision. But is this vision truly utopian or is there a darker dystopian aspect? This chapter examines the transhumanist worldview from a bioethical perspective and offers a critique. Far from the transhumanists' utopian vision of humanity living in a world free from pain, poverty, and death, posthuman existence means the end of the human race, not by some radical apocalyptic global war, but by deliberate social engineering.

A BRAVE NEW WORLD: WHAT IS TRANSHUMANISM?

The term *transhumanism* seems to hint at current debates on gender identity, but it is a distinct term with a separate origin. Transhumanism is a term that has been around since 1923.[1] Specifically, it refers to the merging of the

---

1. British geneticist J. B. S. Haldane was the first to posit the fundamental ideas of

human race and technology. Epistemologically, it is a mechanical worldview, holding that humanity evolved to its present state through some form of Darwinian evolution. This series of random accidents created a flawed system that has no teleological end other than the continuation of the species. Transhumanists believe that the human species rose to the top of the food chain due to the development of superior rational capabilities. Metaphysically, if there is no God and no immortal soul, then, transhumanists posit, humanity must find physical, material answers to the problems facing humanity and must do so in a rational manner.

In his essay "Towards the Morphology of a Genre," John J. Collins defines ancient apocalyptic literature by two primary characteristics: (1) an eschatological salvation, involving (2) an otherworldly existence. Some kind of cosmic transformation is involved. He says, "The existence of another world beyond what is accessible to humanity by natural means is a constant element in all the apocalypses."[2] By this definition, transhumanism is clearly an apocalyptic philosophy, seeing death as the ultimate flaw that needs to be corrected.

Transhumanists divide into two camps at this point. The H+ (Humanity +) camp promoted by Aubrey de Grey sees technology from fields such as genetic engineering and medical science as aiding the natural human body in overcoming disease and aging, while nanotechnology aids the body in self-repair. Immortality is achieved while humanity as a whole remains embodied. H+ is exactly that—humanity plus technology.[3]

In the second camp are the post-humans promoted by Nick Bostrom and Ray Kurzweil.[4] Working in fields such as cybernetics and artificial intelligence, they believe that, based on Moore's Law,[5] humanity will merge with machines in an event called the "singularity," becoming inseparable from technology. Since materialists do not believe that humans have a duality of nature that supernaturally survives after death, their answer is to infuse humanity with a material component that will outlive the human body. In post-humanity, each personality will be downloaded as a

---

transhumanism in 1923, predicting that great benefits would come from applications of advanced sciences to human biology. See Haldane and Hyamson, "Daedalus."

2. Collins, "Introduction," 9.

3. De Grey, *Ending Aging*.

4. Kurzweil, *Singularity Is Near*; Bostrom, "What Is a Singleton"?

5. Moore's Law is the observation that the number of transistors in a dense integrated circuit doubles approximately every two years, increasing the complexity of devices while reducing their costs. While this is an observation rather than a law of physics, it has become the target goal of the semiconductor industry and has proven reliable since 1975. Thus, it is used as a predictive element for the advances of computer technology.

computer program and exist within a worldwide network. The soul, i.e., the "program," can be downloaded into any avatar of choice or remain within the matrix. But the distinguishing characteristic of this view is that humans will no longer be embodied beings. Thus, a post-human is no longer human but a non-embodied electronic soul.

The transhumanists present a new vision, bonding the human mind's creativity and flexibility with the speed and precision of a machine to create a unique form of superbeing never before seen on this world. M. Chorost describes this superbeing as a gestalt of humanity where the Internet would become "a new nervous system for humanity, and humanity would become a new body and executive brain for the Internet."[6] The ultimate transhumanist utopia is that the machine mind will cure all social ills. Transhumanists freely admit that they have no idea as to the specific details as to how these flaws in humanity and society will be solved, but they cheerfully state that not knowing is specifically the point—they have no idea *at this time*. We need to embrace the singularity, become one with technology, and the gestalt of the machine mind will solve these problems, perhaps "in the blink of an eye."[7]

THROW THE BABY OUT WITH THE BATHWATER: A CRITIQUE OF SCIENTIFIC HUBRIS

Nonetheless, the transhuman utopia, while good news for the transhumanists, is bad news for everyone else. Those that embrace the singularity transform into *Homo superior*. Those who reject it remain *Homo sapiens* and go the way of the Neanderthals. As Jeffery Bishop succinctly puts it: "In order to transcend the human condition, they must transgress the human."[8]

Unspoken is the idea that, as Tom Koch says, "the scientifically enlightened know which human characteristics are desirable" and that this agenda will be "pursued in an ethical and value-free manner."[9] Yet, there is no consensus around the relevant ethics, and no technology is value free. One case illustrating this ambiguity was the hostility a significantly large number of deaf parents had to cochlear implants that allowed deaf children the ability to hear and function in the "normal" world. Deaf parents did not want their children "corrected" because they did not believe being deaf was a defect. Being changed in this way would make the children

---

6. Chorost, *World Wide Mind*, 11.
7. Vinge, "Coming Technological Singularity."
8. Bishop, "Transhumanism, Metaphysics," 702.
9. Koch, "Enhancing Who," 686.

outcasts in their community.[10] Another case is explored in Julian Savulescu's discussion of a couple, both dwarves, wanting to use IVF (in vitro fertilization) and PGD (preimplantation genetic diagnosis)[11] to select a child with dwarfism on the grounds of procreative autonomy. They would be producing children in their image and likeness, which is what most parents desire. Savulescu argues that this reproductive technology should be denied to them on the grounds that their autonomy is superseded by the principle of *procreative beneficence*. In other words, being born a dwarf is not in the best interest of the child nor in the best interest of society.[12] I think Peter Dinklage and most *Game of Thrones* fans would strongly disagree with that.[13] Most people would look at Dinklage and say he has a substantial quality of life and quite a lot to offer society. Yet, a recent survey of medical providers showed 75% of respondents believed termination of a fetus should be available for dwarfism at twenty-four weeks.[14]

In the most pervasive case of technological bias, 90% of fetuses PGD diagnosed with Down syndrome are aborted with the reason given "to avoid pain and suffering."[15] My question is, whose pain and whose suffering are being avoided? These fetuses are not being cured and restored to a "normal" life. They are being eradicated and not permitted to exist, and society is being told this is a good thing. Yet, when raised in a loving and caring environment, Down syndrome individuals flourish and are often exceptionally loving people. In a culture of consumerism on steroids, they are countercultural.[16]

---

10. Sparrow, "Defending Deaf Culture." Also, Sparrow, "Implants and Ethnocide"; Sparrow, "Egalitarianism and Moral Bioenhancement."

11. IVF refers to in vitro ("in glass") fertilization, fertilizing an egg outside of the womb. PGD refers to preimplantation genetic diagnosis.

12. Savulescu, "Procreative Beneficence," 524.

13. Dinklage has achondroplasia, a form of dwarfism, and plays Tyrion Lannister in the HBO *Game of Throne* series. He is known both on camera and off as being highly intelligent, having a very dry wit, and was voted unanimously as the funniest cast member by his fellow cast members at a panel at the San Diego Comic Con. In 2011, he made GQ's Men of the Year list.

14. Savulescu, "Ethics," 295.

15. Dixon, "Informed Consent," 5.

16. The media spends billions of dollars researching ways to make us discontented and unsatisfied with who we are. It tells us we need a new phone, a new computer, a particular brand of soft drink or not to drink soda but this health drink, instead . . . and it will make us happy. Down syndrome tells us that we don't have to be the most intelligent, the most beautiful, or have the most "stuff"; we just need to have people in our lives who love us and accept us as we are. And yet, 90 percent of the most loving individuals you would ever meet are not being permitted to be born.

Comparing and contrasting responses from the disabled community with those from the medical science community reveals two incompatible ethical views. Those seeking to bioengineer society are using utilitarian ethics to place cost effectiveness and productivity as primary "quality of life" qualifiers. The disabled and their supporters are following the ethics of intrinsic human dignity: valuing community, tolerance, and embracing variation.[17] Can a utopia really be created based on utilitarian ethics?

Bishop describes a transhuman as "a future being—a person—who constructs herself out of various technologies."[18] The idea that you can be anyone you want to be, any*thing* you want to be, can be intoxicating. But as we have seen, machines excel at mass producing exact replicas of items because making clone-like products is efficient. Far from the intoxicating utopia of radical individualism, transhumanism leads to a dystopia of conformity.[19]

Bostrom sees the rational progression of the singularity resulting in a single universal governing agency he calls the "Singleton." Transhumanists envision this agency to be a beneficent, super-intelligent machine or a gestalt of global humanity: a "transcending upload"[20] that guides humanity based on permutations of all possible value systems and their probable outcome in every conceivable future event. Yet, Bostrom acknowledges that, "Once formed, a future Singleton might be perpetually stable. This could happen if surveillance, mind control, and other security technologies develop in such a way as to enable a Singleton to effectively prevent the emergence of internal challenges."[21] He is in effect admitting that the Singleton will choose only from the limited selection of choices it has preselected, and no dissenting opinions will be heard, as it would have "the ability to prevent any threats (internal or external) to its own existence and supremacy."[22]

James Hughes describes this inconsistency between a vision of utopian individualism being rigidly implemented as mirroring the Enlightenment philosophes'[23] contradictory view of humanity. The philosophes believed that, if individuals were given complete liberty, they would pursue self-perfection.

17. Lee, "Cochlear Implantation," 67.

18. Bishop, "Transhumanism," 701.

19. One has to ask whether conformity would be a good thing. And one has to answer that it would be good only for those who set the standards. For an in-depth discussion on this issue, see Bostrom and Sandberg, "Unilateralist's Curse."

20. Bostrom, "What Is a Singleton," 49.

21. Bostrom, "What Is a Singleton," 54.

22. Bostrom, "What Is a Singleton," 48.

23. The philosophes refer to the French Enlightenment thinkers, such as Voltaire, Diderot, and Rousseau.

However, they also justified a strong, authoritarian government, because they believed that only the elite acted out of rational principle while the common masses continued to act out of emotion and superstition.[24]

Transhumanists operate with this same inconsistency. Koch tells us that bioengineers in genetics and the neurosciences assert an ethical right, if not also a moral obligation, to make "better" people through technologies of genetic selection whose goal is "enhancing evolution."[25] Currently, millions of dollars are spent on research into moral enhancement, in addition to the funding for physical and intellectual enhancement. Transhumanists envision a future where PGD screens out genetic tendencies for antisocial behavior, such as a propensity for violence, alcoholism, and anger issues. Neurologists are researching chemicals within the brain that promote positive behavior like empathy and altruism.[26] Neurologists have also made progress on identifying chemicals linked to memories for potential application in helping individuals with post-traumatic stress disorder (PTSD) by permanently erasing painful memories.[27] Of course, this raises the concern that the same technologies could be used to implant false memories.

When these technologies sufficiently advance, parents would be able to select behavioral characteristics as well as physical. We could see a world overwhelmed (or underwhelmed) with passive, compliant children. And parents would merely be the consumers, not the producers. Bostrom's Singleton would be the agency that decides which kind of people would be produced. With everyone connected directly into the Net, governing bodies would be able to read not only every thought but every emotion as well. Nada Gilgorov states that "the distinction between voluntary and involuntary behavior become harder to maintain."[28] Scientific determinism would replace free will. For the H+ individual, the age-old question of "nature vs. nurture" would be resolved once and for all into "designer's specifications." In the case of the post-human, your software would simply be rewritten.

A TERMINUS EVENT

Is the transhumanist telos a wholesale annihilation of humanity in favor of the success of another species? There is a new branch of law emerging

24. Hughes, "Contradictions," 633. The culmination of Enlightenment concepts of human freedom and government boundaries that shape much of our society today can be found in John Stuart Mill's *On Liberty* (1869).

25. Koch, "Enhancing Who," 686.

26. Agar, "Moral Bioenhancement," 39. Oxytocin is showing promising results.

27. Gligorov, "Applicability," 192. Propranolol has been found to decrease the emotional intensity associated with memories without erasing those memories.

28. Gligorov, "Applicability," 191.

around "climate justice" called *postericide*, the eradication of future generations. These laws seek to make it a crime to intentionally or unintentionally make human populations extinct internationally through pollution, climate change, or bioengineered food.[29] The University of Reading has recently received a £1 million Leverhulme Grant for research into what it calls "crimes against humanity and future peoples."[30] If causing the human species to become extinct through global warming and Frankenfoods are postericide, would not transhumanism also be postericide?

Transhumanists get around this is by redefining the term *species*. In their article "Moral Transhumanism," Persson and Savulescu argue that belonging to the human species is superficial. If a "person" maintained a continuous awareness of his or her own existence, the form that that awareness was housed in would be immaterial to maintaining their personal identity. They claim that membership in a species has no moral quality; it is merely a biological distinction marking which life forms can breed with each other and produce other viable forms. They claim, "It is plausible to take interfertility to be not only a sufficient but also a necessary condition for sameness of species."[31] This leads them to argue that one is a *Homo sapiens* merely because one breeds with and produces other *Homo sapiens*.

> So, our value is not plausibly based upon the fact that we are members of the human species. Furthermore, species membership is not an essential property of us. Therefore, we could lose our species membership without ceasing to exist. Such a loss of species membership would not represent any loss of value. Fear of this loss, then, should not prevent us from wanting to change radically. Sometimes humans who have been radically altered by technology are referred to as transhumans or, if the alteration is more extreme, posthumans. We should not fear a change to transhumans or posthumans even if we ceased to be members of the species H. sapiens.[32]

Askland points out that "the point is that transhumanists do not really seek to 'manage' our evolution. They instead seek to sever us from an evolutionary past and undertake an entirely self-engineered future."[33] While this is a voluntary extinction scenario for those *Homo sapiens* who have become

---

29. McKinnon, "Endangering Humanity," 399.

30. REAPP News, "McKinnon £1m Leverhulme Grant." See also Leverhulme Trust, *Leverhulme Programme in Climate Justice*.

31. Persson and Savulescu, "Moral Transhumanism," 657.

32. Persson and Savulescu, "Moral Transhumanism," 660.

33. Askland, "Misnomer of Transhumanism," 77.

the newly formed *Homo superior*, it remains an involuntary extinction scenario for those who remain unchanged.

So what does transhumanism intend to do with humanity? Since it pursues a utilitarian ethic where the end justifies the means, there would be no sense of moral responsibility in continuing to care for *Homo sapiens*. Equality would never be an option. We have already referred to cases where so-called "abled" people make incorrect assumptions that lead them to "help" disabled people by mistreating them. Thus, it is possible that active euthanasia would be used to eliminate the "suffering" of *Homo sapiens*. Human nature is full of dark surprises. *Homo superior* might keep humans around as pets or in zoos for entertainment purposes. DNA could be kept on file just in case this whole singularity thing turned out to be a bad idea. The whole "retro" look has always been in fashion; even during the Enlightenment, people dressed up like the Greeks. So humans might be kept around as breeding stock for post-humans who wanted to download into a retro body for the day before discarding it in the pile of dirty "clothes." Unfortunately, with transhuman premises, it is easy to imagine dystopia.

CONCLUSION

Transhumanism uses scientific imperatives to make moral choices. Science can be excellent at deriving objective truths about physical reality, but it does not have the metaphysical framework to evaluate moral, ethical, or "ought" questions. Bioengineering and universal compliance raise serious issues about autonomy, identity, ethnic futures, and community.[34] While H+ enhancement can result in goods such as human longevity or overcoming disease, transhumanism is proposing something darker. Post-human existence means the end of the human race, not by some global apocalyptic war or a meteor hitting the earth, but by deliberate social engineering. Even with the singularity promising an eschatological salvation and a messianic Singleton to guide the way, the eradication of "old humanity" is still an act of genocide, for all its good intentions.

BIBLIOGRAPHY

Agar, Nicolas. "Moral Bioenhancement and the Utilitarian Catastrophe." *Cambridge Quarterly of Healthcare Ethics* 24 (2015) 37–47.

Askland, Andrew. "The Misnomer of Transhumanism as Directed Evolution." *International Journal of Emerging Technologies and Society* 9 (2011) 71–78.

Bishop, Jeffery P. "Transhumanism, Metaphysics, and the Posthuman God." *Journal of Medicine and Philosophy* 35 (2010) 700–720.

---

34. Lee, "Cochlear Implantation," 67.

Bostrom, Nick. "What Is a Singleton?" *Linguistic and Philosophical Investigations* 5 (2006) 48–54.

———, et al. "The Unilateralist's Curse and the Case for a Principle of Conformity." *Social Epistemology* 30 (2016) 350–71.

Chorost, Michael. *World Wide Mind: The Coming Integration of Humanity, Machines, and the Internet*. New York: Free, 2011.

Collins, John J. "Introduction: Towards the Morphology of a Genre." *Semeia* 14 (1979) 1–20.

De Grey, Aubrey. *Ending Aging: The Rejuvenation Breakthroughs That Could Reverse Human Aging in Our Lifetime*. New York: St. Martin's, 2007. Kindle.

Dixon, Darrin P. "Informed Consent or Institutionalized Eugenics? How the Medical Profession Encourages Abortion of Fetuses With Down Syndrome." *Issues in Law & Medicine* 24 (Summer 2008) 3–59.

Gligorov, Nada. "The Applicability of Psychological and Moral Distinctions in an Emerging Neuroscientific Framework." *AJOB Neuroscience* 7 (2016) 191–92.

Haldane, J. B. S., and Albert Montefiore Hyamson. *Daedalus, or, Science and the Future: A Paper Read to the Heretics, Cambridge, on February 4th, 1923*. London: Paul, Trench, Trubner, 1925.

Hughes, James. "Contradictions from the Enlightenment Roots of Transhumanism." *Journal of Medicine and Philosophy* 35 (2010) 622–40.

Koch, Tom. "Enhancing Who? Enhancing What? Ethics, Bioethics, and Transhumanism." *Journal of Medicine and Philosophy* 35 (2010) 685–99.

Kurzweil, Ray. *The Singularity Is Near: When Humans Transcend Biology*. New York: Viking, 2005.

Lee, J. "Cochlear Implantation, Enhancements, Transhumanism and Posthumanism: Some Human Questions." *Science and Engineering Ethics* 22 (2016) 67–92.

Leverhulme Trust. *Leverhulme Programme in Climate Justice: Doctoral Scholars Handbook 2016–2017*. University of Reading, 2016. https://www.reading.ac.uk/climate-justice/-/media/project/functions/research/climate-justice/documents/leverhulmeprogrammehandbook.pdf.

McKinnon, Catriona. "Endangering Humanity: An International Crime?" *Canadian Journal of Philosophy* 47 (2017) 395–415.

Persson, Ingmar, and Julian Savulescu. "Moral Transhumanism." *Journal of Medicine and Philosophy* 35 (2010) 656–69.

REAPP News. "McKinnon £1m Leverhulme Grant." University of Reading, Apr. 3, 2017. https://www.reading.ac.uk/spirs/research/spirs-REAPPnews.aspx.

Savulescu, Julian. "Ethics: Conscientious Objection in Medicine." *British Medical Journal* 332 (Feb. 4, 2006) 294–97.

———. "Procreative Beneficence: Why We Should Select the Best Children." *Bioethics* 15 (Oct. 2001) 413–26.

Sparrow, Robert. "Defending Deaf Culture: The Case of Cochlear Implants." *Journal of Political Philosophy* 13 (2005) 135–52.

———. "Implants and Ethnocide: Learning from the Cochlear Implant Controversy." *Disability & Society* 25 (2010) 455–66.

———. "Egalitarianism and Moral Bioenhancement." *American Journal of Bioethics* 14 (2014) 20–28.

Vinge, Vernor. "The Coming Technological Singularity: How to Survive in the Post-Human Era." Paper given at Vision 21: Interdisciplinary Science and Engineering in the Era of Cyberspace, NASA John H. Glenn Research Center at Lewis Field, Brook Park, OH, Dec. 1, 1993. https://ntrs.nasa.gov/citations/19940022856.

The End of (Our) Time
Reflections on Barth's Theology of Dying and the Thereafter

ROGER L. REVELL

INTRODUCTION

WHEN IT COMES TO Christian eschatology—that is, questions about death and eternal life, the end of time, new creation, etc.—the legacy of Karl Barth, at least upon first glance, would appear to be of limited value. This is chiefly because Barth died before producing the volumes of *Church Dogmatics* (hereafter *CD*) earmarked for a fulsome treatment of such topics.[1] Nevertheless, as current scholarship on Barth's eschatological outlook indicates, it is possible to infer from earlier portions of his corpus some general contours of what he might have said on this topic.[2] In this spirit, my essay discusses Barth's treatment of the nature of human time in *CD* III/2, a section which contains some intriguing claims about dying and the hereafter. While this is not the only text that sheds light on these facets of

---

1. When he died, Barth had not yet finished volume 4 and had yet to commence volume 5, which would have been titled *The Doctrine of Redemption*. This fifth volume was meant to treat the person and work of the Holy Spirit and would have devoted substantial attention to eschatology. For some of Barth's own comments on why he was unable to progress as planned, see *CD* IV/4, vii–viii. For an additional, captivating bit of commentary, see Anderson, "Life after Death?"

2. This is what Aaron Smith has nicely done in his recent article, "Perfection of Glory." In this same vein, Princeton's 2019 Barth conference centered on eschatology.

Barth's outlook, it does provide a manageable access point to his settling perspective on such topics.³

In interacting with this text, my overarching objective is to suggest that two elements of Barth's eschatological thought are especially useful for ongoing Christian theologizing about the end of human time (i.e., death) and that which comes after (i.e., eternity). Specifically, I have in mind (1) Barth's reinterpretation of dying within the economy of redemption and (2) his conspicuous accent on the alterity (or radical disparity) between present human existence and human existence in Christ on the far side of death. From one vantage, this call for retrieval may seem strange, given certain shortcomings (treated below) which beset Barth's thought in this arena. Yet, while such shortcomings certainly demand attention, they do not entirely negate the value of his conclusions—or so I wish to argue.

BARTH ON DEATH AND THE HEREAFTER

Death, Horrible Yet Kind

In *CD* III/2, Barth's contemplation of matters eschatological commences with consideration of death; like most of us, he sees this phenomenon as an awful reality that suffuses human existence with "anxiety and care."[4] Ultimately, such terror owes to death's function as a form of judgment, inasmuch as our deaths are tied to the "irreparable guilt" that we have incurred before God "from the beginning our existence."[5] Those familiar with the Christian Bible will, of course, know that Barth's emphasis on the punitive nature of death is well supported by the testimony of Scripture. For example, in the Old Testament, death is depicted as an event to be approached with fear and trembling (Ps 55:4; Ps 116:3), as entry into a realm whereby one is separated from God (Num 16:33, Ps 6:5, Isa 38:18), and as an enemy of human life (Hos 13:4). And in the New Testament, the apostle Paul frequently renders death as a horrible consequence of sin (Rom 5–7) and portrays it as an enemy to be destroyed (1 Cor 15). Accordingly, there is nothing strange about Barth's claim that death "as it actually encounters us" is an unnatural invader that rightly excites dread.[6]

---

3. A more comprehensive study would begin with Barth's *Resurrection of the Dead*, his 1933 commentary on 1 Corinthians. More than 50 percent of the exposition centers on chapter 15.

4. Barth, *CD* III/2:588; cf. 517.

5. Barth, *CD* III/2:596; cf. *CD* IV/2:486–49.

6. Barth, *CD* III/2:596; cf. *CD* IV/2:486–49.

What comes next, however, is somewhat unexpected: he contends that *death-as-judgment* is not the only way to evaluate the phenomenon of dying. In advancing this counterpoint, Barth develops a robust christological argument, premised on the (characteristically Barthian) conviction that Christ's "death, resurrection, and coming again . . . [must be] the basis of . . . everything that is to be said about man and his future, end and goal in God."[7] In this vein, he goes on to assert that the death of Jesus reveals that human dying is not simply a punitive, and therefore *unnatural*, affair but also a *natural*, and even salutary, phenomenon.

In defending this striking statement, Barth argues that Christ's crucifixion reveals another form of death, one that stands as a feature of "original" creation, in contrast to death as a punitive consequence of sin.[8] This claim is grounded in the observation that Jesus died—or *was able to die*—even though he was in fact sinless.[9] That even the sinless Jesus was capable of dying reveals that no human nature, not even an *unfallen* nature such as Jesus's, is immune to being "fundamentally called into question by death."[10] For Barth, it follows from this that the basic condition of human mortality does not have its provenance in the fall. To the contrary, it is part and parcel of original creation—meaning that mortality is in fact *intrinsic* to humanity as originally created by God.[11] Put another way, before and apart from the fall, God allotted (or bound) the span of each human's earthly time.

In advancing this claim, Barth secondarily appeals to a selection of biblical passages that hint at a nonpunitive understanding of dying: "Another form of death is . . . to be seen in the Bible."[12] Here, he cites Ps 90, contending that it distinguishes between human life, human death, and the curse over humanity as a result of sin. Additionally, he appeals to 1 Kgs 2, when David speaks of his death as a natural event, whereby he goes the way of all flesh. And then there are the passings of Moses (Deut 34) and Elijah (2 Kgs 2), both of which are depicted as nonpunitive forms of dying.[13] Such examples signal that, even while death-as-judgment is a

---

7. Barth, *CD* III/2:624.

8. Barth, *CD* III/2:626–27.

9. Barth, *CD* III/2:628. On this question, it is important to remember that the sin for which Christ died was an alien burden, which is to say that he died not for his own sins (there were none) but for the sins of humanity imputed to him, as 2 Cor 5:21 reports.

10. Barth, *CD* III/2:601.

11. Thus Barth writes that a "strict identification of dying and judgment in death" is possible only if we ignore Christ's crucifixion and what it reveals about the nature of death (*CD* III/2:629; cf. 553).

12. Barth, *CD* III/2:634.

13. Barth, *CD* III/2:637–40.

major motif of the Scriptures, death as a neutral creational reality has not been entirely "crowded out."[14]

Barth's reappraisal of death ramifies in several immediate ways, as he subsequently outlines. Most obviously, it means that human subjection to death is not to be regarded as wholly "intrinsically negative and evil."[15] It also induces a revised view of how Christ redresses the "problem" of death, which is to say, *death-as-judgment*. On this theme, Barth stresses that the atoning work of Jesus does not negate death per se; instead, it abolishes the link between death and judgment in a fallen world. It is for this reason that the application of Christ's redemption to humans does not entail some sort of infusion of immortality that negates death but rather effects a return to that mode of (natural) dying which typified original creation.[16] In short, while the phenomenon of death continues, it is no longer a form of judgment, for it is only "sin [which] makes a judgment out of death," and Christ has overcome sin.[17]

These contentions, however, do not complete Barth's discussion, for he goes on to speak of natural death not merely as a *neutral* event but as one that possesses a certain *goodness*.[18] What does Barth have in mind with this rather counterintuitive and even bizarre declaration? Two of his explanations deserve mention.[19]

First, Barth believes that if human existence was temporally unbounded, we would fail to regard our time with a healthy sense of urgency or purpose.[20] After all, if one's years are without number, how could one possibly conclude that one's actions here and now carried any real import? In this sense, it is only in knowing that our time is a limited commodity that we are pressed to examine our choices, so as to conscientiously embrace or reject the opportunities that come in the midst of our days.[21]

---

14. Barth, *CD* III/2:634.
15. Barth, *CD* III/2:631.
16. Barth, *CD* III/2:632.
17. Berkhouwer, *Triumph of Grace*, 334.

18. Somewhat arrestingly, Barth writes that there is a certain *goodness* at play in God's creational determination that "man's ... time should have an end" (*CD* III/2:598).

19. So far as I can tell, Barth makes at least four arguments in support of the salutary nature of death as a feature of original creation. Several of these points, however, are posited merely in passing and thus stand in need of further development in order to be persuasive. For example, Barth enjoins that the atonement is efficacious only if humans are finite beings but fails to expand upon this pronouncement (*CD* III/2:631).

20. Barth, *CD* III/2:633.
21. Barth, *CD* III/4:580.

Natural death, therefore, can be regarded in positive terms in that it infuses our existence with a sense of purpose.

Second, Barth also sees death as a precondition for the possibility of cultivating a meaningful personal identity. This is because a genuine, stable identity is contingent upon having a finite history, given that a person is only "himself . . . in the sequence of his life-acts."[22] This outlook reveals Barth's *actualism* (or "actualist ontology"), that is, the deep-seated conviction that each person's essence is inseparable from their concrete existence (i.e., the concrete actions and events of their lives).[23] As an actualist, he assumes that to "exist as a [hu]man means to act,"[24] such that our identities are constituted by "the possibilities offered by our choices—the wrestling with the possibilities which are offered in our time."[25] In simpler terms, Barth is saying that a proper human identity is unobtainable apart from a personal history that has a terminus. After all, apart from the constraints of time (i.e., birth and death), we would have "no center, and therefore would not be [ourselves]."[26] To the contrary, we "would continue to unfold through a never-ending sequence of actions in time," always emerging and never settling into an identity.[27] Bearing this in mind, natural death is salutary inasmuch as it is an indispensable ingredient for achieving a determinate personal identity—that thing that makes a person who they are.

Eschatological Adumbrations: From Human Time to Divine "Eternalization"

Corresponding to his reevaluation of death, Barth offers several reflections on the nature of eschatological existence, which he portrays as the "eternalization" of those in Christ[28] or as the "appearing of eternal life in our life itself as it is."[29] What precisely does this entail? While his further commentary is frus-

---

22. Barth, *CD* III/2:521.

23. As explained by Paul Nimmo, Barth's actualism stands in contrast to a "substantialist ontology," in which humans are conceived more as "fixed and determinate quantities in a certain abstraction from their histories, acts, and relationships" (Nimmo, "Actualism," 2).

24. Barth, *CD* II/2:535.

25. Barth, *CD* III/3:232–33.

26. Barth, *CD* III/4:573. For Barth, birth and death are the "two events which give to human life its character of once-for-allness" (*Church Dogmatis* III/3:231).

27. Cortez, *ReSourcing Theological Anthropology*, 249.

28. Barth, *CD* III/2:632–33.

29. Barth, *Faith of the Church*, 140.

tratingly vague—manifesting the notorious "elusiveness" of his eschatological ideas—it is possible to pinpoint several characteristics.[30]

First, and in contrast to the position he appears to have espoused in his younger years, Barth makes it clear that eternal existence is nontemporal.[31] This is to say that eternal life is not synonymous with living forever, as he pointedly underscores in writing that "mankind . . . has no beyond."[32] This sentiment, of course, corresponds to Barth's idea that "temporal finitude is necessary for the well-being of the creature."[33]

Second, even while Barth excises any notion of time from his vision of eternity, he does not hold that there is *nothing* that follows natural death. He should not, therefore, be grouped with those modern theologians who have attempted to construe eternal life as a purely *present* possession.[34] To the contrary, Barth is an "eschatological realist," which is why even as he asserts that the eschaton is devoid of time, so too does he insist that it is not empty.[35] This is what he means to communicate in writing that when a human life reaches its earthly terminus, it is raised into "the revelation of its redemption as completed in . . . Christ."[36] The upshot is that although human time does come to an end, it does not perish; rather, one's "biographical lifetime considered as a whole" is placed into eternity.[37]

Although eternalization is properly regarded as an ineffable affair, a few comments can be made about Barth's sense of what it does and does not entail. First, it involves a certain unveiling, which is to say a fuller revelation

30. Gunton, "Salvation," 150. For a commendable attempt to thoroughly index Barth's ideas about eschatological anthropology, see Nathan Hitchcock's *Karl Barth*, esp. ch. 3. Cf. Timo Helenius's paper at the 2019 Princeton Karl Barth Conference, "What I Am Not."

31. The younger Barth, in his more modest *Göttingen Dogmatics* of the 1920s, seems to have advocated a picture of eschatological existence in which humans continue to lead individual lives as personal subjects (Etzelmüller, "Eschatology"). For more on the development of Barth's thought about time and eternity, see Nielsen's, "Karl Barth."

32. Barth, *CD* III/2: 632. Anderson offers an engaging firsthand account of Barth's shifting sensibilities in this arena, recalled from a conversation during his time as one of Barth's PhD students (Anderson, "Life after Death").

33. Cortez, *ReSourcing Theological Anthropology*, 253.

34. For more on this general outlook, see Burley, "End of Immortality," 305, 307, 313–17. For an example, see Jantzen, "Do We Need Immortality." On this topic, it should be noted that other portions of Barth's theology do in fact speak of eschatology in terms of a *current in-breaking* of redemption. In this sense, his ideas about "eternal life" are sometimes (though never exclusively) portrayed in terms of present spirituality (Etzelmüller, "Eschatology").

35. Dalferth, "Karl Barth's Eschatological Realism," 14.

36. Barth, *CD* III/2:633.

37. Burley, "End of Immortality," 313.

of a human's redemption "as completed in Jesus Christ."[38] Second, even while the eschaton will be devoid of human temporality, a person's time—as it comes to exist as a fixed entity through their dying—will somehow experience further redemption. More concretely, Barth envisions this as a sort of "healing" of human time, through which its "imperfection[s] [are] transcended and overcome."[39] This happens as one's allotted, bounded time comes into contact "with the perfection of [God's] love."[40] Third, Barth's thought elsewhere makes it clear that none of this is to be understood in terms of the classical (Eastern) Christian notion of deification or divinization.[41] Instead, he submits that those who die in Christ will experience an "exaltation," through which their history will find its place in God's eternity (as opposed to their essence being joined to God's essence).

In delineating eschatological existence in these ways, Barth believed he was honoring the requirement of Scripture. At the same time, he was well aware that his view was a "far cry" from what many biblical Christians would have long assumed about the nature of eschatological existence.[42]

TWO PROBLEMS WITH BARTH'S CONCEPTION

Before moving to demonstrate how Barth's conclusions about dying and the eschaton offer a fertile resource for ongoing Christian reflection on last things, two shortcomings in his thought need to be identified. These pertain to (1) his handling of Scripture and (2) an internal inconsistency in his christological reasoning.

We begin with Barth's handling of the Bible, for even a cursory reading of germane New Testament passages raises questions about his use of Scripture. For example, in contrast to Barth's repudiation of the idea of a continuing immortal afterlife, do not some of Jesus's parables (e.g., the story of Lazarus and the rich man in Luke 16) suggest that dying might in fact give way to a new form of being that is nevertheless marked by a sense of continuation or progression? Then there are Jesus's remarks on the resurrected life, which imply that it encompasses some form of conscious, continued existence (e.g., Luke 20:27–38). Additionally, one might consider

---

38. Barth, *CD* III/2:633.

39. Hunsinger, "*Mysterium Trinitatis*," 184.

40. In attempting to explain this, Barth writes that through eternalization, God "re-creates" human time and "heals its wounds, the fleetingness of the present, the separation of past and future from one another, as well as their separation from the present" (*CD* II/1 617–19).

41. McCormack, *Orthodox and Modern*, 236.

42. Anderson, "Life after Death."

St. Paul's statements (e.g., 1 Cor 15:20-22, 53-54; 1 Thess 4:16-18) on the future that awaits Christians, as well as those in Rev 21:1-6, which can be plausibly taken to indicate that the life which comes after death is not entirely unrecognizable as compared to present existence. Indeed, 2 Pet 1:10-11 and Heb 8:12-14 bespeak as much when they signal that Christian virtue, cultivated here-and-now, is of value for existence in God's eternal kingdom. Along these lines, in expounding the latter passage, A. W. Tozer avers that present growth in godliness (or godly character) is part of "preparing [Christians] for [their] heavenly home" and readies them for "eternal fellowship with the saints [and] the martyrs."[43]

Of particular significance within this critique is the fact that Barth's nontemporal account of the eschaton fails to sufficiently grapple with the implications of Jesus's own *temporal* and *historical* post-resurrection existence. Passages such as John 21:9-14 depict the resurrected Jesus as having an ongoing personal history.[44] To be fair, Barth acknowledges this aspect of *Jesus's* resurrected existence; however, he refuses to treat Jesus's "further history" as a basis for the possibility that other humans, too, might have some sort of temporal and historical existence on the other side of death.[45]

In light of these observations, certain critics are not without basis in asserting that Barth's hefty emphasis on the disjunction between present and eschatological existence ignores portions of the Bible that sound a different note.[46] Making this point forcefully, G. C. Berkhouwer writes that "it is not the idea of continuity that Scripture opposes but the denial of it."[47] As such, it is valid to question whether Barth's conception of eternalization is in fact governed by the testimony of Scripture to the extent he claimed.[48]

A second problem with Barth's perspective is found in his christological argumentation, as Marc Cortez has perceptively identified.[49] As mentioned above, Barth's reappraisal of death has its basis in the fact that even (sinless) Jesus died. Yet this reasoning is seemingly called into question by his prior assertion that the human nature assumed by Jesus in the incarnation was a *fallen* nature.[50] Consequently, Jesus's ability to die may *not*

43. Tozer, *Jesus*, 87, 90.

44. Other pertinent examples from the New Testament include Luke 24:13-29, 38-40, and also John 20:24-27.

45. Barth, *CD* III/2:440-41.

46. Vogel, "Ecce Homo," 119-20.

47. Berkhouwer, *Triumph of Grace*, 338; cf. 336-39.

48. Anderson, "Life after Death."

49. Cortez, *Resourcing Theological Anthropology*, 252-53.

50. "There must be no weakening or obscuring of the saving truth that the nature which God assumed in Christ is identical with our nature as we see it in the light of Fall.

therefore reveal a neutral form of death encompassing humanity before and apart from the advent of sin. Alternatively, Jesus's dying may simply owe to his assumption of a fallen nature.[51] If Barth's reappraisal of death—and especially his attempt to demonstrate the goodness of natural death—is to prevail, this inconsistency certainly demands attention.

THINKING WITH AND BEYOND BARTH

Notwithstanding the preceding issues, Barth's perspective on last things is not without value. Along these lines, I want to suggest that there are two features of his outlook (as broadly taken) that are gainful for continuing Christian contemplation of the reality of dying and the hope the church carries for eternal life.

I begin with Barth's reappraisal of death, which ultimately portrays human mortality (and dying) as an intrinsic feature of original creation. In contrast to Cortez's more dismissive evaluation, and in spite of the aforementioned glitch at play in Barth's christological reasoning, I am convinced that his more nuanced understanding of death ought to be entertained.[52] Although there are problems with *the way* Barth reaches his conclusion, the *conclusion itself* should be retained.

This assertion is substantiated by the fact that Barth's resolution is amply supported in other ways, chiefly by careful attention to apposite scriptural texts. For starters there is the witness of the Old Testament; recent scholarship continues to challenge the commonplace idea that Gen 2:17 is "an account of the *origin of death* in the world."[53] Against this familiar reading, scholars such as Walter Brueggeman, Iain Provan, and John Walton contend that the Genesis narrative does not in fact attribute death to sin. More accurately, it seems to assume that even though "certain

---

If it were otherwise, how could Christ be really like us? What concern would we have with him? We stand before God characterized by the Fall. God's Son not only assumed our nature but he entered the concrete form of our nature, under which we stand before God as men damned and lost" (Barth, *CD* I/2:153).

51. Moreover, one might also posit that Jesus's death owed to the fact that he willingly gave up his life (Matt 27:50) and is not therefore attributable to his possession of a finite human nature.

52. Says Cortez, "I think we need to challenge Barth's conclusion that . . . death itself is intrinsic to human nature" (*ReSourcing Theological Anthropology*, 252).

53. Brueggeman, *Genesis*, 42. For an example of this view from the Reformation era, see Calvin who, in commenting on Gen 2:17, judges that apart from the advent of original sin, humans "would have passed into heaven without death" (*Commentary on Genesis*, 127). For a more recent instantiation of this same outlook, see Boice's *Foundations of the Christian Faith*, 201.

forms of death may be punishment, death in and of itself belongs properly to the human life God wills for mankind."[54] In sum, it is plausible to conclude that human dying has its provenance in a God-ordained boundary. It is *death-as-judgment*, rather than death per se, that comes as a result of human sinfulness.

Further corroborating Barth's determination is the witness of the New Testament. On this front, we do well to consider St. Paul's exuberant declaration in 1 Cor 15:55–56: "O Death, where is your sting." In this instance, the apostle's remarks intimate that within the economy of Christ's redemption, in which death-as-judgment is negated, death itself remains in place as a correlate to the "mortality of the present age."[55] In other words, it is the *sting* of death that is abolished in Christ; as signaled by v. 56, this "sting" should not be understood as a synonym for death, full stop. Instead, sting can be read as shorthand for dying as a judgment for sin.[56] All this to say, inasmuch as Paul depicts Christ's atoning work as something that counters the *sting* of death (as opposed to death per se), Barth's perspective finds additional corroboration.

Inasmuch as the Barthian reappraisal of death is not as problematic as it might appear at first glance, how might it positively imprint Christian attitudes towards the reality of dying? In this arena, I wish to make two preliminary proposals.

Contemporary Western culture increasingly abhors the prospect of dying (though not necessarily for fear of divine judgment) and ignores the inevitability of death until it happens. This tendency serves to intensify the baseline disillusionment that so many humans instinctively feel in reaction to the prospect of dying.[57] At the bottom of such potent aversions is a

54. Brueggeman, *Genesis*, 42, 48. In his own way, Provan also advances this outlook, arguing that the Old Testament posits a distinction between a form of hardship and suffering that is "intrinsic to living in the place where God has put us to live" and another, increased form that "results from the entrance of evil." Provan's reading also stresses that the prospect of immortality was never intrinsic to humans but rather was presented as a possible option through the image of the tree of life: it is a human's "natural fate to die unless he eats from the tree of life" (*Seriously Dangerous Religion*, 106–7). Walton also takes this view: "Death and suffering can be feasibly inherent in a non-ordered world . . . [so that the] pre-fall human population would be subject to them" (*Lost World*, 159).

55. Fee, *First Epistle to Corinthians*, 804.

56. To be sure, this reading is not the most familiar—at least in the context of twentieth-century North American Protestantism. Yet it is preferable to more familiar (mis) interpretations that attribute dying full stop to sin. Such a determination, as Van de Beek observes, does not square with other biblical testimony suggesting that it is not merely sin that keeps death alive ("Evolution, Original Sin," 213–14).

57. Louw, "*Cura Animarum*," 1. There are, of course, exceptions to the instinctive

deeply embedded assumption (or feeling) that death is somehow *tout court* a violation of our nature and dignity. If Barth is right, however, such a sentiment is not finally theologically intelligible—even if some have thought otherwise. Accordingly, there is a need for our attitudes towards dying to be reconfigured, which is made all the more urgent by the fact that the relentless quest to elude death is one that can lead to a mode of existence that is selfish and rapacious in various ways.[58]

By clarifying that our mortality is part of God's creational vision—and not therefore automatically a deep offense against human dignity—Barth assists Christians in extricating themselves from a selfish and rapacious life-posture. After all, for those in Christ, death is something "which has lost its terror" and functions only as a door from one domain to another.[59] The door itself need not be feared, for any dread associated with passing through it is, strictly speaking, connected to what might await on the other side.[60]

Beyond this, another gain of Barth's revised construal of death is also worth highlighting: namely, its potential for reconciling one of the many ostensible tensions between faith and science.[61] Given that Christians have long maintained that death emerges only as a consequence of sin, the bio-evolutionary claim that dying is a necessary creative force in the proliferation of life has been deemed theologically problematic.[62] This is especially true in the context of twentieth-century North American Protestantism, where the idea that dying predates the fall appears to cut against the plain testimony of Scripture (Gen 3:3; Rom 5:12).[63] In unsettling this determination, Barth's reevaluation of death conduces to a *rapprochement*—one that is theologically driven and thus cannot be accused of mere subservience to the dictates of modern science.

Where death is recognized as an original feature of creation, the basic phenomenon of human dying can be seen in a new light: it is not something that detracts from the world's splendor but rather that is an *integral* part of its emergence. As explained by Rolston Holmes, "There are sorts of creation that cannot occur without death, and these include the highest created

---

aversion to death, as in the case with those who seek to be euthanized.

58. For insightful treatments of this tendency, see Hauerwas, "Salvation and Health," as well as his *Suffering Presence*.

59. Berkhouwer, *Triumph of Grace*, 333.

60. Barth, *Faith of the Church*, 141.

61. For an overview of said tensions, see Rosenberg's, "Making Space."

62. Thus Denis Lamoureux rejects the classical doctrine of original sin in his otherwise theistically-oriented defense of evolutionary theory (Van den Brink, "Questions, Challenges, and Concerns," 122–23).

63. See, e.g., Ham, *Over 35 Questions*, ch. 11.

goods." For this reason, "death [must] be meaningfully put into the biological processes as a necessary counterpart to the advancing of life."[64]

While a more traditional Christian interpretation of the fall would be uneasy with this assertion, Barth's perspective enables Christians to entertain such an outlook for good theological reasons. As such, it is possible for people of faith to affirm one of the seminal lessons of God's "book of nature," namely that an evolutionary process is central in the process of creation's unfolding.[65] In this sense, Barth's legacy pays dividends in ways he perhaps never imagined. Such dividends are win-win, for they allow believers to affirm evolutionary theory in good conscience, and they open up space for nonreligious scientists to consider the Christian faith.

Moving along, another theme of Barth's eschatological intimations is also deserving of retrieval: the *alterity* that characterizes his vision of eternity. As depicted earlier, this theme is vividly manifest in a drive to eschew any inkling of continued, temporal existence from his construal of eternal life. In our sociocultural setting, this stress on disparity is likely to feel unusual, given that Christian eschatological reflection in the context of modernity has evolved "to emphasize the continuity between this world and the next."[66] Otherwise put, ours is an age where the eschaton is commonly envisaged as a mere enhancement of the created order and our lives, as they *currently* are.[67] Accordingly, we speak of transformation instead of transfiguration and of material improvement rather than beatification. While this modernist casting of the eschaton is not without its benefits, it is nevertheless susceptible to certain misgivings.

To begin, there is the question of scriptural integrity. Those who render the eschaton as something that is robustly congruent with present existence often appeal to the Bible for their view.[68] Yet there are reasons to wonder if the perspective they champion is indeed as scriptural as they purport. Here, the work of Charles Taylor is instructive; by Taylor's

---

64. Holmes, *Science and Religion*, 217. In support of this clam, Holmes contends that the story of the fall is not primarily about the provenance of "disease and disaster" so much as a way of depicting "the fracture in relationship between God and the human creature made in his image." While this fracture certainly results in intrapersonal disorder, as well as disorder with our neighbors and our environment, it does not encompass the basic reality of dying (Holmes, *Science and Religion*, 94).

65. For a more in-depth discussion of this point, see J. Smith's "What Stands on Fall?"

66. Boersma, "6 Questions."

67. A variety of factors are at play in this shift. For a succinct genealogy, see Boersma's *Seeing God*, esp. ch. 1. Cf. Boersma, "Becoming Human."

68. For a representative example, see Wright's *Surprised By Hope* as well as Steven James's *New Creation Eschatology*, esp. 1–50.

reading, our age is one that has been heavily *immanentized*, which is to say that we have a lost a meaningful sense of the transcendent.[69] Such a loss does not signal a conscious shift in our beliefs so much as the fact that, at the level of what we take for granted, we now operate in essentially immanent terms. We have come to carry a "vision of life in which anything beyond the immanent is eclipsed."[70]

Within this scenario, it is hardly surprising that eschatological reflection has assumed an immanent coloring, centering on "the earth and its future viability, the material well-being of all its inhabitants, and justice in human relationships."[71] While such goods are to be celebrated and pursued, the dominance they hold in our eschatological imagination can obscure other elements of the Bible's teaching on this subject. Notably, this is exhibited by the fact that our modern ways of imagining eternity are conspicuously different from the way that theologians of the patristic, medieval, and even Reformation eras tended to conceive it.[72] Given that such earlier theologians grounded their outlook in the same Scriptures we use, one wonders why themes that are so prominent in their inheritance have often been elided in our period. Perhaps our eschatological sensibilities owe much to the tacit assumptions about reality that prevail in our immanentized era?

Dovetailing with this point is the tendency towards reification and its accompanying risks. When the eschaton is reduced to something that is exceedingly contiguous with the present age, it is but a small step further to overidentify it with the world as it now exists and some particular order therein. Simply put: immanentizing the eschaton can result in absolutizing politics. Barth himself knew this well, as one who witnessed the rise of the Third Reich, with its horrendous conflation of "God's coming kingdom with [the] realization of German political ends."[73]

This same sort of noxious conflation ever remains at risk. According to Stanley Hauerwas, it can also be discerned in the American context, wherein the nation's progress has been equated with the consummation of the kingdom of God.[74] Indeed, the success and furtherance of American

69. Taylor, *Secular Age*, 359–93, esp. 549–50. cf. 159–212. For a more accessible, concise summary of this facet of Taylor's thought, see J. Smith's *How (Not) to Be Secular*, 20–25.

70. J. Smith, *How (Not) to Be Secular*, 23.

71. Boersma, *Seeing God*, 17.

72. This is the central argument of Boersma's *Seeing God*, which is amply demonstrated along the way with reference to a variety of divines from the broader Christian tradition.

73. A. Smith, "Perfection of Glory," 180.

74. Hauerwas, "Christian Critique."

democracy has assumed a *religious* coloring, such that the salvation of the world is seen to be contingent upon it. Emanating from this coalescence of *God's* eschatological purposes with the vitality of the American republic is the temptation to (grossly) legitimize forms of coercion or violence on theological grounds.[75]

The alterity of Barth's vision of eternity stands as a bulwark against the tendency towards reification and its attendant dangers. Thus, even while his account of the eschaton may itself need some rebalancing in light of the wider revelation of Scripture, it is concurrently poised to rebalance and redress certain liabilities inchoate in the modernist brand of Christian eschatology. By insisting that eternity entails much more than a mere "facelift" of our world but amounts instead to something "absolutely unexpected and inconceivable,"[76] Barth's construal militates against the risk of what has been called premature eschatology. Eschatology that is premature breeds an impatience that hankers to *achieve* the redemption of all things rather than to *wait* for God to do it.[77] It can mutate into Nazism, American exceptionalism, or any number of political ideologies that confuse the kingdoms of humankind with the kingdom of God. Against any such conflations, the otherworldliness of Barth's portrayal of eternity reminds us that while the eschaton is indeed coming, it is *only* coming. And when it dawns, the difference (as Barth was fond of quipping) will be as great as that between Christ at his death and Christ after his resurrection—a "wholly new event."[78]

CONCLUSION

This essay has sought to demonstrate Barth's utility as a resource for contemporary Christian reflection on the end of our time and the thereafter, despite the fact that his doctrines of the last things never came to full expression. As has been shown, an earlier segment of Barth's thought provides access to some of his settling ideas in this arena, especially pertaining to the nature of death and the character of eschatological existence. While his theologizing on these topics is not without its shortcomings, I have argued that it nevertheless offers several worthwhile insights that, as critically digested, prove to be existentially and ethically salutary.

---

75. Hauerwas, "Christian Critique," 459.
76. Eberhard Busch, *Great Passion*, 280.
77. A. Smith, "Perfection of Glory," 181.
78. A. Smith, "Perfection of Glory," 179.

BIBLIOGRAPHY

Anderson, Raymond. "Life after Death? Reflections on the Princeton Karl Barth Conference." *Presbyterian Outlook*, June 28, 2019. https://pres-outlook.org/2019/06/life-after-death-reflections-on-the-princeton-karl-barth-conference/.

Barth, Karl. *Church Dogmatics*. Translated by G. W. Bromiley. 14 vols. Peabody, MA: Hendrickson, 2010.

———. *The Faith of the Church: A Commentary on the Apostle's Creed*. Translated by G. Vahanian. London: Collins, 1960.

———. *The Resurrection of the Dead*. Translated by H. J. Stenning. Eugene, OR: Wipf and Stock, 2003.

Berkhouwer, G. C. *The Triumph of Grace in the Theology of Karl Barth*. London: Paternoster, 1956.

Boersma, Hans. "6 Questions with Hans Boersma." Eerdword (blog), July 24, 2018. https://eerdword.com/2018/07/24/6-questions-with-hans-boersma/.

———. "Becoming Human in the Face of God: Gregory of Nyssa's Unending Search for the Beatific Vision." *International Journal of Systematic Theology* 17 (Apr. 2015) 131–51.

———. *Seeing God: The Beatific Vision in Christian Tradition*. Grand Rapids: Eerdmans, 2018.

Boice, James Montgomery. *The Foundations of the Christian Faith: A Comprehensive and Readable Theology*. Rev. ed. Downers Grove, IL: InterVarsity, 1986.

Brueggeman, Walter. *Genesis*. Interpretation: A Bible Commentary for Teaching and Preaching. Louisville: Westminster John Knox, 2010.

Burley, Mikel. "The End of Immortality!" *Journal of Ethics* 19 (2015) 305–21.

Busch, Eberhard. *The Great Passion: An Introduction to the Theology of Karl Barth*. Translated by G. Bromiley. Grand Rapids: Eerdmans, 2004.

Calvin, John. *Commentary on Genesis*. Translated by John King. London: Banner of Truth, 1965.

Cortez, Marc. *ReSourcing Theological Anthropology: A Constructive Account of Humanity in the Light of Christ*. Grand Rapids: Zondervan, 2018.

Dalferth, Ingolf. "Karl Barth's Eschatological Realism." In *Karl Barth: Centenary Essays*, edited by S. W. Sykes, 14–45. Cambridge: Cambridge University Press, 1989.

Etzelmüller, Gregory. "Eschatology." In *Westminster Handbook to Karl Barth*, edited by Richard Burnett, 61–63. Louisville: Westminster John Knox, 2013.

Fee, Gordon D. *The First Epistle to the Corinthians*. Grand Rapids: Eerdmans, 1993.

Gunton, Colin. "Salvation." In *The Cambridge Companion to Karl Barth*, edited by John Webster, 143–58. Cambridge: Cambridge University Press, 2000.

Ham, Ken, ed. *Over 35 Questions on Creation/Evolution and the Bible*. Vol. 3 of *The New Answers Book*. Green Leaf, AR: Master, 2010.

Hauerwas, Stanley. "A Christian Critique of Christian America." In *The Hauerwas Reader*, edited by John Berkman and Michael G. Cartwright, 459–80. Durham, NC: Duke University Press, 2001.

———. "Salvation and Health: Why Medicine Needs the Church." In *The Hauerwas Reader*, edited by John Berkman and Michael G. Cartwright, 539–55. Durham, NC: Duke University Press, 2001.

———. *Suffering Presence: Theological Reflections on Medicine, the Mentally Handicapped, and the Church.* Notre Dame, IN: University of Notre Dame Press, 1986.

Helenius, Timo. "'What I Am Not': Barth's Negative Phenomenology of Eternity." Paper presented at Princeton Theological Seminary Annual Karl Barth Conference, Princeton, NJ, June 16–19, 2019.

Hitchcock, Nathan. *Karl Barth and the Resurrection of the Flesh: The Loss of the Body in Participatory Eschatology.* Eugene, OR: Pickwick, 2013.

Holmes, Rolston. *Science and Religion: A Critical Survey.* New York: Random, 1987.

Hunsinger, George. "*Mysterium Trinitatis*: Barth's Conception of Eternity." In *For the Sake of the World: Karl Barth and the Future of Ecclesial Theology*, edited by George Hunsinger, 165–90. Grand Rapids: Eerdmans, 2004.

James, Steven. *New Creation Eschatology and the Land: A Survey of Contemporary Perspectives.* Eugene, OR: Wipf & Stock, 2017.

Jantzen, Grace. "Do We Need Immortality?" *Modern Theology* 1 (1984) 33–44.

Karlson, Henry. "The Eschaton Has Been Immanentized: Against the Modern Gnostics." Vox Nova, Aug. 18, 2009. https://www.patheos.com/blogs/voxnova/2009/08/18/the-eschaton-has-been-immanentized-against-the-modern-gnostics/.

Louw, Daniel. "*Cura Animarum* as Hope Care: Towards a Theology of the Resurrection within the Human Quest for Meaning and Hope." *HTS Theological Studies* 70 (2014) 1–10.

McCormack, Bruce. *Orthodox and Modern: Studies in the Theology of Karl Barth.* Grand Rapids: Baker Academic, 2008.

Nielsen, Bent Flemming. "Karl Barth: A Brief Introduction; *Time and Eternity*." NTS Library, Nov. 2002. www.ntslibrary.comPDF%20BooksBarth%20A%20Brief%20Introduction%20Time%20and%20Eternity.pdf.

Nimmo, Paul. "Actualism." In *Westminster Handbook to Karl Barth*, edited by Richard Burnett, 1–3. Louisville: Westminster John Knox, 2013.

Provan, Iain. *Seriously Dangerous Religion: What the Old Testament Really Says and Why It Matters.* Waco, TX: Baylor University Press, 2014.

Rosenberg, Stanley. "Making Space in a Post-Darwinian World: Theology and Science in Apposition." In *Finding Ourselves After Darwin*, edited by Stanley Rosenberg, 3–10. Grand Rapids: Baker Academic, 2018.

Smith, Aaron. "The Perfection of Glory in Humility: What Karl Barth Would Have Had to Say about Redemption." *International Journal of Systematic Theology* 17 (Apr. 2015) 176–93.

Smith, James K. A. *How (Not) To Be Secular: Reading Charles Taylor.* Grand Rapids: Eerdmans, 2014.

———. "What Stands on the Fall? A Philosophical Exploration." In *Evolution and the Fall*, edited by William Cavanaugh and James K. A. Smith, 48–66. Grand Rapids: Eerdmans, 2017.

Taylor, Charles. *A Secular Age.* Cambridge, MA: Belknap, 2007.

Tozer, A. W. *Jesus, Author of Our Faith.* Edited by Gerald Smith. Camp Hill, PA: Christian, 1988.

Van de Beek, Abraham. "Evolution, Original Sin, and Death." *Journal of Reformed Theology* 5 (2011) 206–20.

Van den Brink, Gijsbert. "Questions, Challenges, and Concerns for Original Sin." In *Finding Ourselves after Darwin*, edited by Stanley Rosenberg, 117–29. Grand Rapids: Baker Academic, 2018.

Vogel, Heinrich. "Ecce Homo: Die Anthropologie Karl Barths." *Verkündigung und Forschung* (1949/1950) 102–28.

Walton, John. *The Lost World of Adam and Eve*. Downers Grove, IL: IVP Academic, 2015.

Wright, N. T. *Surprised By Hope: Rethinking Heaven, the Resurrection, and the Mission of the Church*. New York: Harper, 2008.

Belief in the Day of Judgment

Its Impact on the Development of the Human Soul

Syed Nasir Zaidi

INTRODUCTION

IN ISLAMIC TRADITION, THE idea of the end times is expressed in the context of the day of judgment. On that day, life as we know it will end. Everyone who has died will be resurrected and face judgment by God Almighty. Faithful servants of God will immediately be placed in paradise. For many people, the idea of ultimate judgment by God inspires fear. But the Qur'an presents belief in the hereafter as a positive spiritual resource. This belief offers people a way of understanding death and describes moral accountability at the end of life. Thus, it can bring tranquility of heart and peace of mind. It can help believers realize their moral responsibilities and inspire them to persistently examine themselves. In this essay, I present Islamic eschatological beliefs with a focus on their positive spiritual effects. To do so, I present selected verses from the Qur'an, interpret them, and show how taking them seriously can change a person's mind and heart.

THIS WORLD AND THE HEREAFTER

The Qur'an rejects a view of life as merely worldly. In a way, life in this world is a test of virtues and deeds for each individual (67:2). This test gives us the opportunity not to enter empty handed through the gate of death. The Qur'an says, "Every soul shall have a taste of death" (2:185). This verse signifies that death is inevitable for every human being. At the same time, however, this verse speaks of a "taste" of death. To "taste" a death is to experience it as a temporary feeling or flavor which disappears like a food, after which you move on to a deeper life. The Qur'an also says, "The death from which you try to run away will definitely visit you, then you will be sent back to the Knower of the unseen and the seen, and He will tell you what you used to do" (62:8). This verse means that after facing death, a human being will leave it behind and continue his or her journey to the next world.

We understand from the Qur'an that death is not a point of termination. Rather, life is eternal and extraordinarily vast, and death is a transfer of life from one stage to another. In the view of the Qur'an, death is the start of a "real" life. The Prophet Muhammad stated, "Death is the first stage in the stages of the hereafter and the last stage from the stages of the world."[1] The Qur'an states that everyone has to return to God (3:28), because death is part of life. A human being goes through a deep process of spiritual changes and transfers these changes into the next life.

Here is a helpful analogy. When we are in our mother's womb, that alone is our world and we know nothing beyond it. But our development in that environment advances us, so that we are prepared when we exit the womb and enter this world. Similarly, death is an exit from this world into another world. We cannot return to this world to develop the qualities and strengths we need to face the next stage in life. But the effect of every act, effort, hardship, feeling and thought manifests its nature onto the soul (84:6).

People might be tempted simply to enjoy life in this world. To such people, the Qur'an says, "The life of this world is nothing but an amusement and a (childish) game, and a show of beauty and exchange of boastful claims between you, and a competition of increase in riches and children" (69: 20). But there is no pleasure in the world which is not surrounded by hundreds of pains and troubles. If there is youth, then old age and weakness is bound to follow it anyhow. If there is health, which is primarily essential for enjoying every pleasure of life, then there are several ailments and illnesses which pose threats to it. If there is wealth, which makes it possible to get comfort and ease, then it is not possible to gain wealth without doing hard labor. No high position is attained without laboring hard and facing deterrents and oppositions. Besides, all such worldly gains, benefits, comforts, and positions are bound to perish one day.[2]

According to the divine worldview, humanity is not created for this material world; rather, the material world is created for humanity. This gives

---

1. Majlisi, *Bahār al-Anwār*, 133.
2. D. Shirazi, *Hereafter*.

humans insight on what our relation to this world is, and how we can bring real worth to the material around us. Ideally, humans see their worldly life as a tool to attain higher objectives. Belief in resurrection day helps a person know not to trade the permanent and elevated happiness of the hereafter for what they "enjoy" in their present life (2:86).

Renowned Muslim scholar, historian, and hadith narrator Sheikh Abbas Qummi says that love of this world is the outcome of an ignorant person's mind. Such a person thinks that prosperity and good fortune in this world bring happiness. But this happy world is actually beset with numerous troubles and anxieties. It is about to end and does not enjoy eternity, perpetuity and sincerity. About this, a poet has said, "Do not give your heart to this world, for its example is of an unfaithful bride who has never loved you, even for a night." Along these lines, the holy Qur'an says that love for this world is a characteristic of the disbelievers (10:7).[3]

Because revelation is our only source of knowledge for what will happen after death, the Qur'an delicately describes many attributes of hereafter. The hereafter will be eternal and absolute, with no other "transfers" or "deaths" into another stage. Similarly, the pleasures of the hereafter will not be accompanied with pain and suffering, and its prosperity will be without misfortune and calamity.[4] Some Qur'anic verses suggest that the relation between this world and the hereafter is one of cause and effect. Other Qur'anic verses suggest that the two worlds are more like synonyms, reflecting a person's deeds in two different but related ways. Whatever we do in this world, its true nature will be manifested in the hereafter. As the Qur'an says, "They know something superficial of this worldly life, but of the Hereafter they are negligent" (30:7). Only on the day of judgment will each human be resurrected with their true perfection, one that they acquired through their faith and deeds. On the day of judgment, humans will see and experience the true psyche of worldly life (50:22).

MORAL PURPOSE AND THE HEREAFTER

If the day of judgment did not exist, says the Qur'an, the creation of this world would have been without a purpose (23:115). How would creation lose purpose if we denied the existence of the day of judgment? Makarim Shirazi, a renowned Muslim scholar and jurist, says that our world is vast, glorious, and marvelous. The number of galaxies and the distance between them are outstandingly immense. Most of ordinary human life is concerned

---

3. Qummi, *Manazelul Akherah*, 12.
4. Tabatabai, *Tafseer Al-Mizaan*, 16:225.

with fulfilling such simple purposes as finding food, wearing clothing, sleeping, walking and procreating. Could humanity have been created for such simple purposes? No, Shirazi says; animals already fulfilled those purposes.[5] Could such a complex and vast system be created for such simple purposes? No, Shirazi says; the study of this great world merely indicates that this life is an introduction to a greater, vaster, eternal world. It is only the existence of such a world that makes our lives meaningful.[6]

Further, the universe has a moral purpose. God says that he is the One who created the heavens with truth (6:73). If the day of judgment did not exist, we might easily assume that we were given free hand to do whatever we desired, without repercussions. Aggressors and tyrants would not be answerable for their aggression and tyranny. If the pain and suffering faced by oppressed and deprived people were left unanswered, this existence and the creation of this world would have been considered meaningless.[7]

Every human heart has a strong desire for justice, where people are held accountable for inhumane behavior and widespread corruption, and where full reward is given to those who serve humanity. However, this justice does not come about fully in our material world. The Qur'an says, "You certainly have known your first creation [when you were in the material world] then why did you not admonish" (52:62). In this physical world, every creature is guided towards prosperity and perfection; human beings are guided towards its success and prosperity through prophets, religions and wisdom. But these ends cannot be achieved without accountability and reward. And, for that, given the limitations of our world, another world is required.

A person can prepare for this next world by developing a kind of inner justice system. In the beginning of Qur'an chapter 75, God swears by the day of judgment. Immediately in the next verse, God swears by the self-reproaching self. Human beings have a conscience to enlighten them on the wrong doings for which they will be judged. The conscience is knowledge of our own acts and feelings of right or wrong. It is a sensitive balance to weigh actions, a gauge of truth, a guiding voice from within. Normally people experience a stage of self-awareness where they listen to the inner voice of their conscience that judges their behavior. This moral compass governs a person's thoughts and actions. If the voice of conscience is continuously ignored, a person goes back to the prior stage of self, which incites evil (12:53). But if a person listens to this inner voice of self, they can reach

---

5. D. Shirazi, *Hereafter*.
6. M. Shirazi, *Tafseer-e-Namuna*, 347.
7. Amoli, "Tafseer-e-Surah Muminun."

the highest stage of self, which is the stage of happiness and satisfaction (89:27). Hence, the self-reproaching stage is a small scale of justice placed in the human soul. On the day of judgment, a bigger scale of justice will be used—a conscience of the whole universe.[8]

Some people, however, do not have the wisdom to contemplate truth that comes from an inner messenger. Nor are they able to receive it from an outer messenger, i.e., a prophet. The Qur'an teaches that, on the day of judgment, people will be held accountable only for what they were capable of doing. In addition, on the day of judgment, no person shall carry the load of another. No one will be punished until a messenger is sent for him or her (17:15). In other words, God will not punish anyone without first conveying his commandments and responsibilities through another medium.[9] It is also important to note that God alone is aware of whether and how a person received the message.[10]

The Qur'an teaches that one should always be hopeful about the mercy of God. At the same time, one should also be afraid of God—meaning we should be afraid of how God will judge our own bad deeds on the day of accountability. This important principle is reflected in the verse describing the story of the prophet Zacharias. The Qur'an says: "The family of Zacharias would call to us with hope and fear and they were humble before us" (21:90). Islamic scriptures recommend that one should find an inner balance between hope and fear. Excessive hope without fear can give a person courage to conduct wrongful acts. Excessive fear without hope can also affect a person's psychological wellbeing. Speaking about this balance, Allama Husayn Fadhlullah, a renowned jurist and scholar, says, "We inspire the child or youth to move forward through encouragement and push him back through threats."[11]

REMEMBERING GOD AND PURIFYING THE HEART

In the Qur'anic worldview, the day of judgment cannot be conceptualized without the existence of God. The hereafter is also a day of return to God, the originator of the universe. The Qur'an says, "He is the first and the last, and the manifest and the Hidden and He is all knowing about anything" (57:3). Almighty God, says this verse, is the origin of the universe who shall continue

---

8. Mutahari, *Majmua-e-Aasaar*, 147.
9. M. Shirazi, *Tafseer-e-Namuna*, 57.
10. Maududi, "Towards Understanding the Quran."
11. Fadlullah, *World of Our Youth*, 134.

to exist following the annihilation of this world. God is more manifest than anything and also more hidden than anything. Thus, the remembrance of the day of judgment will have the same effect as the remembrance of God. In the Qur'an, believers are highly encouraged to remember God abundantly. About those who forget God, the Qur'an says, "He made them forget their own selves" (59:19), in the sense that they will act against their own interests and bring themselves to punishment in the hereafter.[12]

On the day of judgment, the Qur'an teaches, neither wealth nor children can help; instead, one must come to God with pure heart (26:88-89). From this verse we learn that our success in the hereafter depends upon the purification of our heart in this life. We must purify our hearts from spiritual sins such as greed, malice, envy, arrogance, and worldliness. Success in the hereafter lies in the purification of self, which is interconnected with the remembrance of God and with prayer (87:14-15). The story of the prophet Moses, as narrated by the Qur'an, illustrates this, too. Moses was ordered to go to Pharaoh who has crossed all bounds, and say: Would you like to purify yourself? (79:17-18).

Commander of the faith Ali Ibn Abi Talib, the fourth caliph of Islam, says that those who remember the day of judgment will make themselves ready for the accountability of their souls. To do so, they gradually get control over their soul until they are spending most of their time in remembrance of God.[13] The remembrance of the day of judgment helps a person pay close and continuous attention to their deeds and behavior. Thus, it helps them try their best to seek the pleasure of God, take distance from worldly desires, and purify their heart and soul.

The Qur'an says, "Indeed, we exalted and purified our prophets with the pure quality which is a remembrance of their [final] dwelling place" (38:46). According to this verse, God inspired his prophets Abraham, Isaac, and Jacob to establish a strong connection with the day of judgment, so that all their mental and physical efforts would be focused towards the hereafter. Due to the remembrance of the day of judgment, Abraham, Isaac, and Jacob became men of strength and vision (38:45). Their knowledge of God reached a level of perfection, at which they were able to distinguish between true and false beliefs. Unwaveringly, they travelled on the right path. They were not distracted or obstructed by the apparent aspects of this world.[14] Along these lines, the Qur'an also says, "O Muhammad, stay away from those who turn away from our guidance

---

12. Usmani, *Tauzeeh ul Qur'an*, 1708.
13. 'Ali, "Richest Treasure."
14. Tabatabai, *Tafseer Al-Mizaan*, 16:322.

and who do not desire anything except the worldly life. This is what the extent of their knowledge amounts to" (53:29–30).

Remembrance of the judgment day can make an individual's heart humble and soft. The Qur'an says, "Seek help through patience and prayer. It is indeed difficult and exacting, but not for those who are humble in their hearts, who conceive that they are to meet their Lord, and that to Him they are to return" (2:45–46). According to this verse, overcoming difficulties and problems in life requires two fundamental principles. The first principle is a patience, i.e., a strong inner will, and the second is prayer, i.e., a firm outward refuge (prayer). To gain these two spiritual powers, one needs a humble heart, which can only be acquired by paying attention to the day of return. Hence, these three powerful principles; patience, prayer, and humility are derived through remembrance of the day of judgment.

Even imagining the circumstances around the day of judgment is enough to make a heart humble. Allama Tabatabai, a renowned exegete of the Qur'an, says that instead of using the words *certainty* or *full knowledge* of the day of return, it was sufficient for the Qur'an to use the word *imagine* or *conceive*. If an individual realizes and accepts that one day they have to meet God and return to him, they will not require full knowledge of that meeting to relinquish disobedience and behave with caution.[15]

OVERCOMING FEAR

The Qur'an tells several stories about people who overcame their fears of violence and poverty through their belief in the hereafter. These stories show that faith in the day of resurrection is a tool that allows us to resist the severest of tortures. For example, Pharaoh believed his magicians had entered into a conspiracy with Moses. Thus, he threatened the magicians with torture and death (26:49). Pharaoh was sure the magicians would confess the plot, not fall into prostration before God in front of thousands of spectators.[16] Previously such threats had affected them because they did not know themselves or God. They had lost the path of truth and were wandering in the desert of life. But this time the magicians found what they had lost.[17] They now feared only their former sins and hoped for salvation under the auspices of faith and Allah's mercy. So they said to Pharaoh, we must return to our Lord in any case. If you kill us now, we shall present ourselves before him, and we have nothing to worry about. We rather expect that we shall be

---

15. Tabatabai, *Tafseer Al-Mizaan*, 16:229.
16. Maududi, "Towards Understanding the Quran."
17. M. Shirazi, *Tafseer-e-Namuna*, 232.

forgiven our sins and errors because out of this entire gathering we were the first to believe the truth (26:50–51).

When Pharaoh's wife revealed her love for God, Pharaoh warned her against it and threatened her with severe punishment. But still she prayed to God, "My Lord, build a home for me near You in Paradise, and save me from Pharaoh and his works; save me from the transgressing people" (66:11). She rejected the great palace of her husband in all its materialistic beauty and greatness. Instead, she preferred a palace in paradise along with proximity to God. She refrained from the worldly pleasures available for her and overcame a fear of harsh punishment by remembering the rewards of the day of judgment.

Fear of death is part of human psychology. The root cause of this worry is love of life and love of eternity. Because we hope to live forever, we avoid death. We see it as destructive. But belief in the day of judgment can fulfill our desire for an everlasting life. Through it, we learn that death is an opportunity to meet with the Almighty.[18] To prepare, one should ask forgiveness from Allah for their sins and learn to tame the rebellious self. The Qur'an says: "He created death and life that He may try you, [to prove] which of you is best in deeds" (67:2). When the call of the Lord comes, one should welcome it with open arms, accepting it as a blessing from Allah.

BIBLIOGRAPHY

'Ali. "The Richest Treasure, Imam 'Ali's Letter to Malik al-Ashtar, the Governor of Egypt." Translated by Rasheed Turabi. Al-Islam, n.d. https://www.al-islam.org/richest-treasure-imam-ali.
Amoli, Javadi. *Naseem-e-Andishe*. Qom, Iran: Esra Foundation, 1968.
———. "Tafseer-e-Surah Muminun." Esra International Foundation of Revelatory Sciences, n.d. http://www.portal.esra.ir/Pages/Index.aspx?kind=2&lang=fa&id=NTM5Ng%3d%3d-sS61tiPdG6Y%3d. Site discontinued.
Fadlullah, Sayyid Muhammad Husayn. *World of Our Youth*. Translated by Khaleel Mohammed. Montreal: Organization for Advancement of Islamic Knowledge and Humanitarian Services, 1998. http://english.bayynat.org/Books/World_Of_Youth.pdf.
Imani, Faqihi. *An Enlightening Commentary into the Light of the Holy Qur'an*. Isfahan, Iran: Imam Ali Library and Research Centre for Islam and Scientific Studies, 1996. https://www.al-islam.org/printpdf/book/export/html/29612.
Majlisi, Baqir. *Baḥār al-Anwār*. Vol. 6. 2nd ed. Beirut: Al-Wafa, 1983.
Maududi, Abul A'la. "Towards Understanding the Quran: Surah ash-Shu'araa 26:34–51." Islamic Studies, n.d. http://www.islamicstudies.info/tafheem.php?sura=26&verse=34&to=51.
Mutahhari, Murtadha. *Majmua-e-Aasaar* [Murtadha Mutahhari's Collection of Writings]. Vol. 28. 8th ed. Qom, Iran: Sadra, 1952.

18. Qummi, *Manazelul Akherah*.

Qummi, Abbas. *Manazelul Akherah (Stages of the Hereafter)*. Mumbai: Madinatul Ilm Islamic Centre, 1999. https://goaloflife.files.wordpress.com/2011/08/manazil-ul-aakhira.pdf.
Shirazi, Dastghaib. *The Hereafter: Ma'ad*. Qom, Iran: Ansaryan, 2012.
Shirazi, Makarim. *Tafseer-e-Namuna*. 10th ed. Qom, Iran: Dar al-Kutub al-Islamia, 1951.
Tabatabai, Mohammed Hussain. *Tafseer Al-Mizaan*. 27 vols. 5th ed. Qom, Iran: Office of Islamic Propagation, 1954.
Usmani, Taqi. *Tauzeeh ul Qur'an*. Karachi, Pak.: Qur'anic Studies, 1951.

"Do You Not See How Powerful He Is?"
The End, Metanoia, and Visual Imagery in the *Shepherd of Hermas*

Giulia Marchioni

THE SHEPHERD OF HERMAS fits well with the topic of "visions of the end times." The author-protagonist, Hermas, describes the five visions he has. And the "end times" is a leitmotiv in a book that, if not properly apocalyptic *strictu sensu*, seems to be largely concerned with the idea of end times. The shepherd, after whom the work is named, is one of the writing's chief revelators. He is the object of the fifth vision of Hermas. He also has a role that transcends the widespread idea of a guide—although he definitely is one, too. We shall see that the power of the shepherd is deeply connected with the idea of metanoia and its urgency, against a background of the end times. Moreover, the connection of the shepherd figure with end times also takes place in the artistic field. In central Italian funerary iconography, specifically in funerary hypogean or underground chambers, the shepherd figure is often painted in the central tondo or circular depiction of the ceiling.

The *Shepherd* was written in Greek in the first half of the second century. Its author was almost certainly an otherwise unknown freedman named Hermas in Rome.[1] Three sections comprise the work: five visions, twelve mandates, and ten parables or similitudes. Each section warns that a judgment is near and that God has given the work's audience a limited time to repent before the end. The shepherd exhorts Roman Christ-followers to greater obedience to God's commands and to stronger community

---

1. Batovici dates the book 70–150 CE.

solidarity. The *Shepherd* became very popular from the second century onwards. It was quoted and appreciated by early Christian authors, with the sole exception of Tertullian.[2] Later, it was plagiarized by some authors in seventh-century Palestine, proof perhaps of a serious decline in use of the book. Despite its popularity, the *Shepherd* was rejected by the Muratorian Canon (a second- or possibly fourth-century list endorsing Christian canonicity), arguably because of its length. Nevertheless, this refusal is coupled with the approval of reading the *Shepherd* privately. In their lists of canonical books, Athanasius (296/98–373 CE) and Eusebius of Caesarea (265–339 CE) acknowledge that the book was used for catechesis and read in public for those who needed basic instruction.[3]

The geographical coincidence of the book (Rome) and paintings (Italy) led scholars to argue the possibility of an influence of the book on the creation, or at least the interpretation, of some funerary decorations. This chapter explores the representations of emblematic shepherds in funerary contexts. It leaves aside the iconography of bucolic idylls and pastoral scenes. Instead, it focuses on the image of the shepherd portrayed in frontal view, framed and isolated, with no other features but a few sheep, trees, or birds. This emblematic representation of the isolated shepherd is one of the most popular images in tomb paintings and sarcophagi in second- to third-century Italy.

The *Kriophoros* shepherd, center of the ceiling of the Velatio cubicle in the catacomb of Priscilla, Rome[4]

2. Tertullian (*De pud.* 10, 20), Irenaeus (*Adv. haer.* 4.20.2), Clement, Origen. See Osiek, *Shepherd of Hermas*, 4.

3. *Hist. eccl.* 3.3.6; Calvino, *La catacomba*; Fasola, *Le catacombe*; Cacitti, "Da Rode alla tore."

4. Image obtained from Wikimedia Commons, https://commons.wikimedia.org/

Some scholars, including Carolyn Osiek, have already raised the question whether some of the earliest shepherd depictions in emergent Christianity could be images of Hermas's shepherd. The problem has been left unresolved because of insufficient preserved evidence that correlates early Christian literature and art. I would express the question in broader terms. Could the *Shepherd* have *inspired* the interpretation and the use of the Greco-Roman shepherd? This kind of question argues for a more structural relation between texts, imagery, and emblematic images. It does not see image-text relations as a simple matching of narrative episodes and sources. Thus, this essay focuses on the question of the influence of the *Shepherd* on funerary representations of emblematic shepherds.

As the shepherd in the work is the appointed "angel of metanoia," can the shepherd figure in funerary images be read as a figure of metanoia (i.e., conversion)[5] (*Vis.* 5.1.7; *Sim.* 9.1.1; 14.3; 23.5; 24.4; 31.3; 33.1)? To answer, it is necessary to keep in mind two definitions of metanoia. The first is an eschatological definition: conversion to secure salvation in the afterlife. The second is a more social definition: metanoia as an individual interior change, sometimes undertaken for the sake of the social cohesion of the community of the church. With those definitions in mind, I will connect several key motifs found in both the text and the funerary images, such as the eschatological tower, the "cleaner" of stones (*Sim.* 9.7.2), and the redeemer of sinners.

ESCHATOLOGY IN THE *Shepherd of Hermas*

There is some limited evidence of a contact between the *Shepherd of Hermas* and funerary paintings. In the catacombs of San Gennaro in Naples, there is a famous early third-century fresco of three women building a tower, almost undoubtedly representing an episode of *Sim* 9.[6]

---

wiki/File:Good_shepherd_01_small.jpg.

5. I agree with the translation of the word given by Carolyn Osiek, who prefers "conversion" or "change of heart" to "repentance" (Osiek, *Shepherd of Hermas*, 28–29).

6. Fasola, *Le catacombe*. This is the only sure depiction of Hermas in art. Some other pictures may be representations from the *Shepherd*, e.g., a man watching a tree that probably represents the vine; a man with a billhook carved on a gem, probably the man of *Sim.* 8 (Leclercq, "Gemmes," 851, fig. 5114); a square rock with a door in the catacomb of Callistus; the coronation scene in Praetextatus, which could represent *Sim.* 8. 2.1 (Cagiano de Azevedo, "Cosidetta 'Coronatio,'" 6).

Catacombs of Saint Gennaro, Naples[7]

This fresco is not alone in recalling an eschatological dimension. For example, according to Michelangelo Cagiano de Azevedo, the so-called scene of *coronatio* in the Praetextatus catacomb (which Azevado calls the "palm twigs coronation") speaks in favor of the eschatological reward of eternal life (*Sim.* 8.2.1–3). The representation of the tower in the Saint Gennaro funerary complex shares the same sense of eternal life, the reward waiting for those who will convert.[8]

---

7. Image obtained from Wikimedia Commons, https://commons.wikimedia.org/wiki/Category:Catacombs_of_San_Gennaro_(Naples)?uselang=it#/media/File:Catacombe_di_San_Gennaro_052.jpg.

8. Cagiano de Azevedo, "Cosiddetta 'Coronatio,'" 5.

Crown of thorns, catacomb of Pretextatus[9]

Umberto Maria Fasola goes further. He found in *Sim.* 9.16.1–3 the reasons for the location of the tower's representation in a funerary context: death is a crucial topic for the *Shepherd*.[10] The book of *Similitudes* insistently repeats that the absence of conversion leads to "the death[11] that brings eternal destruction" (*ho de thanatos apōleian echei aiōvion*).[12] *Similitude* 8.7 appears to be fully framed by the life-death contrast.[13] Those who repent will save their lives and live in the tower. However, those who will not change their heart will "die the death" (*Sim.* 8.7.3).[14] This kind of "deadly death" returns in opposition to "life" in *Sim.* 8.7.6. "Life is for all who keep the Lord's commandments . . . life in the Lord consists of things like these, but for promoters of dissension and outlaws there is death." In the *Shepherd*, death is the threat of a definitive condition, just as life is meant as the eternal gift (*Vis.* 2.3.2, *Vis.* 3.8.4, *Sim.* 9.27; *Sim.* 9.28.8), or life from the

---

9. Image obtained from Wilpert, *Pitture delle catacombe romane*, 350.
10. Osiek, *Shepherd of Hermas*, 8n76.
11. *Sim.* 8.6.6 (Osiek, *Shepherd of Hermas*, 207) and 6.5.7; 8.3; 9.19; 9.23.5; 10.2.3.
12. *Sim.* 6.2.4 (62).
13. Osiek, *Shepherd of Hermas*, 207.
14. *Thanato apothneskein* (*Sim.* 8.7.3).

Lord (*Sim.* 8.7.6.).[15] Thus, eternal life or death are eschatological effects of metanoia; they belong to an otherworldly time dimension.[16]

The tower in the *Hermas* text, also seen in funerary art, represents the eschatological dimension. It may be connected to the role of the church in eschatology, but it is not clear exactly how. *Vis.* 3.8.9 says, "Whenever the construction of the tower is completed, that is the end." In *Sim.* 9.5.2, the shepherd reminds us that "the tower cannot be completed until its lord comes to inspect this building."[17] *Sim* 8.8.2 says that until the end times, i.e., before the tower is completed,[18] "for those who were converted, their dwelling is in the tower."[19] Through the voice of the old woman-church, in *Vis.* 4.3.5, Hermas speaks of the world that is coming and of eternal life. In Sim. 9.26.6, he warns people about a devastation to death in case of a lack of conversion. After the construction of the tower, after the end (*telos*),[20] there is eternal life or death, and those who did or did not repent will be set forth.

ROLE OF THE SHEPHERD

The eschatological preoccupation with eternal salvation or damnation is why the shepherd urges Hermas to conversion (*Sim.* 8.9; *Sim.* 9.26.6). Metanoia is the last and only chance of salvation. It is entrusted only to the shepherd. The shepherd-angel, "the angel of conversion" (*ho angelos tēs metanoias*) (*Vis.* 5.7), is the teacher who gives commandments to Hermas. He is Hermas's guide and overseer in the process of metanoia. In *Sim.* 10, Hermas insists on relying exclusively on the shepherd and his authority:

---

15. A person enters in the reign of God (*Sim.* 9.16.2) upon receiving a seal of water with baptism: this is the very moment a person puts aside deadliness and takes on life. For what concerns the theology of "repentance," I agree with Osiek who argues that the author "uses eschatological expectation as the occasion to proclaim an exceptional 'jubilee' release from sin" (Osiek, *Shepherd of Hermas*, 29n221), a more moderate position concerning the question of forgiveness after baptism in Hermas.

16. The binomial relation of life and death is an apocalyptic feature because of the dimension of time it involves—the eternal otherworldly time.

17. The interpretation of the arrival of the lord of the tower as the coming of Christ (*parousia*) and the inspection of the building as the final judgment would be tempting, and hazardous as well. This question would be worth a deeper investigation.

18. *Vis.* 3.7.1; *Vis.* 3.9.5.

19. See also *Mand* 4.3.4; *Sim.* 8.9.2. Batovici says, "The believer should repent, for the opportunity is offered. And when fulfilled, metanoia might secure a place in the eschatological tower" (Batovici, "Apocalyptic and Metanoia," 167).

20. Osiek translates *eis telos* as either "completely" or "finally," comparing *Sim.* 8.6.4, *Sim.* 9.19.1, and John 13:1 (Osiek, *Shepherd of Hermas*, 74).

> I have handed over you and your household to this shepherd so you can be protected by him. "Yes, sir," I said. "So if you want to be protected from all annoyance and trouble, and to have success in all your good deeds and words and in every truthful virtue, proceed according to the commandments that I gave to you . . . . To him alone throughout the whole world conversion [*metanoia*] is entrusted. Do you not see how powerful he is? Yet you do not respect the fullness and forbearance he has toward you. (*Sim.* 10.1.2–3)

The herdsman's role as guide and leader has a long cultural tradition. In the ancient Near East, shepherd imagery was often associated with kingship and guidance.[21] For example, in the Hebrew Bible, gods and kings were called "shepherds of the people."[22] In Ps 23, the roles of guidance, protection, loving care, and sovereignty are bestowed upon the Lord-shepherd.[23] Early Christianity also reinterpreted shepherd metaphors for new purposes and original meanings. For example, shepherds witness the birth of Jesus (Luke 2), and Jesus himself is understood as a shepherd (John 10).

This literary and cultural tradition helped to establish a connection between shepherds and leadership. While it did not give birth to any particular iconography, it likely inspired people to recall the idea of guidance when they glanced at the image of a shepherd. In other words, there is a correspondence between the *idea* of leadership and the *mental image* of the shepherd. This mental image found its *material* expression in a particular set of images. These images have no fixed narrative character; rather, they are emblematic.[24] Along these lines, Carlo Ginzburg described how early Christ-followers summarized in concise formulae long literary traditions of concepts and ideas, giving birth to iconic representations.[25]

---

21. Chae, *Jesus*.

22. See Gen 49:24; Jer 23:1–4; 31:10; 49:20; Mic 5:4; 7:14. The shepherd's role is especially prominent in exilic salvation prophecies. In Gen 49:24, Yahweh is called the "shepherd" for the first time (also in Ps 23; Zech 11; Mic 2).

23. The archetype shepherd-king is used with regard to King David too. For discussion, see Antony, "God the Shepherd." Moses, too, is called "shepherd" (Exod 14:31). "In Israel the title evoked special memories of God's own leading and protecting role in the wilderness (Ps 77:20; 78:52–53; 80:1) and in the return from the exile (Isa 40:11; 49:9–10). With this background, the thought of God as shepherd would flood the informed and sensitive reader's mind with evocations too deep for words" (Antony, "God the Shepherd," 62).

24. This conceptualization of mental and material images follows Schmitt et al., "Immagini."

25. Ginzburg, "Ecce."

Thus, early Christian viewers would have recognized in the emblematic shepherd of tomb decorations a figure of leadership. Likely, the *Shepherd of Hermas* added to this interpretative framework the idea of a shepherd who powerfully guides sinners through the process of conversion. By the end of the second century, no other noncanonical Christian writing was as popular as the *Shepherd*. Christians shopping for tomb decorations probably knew of the *Shepherd*, as did Christians who viewed tombs. The *Shepherd* was most popular in central Italy, where it was written. This region has the highest presence of emblematic funerary shepherds.[26] The framed shepherd in a burial context was probably a wish for eternal life for the deceased, gained after metanoia. Simultaneously, it was also a "sign" of the deceased's identity as a member of God's flock, guided by the angel-herdsman.

SOCIAL COHESION

The widespread diffusion of the *Shepherd of Hermas* also had effects on social life in the church. In the *Shepherd*, the call to conversion[27] leads to eternal life in the tower, which is a metaphor for the church. From this standpoint, metanoia outlines conditions for being a member of the church. Thus, it has the additional purpose of creating cohesion and unity in the social group. Some scholars have pointed out that the writing's purpose was to respond to a particular social crisis. For example, Carolyn Osiek argues that the *Shepherd* tried to face a crisis of community division and loss of good spirit. She writes, "Hermas' strategy is to reshape the church by bringing listeners to the point of open-heartedness in which they can change."[28] Adela Yarbro Collins speaks of the "social character" of Hermas's *paraenesis* (warning) when she says that the *Shepherd* is an apocalypse of cosmic and/or political eschatology.[29] Harry Maier stresses the social aim of *Hermas*, arguing that the problems in Hermas's community are due to inappropriate social attitudes. The calls to "repentance" are "attempts to re-establish the purity of the group."[30] The exhortation to conversion, however, is not directed to the whole community, because metanoia is not a mass phenomenon or a ritual. It is, according to the *Shepherd*, a personal change rooted in a social context. "Just as the tower came to be as if made of one stone after it was cleansed, so will the church of God be after its

---

26. Bellucci, "Notizia a Napoli"; Carlini, "Cuma cristiana."
27. *Sim.* 8.3; 9; 10.3; *Sim.* 9.19.2; 20.4.
28. Osiek, *Shepherd of Hermas*, 29.
29. Batovici, "Apocalyptic and Metanoia," 158n27.
30. Maier, *Social Setting*, 69.

cleansing and purging of evildoers, hypocrites, blasphemers, doubleminded, and doers of all kinds of evil" (*Sim.* 9.18.3).

The *Shepherd* also influenced the social context in which metanoia takes place. The role it gives to the shepherd contributed to the metaphorical view of the bishop as a shepherd. It also contributed to the identification of church pastors with shepherds. This metaphor began to appear in first- and second-century Christian writings. In the New Testament, for example, Acts 20:28 expressly associates sheep, shepherds, and overseers.[31] In Ignatius of Antioch's *Epistle to the Philadelphians*, the earliest surviving Christian text,[32] we also see the designation of bishops as shepherds. In *Hermas*, the shepherd is an intermediate character between humankind and the most venerable angel. In *Sim.* 10.2.2, for example, the shepherd is placed at the top of a hierarchical order. This hierarchical leadership speaks in favor of the overlap of bishops (called *epi-skopoi*, "overseers") and shepherds. Over time, this tradition grew. Augustine of Hippo (354–430 CE) in his "Sermon on Pastors" deploys shepherd imagery from the Hebrew Bible (Jer 13:1–4; Ezek 34:1–8) to justify bringing North African believers critical of the imperial church's corruption back into its assemblies by force, if necessary.[33] Augustine's view contrasts with Hermas's *Visions*. In *Hermas*, the shepherd orchestrates the growth of the church as the end of all things. Augustine, however, was motivated to make the imperially sanctioned church a fuller participant in the soteriological process and a means to realize the eschaton.

In this essay, I have read the *Shepherd of Hermas* together with the funerary imagery it inspired. Here, the figure of the shepherd guides humans to metanoia, or conversion, in two senses. In the eschatological sense, metanoia leads to eternal life and away from "deathly death." In the social sense, metanoia is a process of personal and social purification that helps a community cohere. The figure of the shepherd continues to influence Christian conceptualizations of the roles of pastor and bishop.

BIBLIOGRAPHY

Antony, Abraham M. "God the Shepherd in the Book of Psalms, with Special Reference to Psalm 23." In *Shepherding: Essays in Honour of Pope John II*, edited by Paul P. Vadakumpadan and J. Varickasseril, 50–107. Shillong, IN: Vendrame Institute & DBCIC, 2005.

Batovici, Dan. "Apocalyptic and Metanoia in the *Shepherd of Hermas*." *Apocrypha-International Journal of Apocryphal Literatures* 26 (2015) 151–70.

---

31. See also John 21:15–17; 1 Pet 5:1–4.

32. It is the earliest, even if we date it to the second quarter of the second century, as many are now inclined to do.

33. Gomola, "Conceptual Blends," 278–79.

Bellucci, Antonio. "La notizia a Napoli del Poimen di Erma e la datazione delle più antiche pitture del cimitero di S. Gennaro." In *Atti del IV congresso nazionale di studi Romani*, 109–18. Rome: Istituto di Studi Romani, 1938.

Cacitti, Remo. "Da Rode alla torre. La catechesi delle Visioni I–IV del Pastore di Erma." In *Antiche vie all'eternità: colloquium internazionale sugli aspetti dell'ascesi nei primi secoli del cristianesimo*, edited by Aldo Magris et al., 36–80. Udine, It.: Gaspari, 2006.

Cagiano de Azevedo, Michelangelo. "La Cosiddetta 'Coronatio' di Pretestato." In *Studi sull'Oriente e la Bibbia*, 117–22. Genoa: Studio e vita, 1967.

Calvino, Raffaele. *La catacomba di San Gennaro in Napoli: guida illustrata*. Naples: Catacomba di san Gennaro, 1970.

Carlini, Antonio. "Cuma cristiana e il Pastore di Erma." In *Roma: La campania e l'oriente cristiano antico*, edited by Luigi Cirillo and Giancarlo Rinali, 129–37. Naples: Università degli studi L'Orientale, 2004.

Chae, Young S. *Jesus as the Eschatological Davidic Shepherd: Studies in the Old Testament, Second Temple Judaism, and in the Gospel of Matthew*. Tübingen, Germ.: Mohr Siebeck, 2006.

Fasola, Umberto M. *Le catacombe di S. Gennaro a Capodimonte*. Rome: Editalia, 1974.

Ginzburg, Carlo. "Ecce. Sulle radici dell'immagine di culto Cristiana." In *Occhiacci di legno: Nove riflessioni sulla distanza*, 100–117. Turin, It.: Feltrinelli, 2011.

Gomola, Aleksander. "Conceptual Blends with Shepherd(s)/Sheep Imagery in Selected Patristic Writings." *Studia Religiologica* 47 (2014) 275–84.

Leclercq, Henri. "Gemmes." In *Dictionnaire d'archéologie chrétienne et de liturgie*, edited by Fernand Cabrol, 6:794–864. Paris: Letouzey et Ane, 1907–1953.

Maier, Harry O. *The Social Setting of the Ministry as Reflected in the Writings of Hermas, Clement and Ignatius*. Studies in Christianity and Judaism 12. Waterloo, Can.: Wilfrid Laurier University Press, 2002.

Osiek, Carolyn. *The Shepherd of Hermas: A Commentary*. Hermeneia. Minneapolis: Fortress, 1999.

Schmitt, Jean-Claude, et al. "Immagini." In *Dizionario dell'occidente medievale, temi e percorsi*, edited by Jean-Claude Schmitt et al., 517–31. Turin, It.: Einaudi, 2014.

Wilpert, Joseph. *Le pitture delle catacombe romane*. Roma Desclée Lefebvre, Universitats Bibliothek Heidelberg, 1903.

Leonard Cohen
Dance Me to the End of Love

Lorraine Ashdown

This chapter joins others in a collection of ideas, musings, and visions of the end times. The work of poet, writer, musician, and prophet Leonard Cohen is the focus of my chapter. I shall look at his body of work and explore how and where he applied apocalyptic framing to his music and words. I shall also look at different versions of the meaning of the word *apocalypse* with an attempt to understand how Cohen interpreted the concept of the "end times."

The human condition is not simple. We are complex beings. As infants, we arrive into the world fully formed and mysteriously made. If we are fortunate enough to live until we are elders, we experience decades of responding and relating to other humans and to creation. From our first breath, we remain in relationship with others as we do our best to understand the entanglements of day-to-day living.

Music is a way to express some of the joys and pains of living when ordinary words will not do. Leonard Cohen's music, in particular, provides a pathway to the heart and encourages beauty, amazement, grace, love, sorrow, and more. As a revealer of the truth, Cohen was also political. His deep understanding of the human spirit and ability to express its significance and its connections to the divine is what draws me to his music.

APOCALYPTIC SONGS

When I began reading Cohen's words; reading many other writers' words about Cohen; and listening to Cohen's songs, poems, and interviews, my early conclusion was that perhaps the joke was on me. Cohen really did not have an apocalyptic vision of how the world might end. He did not have a consistent conclusion to any of his unveilings or revelations. As Cohen himself said, "Everybody would like an apocalyptic solution to the ending of their lives, but the apocalyptic solution doesn't come, and we are left with daily events that are much more complex than any apocalypse."[1] But then I took a deeper look into his songs.

One particular understanding of apocalyptic literature is that it tells the story of calamity and collapse and indicates that human civilization is coming to an end. His song, "First We Take Manhattan," fits right into that definition. Written by Cohen in 1988, it was recorded by singer Jennifer Warnes. Her version starts out with excerpts from a German radio station addressing the fact that US servicemen were killed in a local nightclub. This violent event happened only a few months before the song was recorded. Little did they know that 9/11 was on the horizon. "First We Take Manhattan" is a song about terrorism. It is a song about protesting capitalism and how seductive the big, uncontrolled money-making machines are. This composition unveils and reveals the underbelly of the finance-focused, paternal society we inhabit. Cohen is warning us about nihilism and about idolatry. There is no mention of worshipping a god of love here. The song speaks of greed, selfishness, and the dangers of feeding the beast that we call the *empire*. Cohen sings, "I'm guided by the beauty of our weapons." Those weapons are not just guns and ammunition. The weapons of mass destruction Cohen refers to are egocentric, systemic malaises that lead to poverty, addiction, hunger, loneliness, and the breakdown of society.

Cohen's song "The Future" also takes on a political tone. He thinks of the future as a joke made in poor taste or a made-up ghost story designed to scare children. He says that the future is murder, and he paints a bleak picture of what lies ahead for humanity. Cohen uses words such as "torture" and "murder," and he references mass murderer Charles Manson. Certainly, if the apocalypse is defined as the end of civilization and the beginning of devastation without hope, this song is in that key, too.

A second definition of the apocalypse is not as a cataclysmic world-ending event, but as a warning or a wake-up call at the edge of time. It is a time when we are called to attention, because it is quite possible that we may be at the gripping edge of our own time. An apocalypse may be

---

1. Cohen, "Ain't No Cure."

understood as an unveiling or a revelation. Leonard Cohen reveals and unveils truths about humanity, about God, and about the relationship between God and humanity. Cohen allows us to see ourselves and the labyrinthine world we have built, and he probes deeply into our psyches and the pathos and poignancy of our lives.

If we understand the apocalypse to be an unveiling or a revealing, the song "Dance Me to the End of Love" is a fit for this definition. In this rhythmic, romantic song, Cohen uses words such as "gathered safely in," "homeward dove," and "a tent of shelter." The language reveals the nature of love, of one heart connecting to another heart. It opens up the vulnerability and joy that erupts when humans connect through their bodies, minds, and spirits. There is an intensity to the song, provided by both the lyrics and the rhythm, that allows us to celebrate the delights of romantic love. The title of the song "Dance Me to the End of Love" has an apocalyptic ring to it as it speaks of the end of love. Yet, if that end is understood as death, then love is revealed as triumphant and stronger than death.

Apocalypse can also have a redemptive dimension. As our times are now so uncertain and treacherous, we may have a yearning for an apocalyptic ending. We may want a dramatic intervention of divine energy and then a rush of hope. Just before Cohen's own death in 2016, he wrote the song "You Want It Darker." It is a personal lament to the world and a cry to God, as Cohen says that he is ready to die. He proclaims to God, "*Hineni, hineni,*" meaning "here I am" in Hebrew. This song presents an apocalyptic yearning. Cohen breathes a breath of faith before he dies.

Writer Richard Gehr wrote an article for *Rolling Stone* in 2014 called "Leonard Cohen: 20 Essential Songs." In it, Gehr refers to Cohen as the "late blooming gloom-monger."[2] I do not fully agree. Many of Cohen's poems and songs are dark. But they are also truthful. Cohen has the heart of a romantic prophet. He believes in love, tenderness, beauty, and surrender, and he steers far from superficial engagement. He discloses the underbelly of depression, loneliness, disconnectedness, brokenheartedness, and fear. Cohen was a wise, mystical prophet with a deep reverence for humans as spiritual beings. He had a claim to the mysteries of God, yet he did not put much faith in any life after this one. He wove his own eclectic faith, drawing on three traditions: Judaism, Buddhism, and Christianity.

---

2. Gehr, "Leonard Cohen," para. 2.

AN ECLECTIC FAITH

Leonard Cohen was born a Jew in Montreal on September 21, 1934. His father died when Cohen was just nine years old. Shortly after his father died, the young Leonard, in his grief, went into his room and found one of his father's bowties. He wrote a line or two, opened up the tie, and slipped the words into the tie. Then, he buried the tie in the backyard. Cohen's father's death left a lasting scar. In his first novel, *The Favourite Game* (1963), he describes that scar as, "What happens when the word is made flesh."[3] Cohen said he did not know where he had buried the tie nor the words, and he spent his lifetime trying to find it again. He felt that the act of writing something crucial, burying it, losing it, and then spending the rest of his life trying to find the lost words, was what writing was all about.

Cohen went to McGill University, spent a year in graduate school in New York City, and then came back to Montreal. He traveled the world as a musician and poet. He lived on Hydra, an island in Greece, for twenty years. He spent five years in a Buddhist monastery where he was ordained a monk. His Jewish roots and his Jewish heritage and culture never left him. He says,

> Being Jewish has given me my ancestors, and its Kabbalistic imagination has influenced me; socially, however, it has marginalized me, placing me with other alienated forces in Canada and elsewhere.... But Judaism did give me a sense of tradition and spirituality which I have taken into new directions.... There was something in Judaism for me. I still had to go whoring after false gods, and maybe I'm still in the bed of one, but there was something about what I saw.[4]

Cohen spent five years at a Zen Buddhist retreat at Mount Baldy, California. There was a time in his life when he was drinking four bottles of wine a day and leaving behind him a string of women who had no true significance in his life. He became aware that his depression, his anxiety, and his related lifestyle were slowly killing him. He says,

> I wasn't looking for a religion. I already had a perfectly good one [his Jewish faith]. And I certainly wasn't looking for a new series of rituals. But I had a great sense of disorder in my life, of chaos and depression, of distress. And I had no idea where this came from. The prevailing psychoanalytic explanations of the time didn't seem to address the things I felt. Then I

---

3. Cohen, *Favourite Game*, 1.
4. Nadel, "Ten or More Questions."

bumped into someone who seemed to be at ease with himself and at ease with others.[5]

That person was Kyozan Joshu Sasaki Roshi, the founder of the monastery. In 1996, Sasaki gave him the monastic name Jikhan, meaning "silence."

Cohen claims his time in the monastery strengthened his Judaism, which he called "a four-thousand-year-old conversation with God and his sages."[6] While at Mount Baldy, Cohen broke through his depression and pronounced that the mist of sadness and despair lifted from him. The prevailing sense of anguish ceased to exist. He had been released.

Cohen was also drawn to the iconography of Christianity.

> I'm very fond of Jesus Christ. He may be the most beautiful guy who walked the face of the earth. Any guy who says, "Blessed are the poor. Blessed are the meek" has got to be a figure of unparalleled generosity and insight and madness.... A man who declared himself to stand among the thieves, the prostitutes, and the homeless. His position cannot be comprehended. It is an inhuman generosity. A generosity that would overthrow the world if it was embraced because nothing would weather that compassion. I'm not trying to alter the Jewish view of Jesus Christ, but to me, in spite of what I know about legal Christianity, the figure of the man has touched me.[7]

In one of Cohen's biographies, I read that Cohen owned a small bracelet that he wore often. It held twelve tiny cameos of Jesus, Mary, and the saints strung together with elastic.

CONCLUSION

If we define the apocalypse as a cataclysmic end to human civilization, I believe Leonard Cohen is not actually in alignment with that definition. If we consider the apocalypse to be a revelation and unveiling of the human condition that can lead to hope and change and growth, Cohen shows up there. In his most prophetic voice, Cohen sings about democracy; about the power of individuals; about God; about compassion, forgiveness, love, sex, brokenness, sin, and danger. He places the entire human condition in front of us, asking us to look carefully at one another while we scrutinize ourselves in the mirror. He is the revealer and the discloser of our truest, deepest selves. He articulates, with clarity and depth, what it is like to feel

5. Cohen, "Leonard Cohen on Poetry."
6. Devlin, *Leonard Cohen*, page number unavailable.
7. Devlin, *Leonard Cohen*, page number unavailable.

love, to feel sorrow, and to experience the spectrum of emotions that belong to us all. This Jewish man embraces his roots and assimilates the beauty and teachings of Christianity as he also weaves in the truths of Buddhism. He does not exclude nor diminish anyone's spiritual path.

As a result of exploring Cohen's work, I have been challenged to join him as he dives deeply into the human journey. I have learned, and been reminded of, the value of spiritual and religious integration. The flame of the revealer and of the life of the man who disclosed so much has gone out. Yet, all his yearnings, learnings, lust and longings, love and lessons live on. Cohen needs us to stay here to honor his work. He knows it is hard work. And he knows that staying here in the game is much harder than being taken out by an apocalypse.

Perhaps apocalypse as calamity and apocalypse as a revelation are similar in some ways. They both indicate an ending of epic proportions. Yet, the devastation associated with the radical apocalypse, destroying life in all forms, does not fit with my vision of the end times. Mine, perhaps similar to Cohen's, is more gentle and more hopeful. Unanswered questions lie before me like an overgrown forest, yet, I feel there is hope for the future.

Leonard Cohen was a gift to us. I sincerely hope that as your life drew to a close, Mr. Cohen, you truly did dance to the end of love.

BIBLIOGRAPHY

Cohen, Leonard. "Ain't No Cure for Love." Interview with Hans Pfitzinger. YouTube, Aug. 18, 2013; interview from 1998. https://www.youtube.com/watch?v=OzsfSVybhRA.

———. "Dance Me to the End of Love." Recorded 1983. Track 1 on *Various Positions*. New York: Columbia, Passport, 1984.

———. *The Favourite Game*. England: Secker and Warburg, 1963.

———. "First We Take Manhattan." Recorded by Jennifer Warnes, 1986. Track 1 on *Famous Blue Raincoat*. Munich: Ariola, 1987.

———. "The Future." Recorded 1992. Track 1 on *The Future*. New York: Columbia, 1992.

———. "Leonard Cohen on Poetry, Music and Why He Left the Zen Monastery." Interview with Terry Gross. *NPR*, Oct. 21, 2016. https://www.npr.org/2016/10/21/498810429/leonard-cohen-on-poetry-music-and-why-he-left-the-zen-monastery.

———. "You Want It Darker." Recorded 2016. Track 1 on *You Want It Darker*. New York: Columbia, 2016.

Devlin, Jim. *Leonard Cohen in His Own Words*. White Marsh, MD: Omnibus, 1998.

Gehr, Richard. "Leonard Cohen: 20 Essential Songs." *Rolling Stone*, Nov. 11, 2016. https://www.rollingstone.com/music/music-lists/leonard-cohen-20-essential-songs-114187/.

Nadel, Ira B. "Ten or More Questions I *Should* Have Asked Leonard Cohen." Canadian Poetry, July 2, 1993. http://canadianpoetry.org/volumes/vol33/nadel.html.

The Eschatology of Everyday Life
Creation, Confession, and Friendship in Saint Augustine

Dylan Harvey

INTRODUCTION

THE ESCHATOLOGY OF EVERYDAY life refers to the tension between being and nonbeing, a tension with which we live from moment to moment. In this context, the "end times" have little to do with a distant, chronological event on the horizon. The horizon of my being is always *here* and *now*, where I find myself burdened with the possibility that I—or my relationships—may not live to see the next moment. Deep down, my heart dreads the inevitability of death and loss, the flash of darkness that overcomes my being. As Saint Augustine of Hippo expresses it,

> I am unable to live in such a state yet powerless to escape from it. Where could my heart find refuge from itself? Where could I go, yet leave myself behind? Was there any place where I should not be a prey to myself? None.[1]

Augustine himself finds his place through confession, an ongoing dialogue with God. He adopts an everyday confessional mode of being, finding rest in God in each successive moment. In the *Confessions*, he tells how his own dear friends helped him find his way to confession. Thus, those whose loss he most feared pointed him towards comfort in God's unchanging nature. Below, I present a theology of confession, drawing in part on Augustine and

---

1. Augustine, *Confessions*, 1.7.

his interpreters Étienne Gilson and Jean-Luc Marion, and show how it is at work in his own stories of confessional friendships.

CREATION AND *Nihil*

> In the beginning was the Word,
> and the Word was with God,
> and the Word was God. (John 1:1)[2]

Through the Word, God created heaven, earth, and incarnated souls. They do not share in God's immutable substance; rather they are mutable. God created them out of nothing (*ex nihilo*)—or as some philosophers say, *with* nothingness. This "nothing" is itself not a positive "thing" or a substance. It is a negative (or lack of) "foundation." Nothingness or *nihil* is a part of our constitution as created beings,[3] present in us such that we remain imperfect. As created beings, we exist precariously as a synthesis of God's power and *nihil*.

Due to our partial origin *ex nihilo*, we created beings lack the power to sustain ourselves in our own right. This power comes from God alone, who preserves our existence at every moment by continuously recreating us. Creating and sustaining the universe is a free and contingent act of God's will. (To see it otherwise would suggest some cause or reason greater than God's own will that would necessitate God's decision, implying that God alone could not sustain the world.[4]) In describing our dependence on God, Rene Descartes focuses on our lack as created beings. He writes that

> from the fact that we now exist, it does not follow that we shall exist a moment from now, unless there is some cause—the same cause which originally produces us—which continually reproduces us, as it were, that is to say, which keeps us in existence.[5]

Saint Thomas Aquinas focuses on God's role, saying, "God not only gives things their form, but He also preserves them in existence, and applies them to act, and is moreover the end of every action."[6]

---

2. Scripture quotations in this chapter are from the NABRE.
3. Drever, "Creation and Recreation," 76.
4. Tanner, "Creation," 155.
5. Descartes, *Principles of Philosophy*, §21.
6. Aquinas, *Summa theologica*, I, q. 105.5, a. 3.

RELATIONSHIPS AND *Nihil*

Relationships, like creatures, are mutable, sharing the attributes that come with creation *ex nihilo*. The possibility of a relationship's failure is rooted in its mutability.[7] Misunderstanding this feature of relationships compounds our grief. To explain this, the philosophical language of "privation" is helpful.

Good human relationships may exhaust themselves through a kind of "natural privation." Sometimes friends grow apart and go their separate ways because something is lacking, e.g., common interests or life goals. In this way, the mutable nature of our relationships can provide the time and space for new good qualities to emerge, developing unforeseen possibilities between two persons or the community at large. Over time, this makes way for new good relationships and thus guarantees celebration as much as it does mourning.

Sometimes, however, our response to loss can become a kind of "moral privation." As imperfect creatures with free will, we sometimes turn away from God's perfection.[8] Evil acts are an obvious example of this. But there are other, more subtler examples. For instance, when Augustine laments the death of his friend, his wish is that his friend be immutable and everlasting—that is to say, something that God's creation is *not*.[9] It follows, then, that the friendship itself is also misrecognized. Augustine improperly elevates God's works to the level of the Worker himself, wishing that these works were equal to God's substance rather than being an effect of God's power.[10] But for Augustine to wish such a thing would be to wish that his friend be a different kind of being altogether. Generalized broadly, it would be to eschew the coming into being of new good creatures.[11] The goodness of created beings is announced through their very mutability and temporality, much like the succession of musical notes that form a melody by appearing and disappearing. It would thus be a mistake to misrecognize the proper relationship between the goodness of creation and this natural privation. The failure to recognize this truth of creation could even be considered a moral privation. Coming from Augustine, it is a neglect of the nature of God's good works and thus a turning away from God himself.[12]

Relationships—whether they continue or end abruptly—can draw us away from recognizing the *nihil* in us in so many ways. There is, for

---

7. Gilson, *Christian Philosophy*, 208–9.
8. Mann, "Augustine on Evil," 44.
9. Augustine, *Confessions*, 4.6.
10. Gilson, *Christian Philosophy*, 214.
11. Mann, "Augustine on Evil," 45.
12. Gilson, *Christian Philosophy*, 208.

example, the wish for someone close to you to be something they cannot be by their very nature, that is, a perfect being. The refusal to accept the fact of the other's limitations as they are is the refusal to observe the limitation in oneself. This desire to know nothing about *nihil* as a part of one's own constitution is a mistake. As the Gospel of John says, "If we say that we have no sin, we deceive ourselves, and the truth is not in us" (John 1:8). When relationships end abruptly, the pain of abandonment is amplified because it can be hard to know the reasons why someone left us. But, as Gilson observes, the possibility of a relationship's failure is rooted in its mutability, its creation *ex nihilo*. And one cannot know anything about the origin of something that comes from nothing.[13] One must disturbingly behold this *nihil* for what it is and learn to live with uncertainty.

CONFESSION

This restless burden of nonbeing is a permanent feature of our everyday experience. Augustine describes this sense of never feeling at rest, always tempted by anxiety, grief, and despair.

> When I am in trouble I long for good fortune, but when I have good fortune I fear to lose it. Is there any middle state between prosperity and adversity, some state in which human life is not a trial? In prosperity as the world knows it there is twofold cause for grief, for there is grief in the fear of adversity and grief in joy that does not last.[14]

As Marion summarizes it, "Never decided, always to decide, the *vita humana* has no other state besides its indetermination in determining, its always pending possibility."[15] One cannot escape this state, but, to constitute a "self," Marion says, one can turn towards a confessional "mode" of being.

As Augustine sees it, confession becomes urgent precisely when propositional knowledge meets its greatest resistance. For Augustine, confession is a mode of cogitation beyond philosophy. To borrow language made famous by Descartes, is not the *cogito* ("I think") that thinks about its *sum* (being) but the *cogito* that thinks insofar as it is *confessio* (in dialogue with God).[16] Thus, when I find myself in the throes of anxiety in the confessional mode, I do not ask "why there is something rather than nothing," as

---

13. Gilson, *Christian Philosophy*, 208–9.
14. Augustine, *Confessions*, 10.29.
15. Marion, *In the Self's Place*, 149.
16. Marion, *In the Self's Place*, 13.

the philosopher Heidegger did.[17] My question is closer to "why have you forsaken me" (Ps 22:1), the voice of human weakness born from the human fear of abandonment. I behold *nihil* as part of my own constitution such that I am able to recognize my relation to God's substantiality and confess myself, a non-god, as a part of his good creation. I rediscover the place of self, and therefore creation, as first and foremost a relationship to God.[18] The eschatological moment that follows is both the dark moment where I confront that which I may despise within me and what I may hope for in eternity, revealed to me as his grace where I find rest.

Through confession, I find myself in the world before God precisely where my language fails. This failure of my own inner dialogical space puts me in relation to God—provided that I speak to him. But as I speak before God, my privation prevents me from speaking to him fully.[19] The *nihil* resists my ability to speak, interrupting the flow of my words. I realize I have no fully subsistent "self" available to me as I recognize "the nature of my sickness."[20] But this inner torment can also return me to God, who already knows what I will confess. This is because confession is already latent with the understanding that God spoke first. In the beginning, the Word brought about the original encounter, to which my confession is already uttered as a response.

The nature of this response is key to the role confession plays in recreation. In this moment of darkness, wherein the self rails against the self, I no longer have my own words and so I may cite Scripture. Yet citing Scripture is not merely my speaking to God but is already God speaking to me. Scripture is, Marion writes,

> the words first said *to* Saint Augustine by the very one *to* whom the confession now *re*says them—words said in the beginning by God, who was first to say His word, or rather who said the first word, as He created the world by it.[21]

In confession, God's own word, which came first, is now spoken through me and back to him as a response. For this reason, the content of my confession is irrelevant because my self and that of which I speak are already known to him.[22]

---

17. Marion, *In the Self's Place*, 233.
18. Marion, *In the Self's Place*, 237.
19. Marion, *In the Self's Place*, 25.
20. Augustine, *Confessions*, 8:11.
21. Marion, *In the Self's Place*, 21.
22. Marion, *In the Self's Place*, 31.

Through this confessional mode I am continuously recreated as the word passes through me and back to him. It is as though the *nihil* in me is the opening through which the word may pass, like a tailor passes a needle through the empty spaces that allow the weaving of a scarf. How I find myself in the world is confirmed through this confessional mode that establishes my place as a created being in relation to God. As Marion writes,

> Creation does not render *confessio* possible, as the ontic place for its enactment, but it itself becomes possible only starting with *confessio*, its liturgical preliminary. In short, in and through God, *confessio* gives its first place to the creation of heaven and earth, not the inverse.[23]

FRIENDSHIP AND CONFESSION

Much of what Augustine recounts in the *Confessions* are everyday life experiences, carrying with them eschatological characteristics that Augustine comes to recognize only in hindsight. In these memories, other people's views, words, and actions come to shape the person Augustine would become. As the narrative of the *Confessions* progresses, the experience of friendship comes to play a greater role in confession. Augustine reflects on what he, as a youth, initially took friendship to be and what he knows it to be as he approaches his baptism many years later.

In an early account of friendship, Augustine confesses his complicity in stealing fruit and feeding it to the pigs out of the thrill of transgression. However, Augustine writes that he would not have committed the act without his friends and emphasizes the importance of companionship.[24] This memory of having "partners in sin" becomes a foil for a later account of friendship in book 8, where the confessional mode forms the partnership. In a conversation with Ponticianus, Augustine and his friend Alypius are moved by a story of two unnamed friends. These unnamed friends, officials working for the Roman state, come to question their sense of purpose while reading a book about the life of Antony. The first friend confesses his uncertainty about the meaning of their shared career. They hope to become friends of the Emperor, yet is that attainable or even valuable? "But if I wish," says the friend, "I can become a friend of God at this very moment." He turns back to the book, "laboring under the pain of the new life that was taking birth in him."[25] After this confession and confirmed dedication to God, the second unnamed

23. Marion, *In the Self's Place*, 237.
24. Augustine, *Confessions*, 2.8.
25. Augustine, *Confessions*, 8.6.

friend insists he will stand by his comrade and join him on his journey. After Ponticianus, the storyteller, leaves, a similar event immediately plays out for Augustine. He confronts his friend Alypius about their sinful enjoyment of the games at the colosseum. Augustine recounts,

> In the heart of the fierce conflict which I had stirred up against my soul in our common abode, my heart, I turned upon Alypius.... I exclaimed, "What is the matter with us? What is the meaning of this story? These men have not had our schooling, yet they stand up and storm the gates of heaven while we, for all our learning, lie here groveling in this world of flesh and blood!"[26]

Here, the testimonies of friends play a crucial role in the facilitation of confession. The role of the friend is like that of the midwife, helping give birth to new life through the confession. One friend's feelings of misery and need to confess emerge spontaneously because another friend is present to receive them. The social bonds of friendship, grounded in our everyday experiences, ground confession. They open up the space for the confessor to confront their own "house divided against itself."[27] Later Augustine and Alypius would be baptized together; this underscores the kind of confessional mode through which their friendship developed.

In a miraculous way, the confessional mode of friendship relieves the tension between the being and nonbeing of everyday social relationships. These relationships may vanish before our eyes in an instant, but they can also point us towards the immutable Creator, God. Confessional friends do not turn away from the *nihil*; rather, they turn towards it together. The friend who listens helps us establish a relationship with God, the one who listens and already knows what we are going to say. By drawing us out of our temporary existence, lived at the edge of nonbeing, it is as if our friends say, "Lo, I am with you always, even unto the end of the world" (Matt 28:20).

BIBLIOGRAPHY

Aquinas, Thomas. *Summa Theologiae: Latin Text and English Translation, Introductions, Notes, Appendices and Glossaries*. Edited by Thomas Gilby. Cambridge: Cambridge University Press, 2006.
Augustine. *Confessions*. Translated by R. S. Pine-Coffin. London: Penguin, 1961.
Descartes, René. "Principles of Philosophy." Translated by Johnathan Bennett. Early Modern Texts, 2017. https://www.earlymoderntexts.com/assets/pdfs/descartes1644part1.

---

26. Augustine, *Confessions*, 8.8.
27. Augustine, *Confessions*, 8.8.

Drever, Matthew. "Creation and Recreation." In *The Cambridge Companion to Augustine's "Confessions,"* edited by Tarmo Toom, 75–91. Cambridge: Cambridge University Press, 2020.

Gilson, Étienne. *The Christian Philosophy of Saint Augustine*. Providence: Cluny, 2020.

Mann, William E. "Augustine on Evil and Original Sin." In *The Cambridge Companion to Augustine*, edited by Eleonore Stump, 40–48. Cambridge: Cambridge University Press, 2010.

Marion, Jean-Luc. *In The Self's Place: The Approach of Saint Augustine*. Translated by Jeffrey L. Kosky. Stanford, CA: Stanford University Press, 2012.

Tanner, Kathryn. "Creation." In *The Cambridge Companion to the "Summa Theologiae,"* edited by Philip McCosker and Denys Turner, 142–55. Cambridge: Cambridge University Press, 2016.

www.ingramcontent.com/pod-product-compliance
Lightning Source LLC
Chambersburg PA
CBHW051641230426
43669CB00013B/2398